# BRUJO: GRIMOIRE OF A PUERTO RICAN WITCH

## Philip Ryan Deal

**Self-Published**

*For my daughter Lu*

# CONTENTS

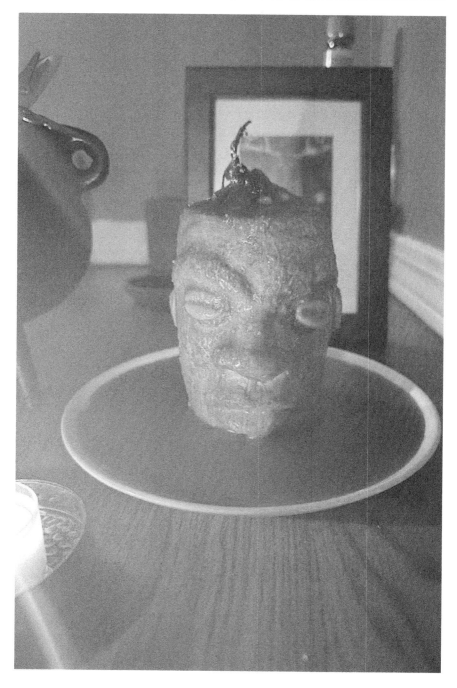

# BRUJO

By Philip Ryan Deal

## Introduction

My name is Brujo Ryan and I am a traditional witch and spiritualist. Today, young witches have lost the occult secrets of practicing astrological magic combined with medicinal / magical herbalism. That means doing spiritual work in harmony with the celestial powers. Witchcraft is an art and a science because real witches experiment with and test the effectiveness of their work using the scientific method. Real witchcraft is not woo woo, it produces real life effects. That's because the first witch was the first woman who went out into Nature and discovered there were herbs that could ease her menstrual cramps. The first witches were women and they were herbalists and healers. They understood how to increase the likelihood of a successful pregnancy or cure erectile dysfunction with plant medicine. They also performed herbal abortions and knew how to concoct poisonous potions that would take care of a cheating, abusive, or violent husband. These are the "mothers" and they were feared for holding herbal secrets that were passed down from mother to daughter or granddaughter since time immemorial. Male allies who ran with these women learned witchcraft from them. A lot of them were queer and gender non-conforming. Men that fell under the influence of the Divine feminine were also referred to as witches. Not much has changed over the last several thousand years. Everything we know in modern medicine comes from this body of knowledge that continues to evolve and expand even today.

Men who practiced traditional magic and sorcery, for good or ill, started the Grimoire Tradition. First by writing spells and incantations on cuneiform tablets and now self-publishing them on Amazon. The Atharvaveda (composed circa 1200 to 1000 BC) is one of the oldest scriptures in Hinduism. And it is full of magical formulas and incantations (mantras) used to change subjective reality using sacred psychology. The Greek Magical Papyri (a collection of rituals, hymns, and spells composed 100 BC to 400 CE) were used by the Egyptians, Greeks, and Romans to make contracts with the spiritual world. These manuals become the foundation of the Magical Grimoire Tradition. Medieval Grimoires are textbooks of magic that contain instructions for creating magical objects, performing spells, and summoning spirits. They also contain symbols, incantations, and charms.

When you study magical history you will see men have always taken a more ceremonial role in traditional magic. They were the master of ceremonies, conducting rituals and animal sacrifices as ritual specialists. They were not as psychic as women so they came up with methods to tap into the binary code and algorithm of physical reality using mathematics and numerology. In the IFA Orisha religion that comes from West Africa a male priest is called a Babalawo while female priestesses are called Iyanifas. When a person is suffering from maladies they will find one to perform divination for them. After the spirit world is consulted they recommend sacrifices and provide the "medicine" the client needs to resolve their problem.

The Root Doctor or Rootworker practiced medicinal and magical herbalism before, during, and after slavery in the American South. Hoodoo is African American slave magic. It was not only a method of blocking energetic and psychic attacks from their colonizers, but also how they stayed alive. Hoodooist, like their African ancestors, would sing songs while making herbal preparations sometimes with a Bible turned open to a Psalm that corresponded with their intent. The Africans that were brought from the Kingdom of the Kongo to the Caribbean developed their own system of working with the spirits of nature and the dead. They created a spiritual system based on the magical and medicinal herbalism taught to them by the Indigenous Taino people, the first Native Americans to be colonized in the new world. The Kingdom of the Kongo was a Catholic nation before Christopher Columbus discovered America. The Ngangas (shamans and ritual specialists) had already started syncretizing Christianity and traditional religion before they got to Cuba. Rootwork and Palo would be considered witchcraft to many people in the diaspora community.

Another thing is it was a lifestyle. For a traditional practitioner life is magical and not something separate from their mundane affairs. To us everything is alive and contains spirit. Now I feel the need to list my credentials to recommend myself and my training for you. My priestess in the IFA Orisha religion is Iya Daniyah Fa Omi Sango. My Manbo in Haitian Vodou is Lalune Bwiye Bon Manbo and I am a member of her fraternity Lod Mayifado Sakre. Almost 25 years ago I self initiated as a Wiccan. Eventually I was initiated into the Palo Mayombe tradition. I had no idea how rich, deep, and satisfying my life would become studying the occult wisdom of the world. People have to talk and if you do not state your credentials they try to discredit you. My best friends are the infamous Witchfoot and the Hoodoo Queen Mama Sunfiyahh from TikTok. I run with old school witches and rootworkers that seek to preserve traditional ways, the way of our magical practicing Ancestors. If you have a problem with anything I say in this book, you can go talk to those four women about me. Just remember everyone else's opinions about you do not matter, and their feelings dont matter either. Because you are on your journey and no one can tell you how to worship God. No one can tell you how to handle your own ancestors. You are the only person who dreams your dreams. And in the end it's all about you. We need to address the elephant in the room, the one I anger people on most frequently on TikTok:

## Intention is not enough to practice witchcraft

No, your intention is not all you need to practice witchcraft. It is called witchCRAFT because it's a craft, something you do manually. If you are a witch you use magical, medicinal, and poisonous herbs and oils in your practice. Putting a statue of a god or goddess on an altar and praying to it is not witchcraft, that's neo paganism. Witchcraft in of itself does not require the cooperation of a deity. Witchcraft is not performed by doing meditation. That is mentalism. You might have psychic abilities, that still does not make you a witch. Talking to the dead does not make you a witch, that is mediumship or spiritism. Only practitioners that work with nature... and I mean trees, plants, herbs, oils, rocks, crystals, dirt, bones, blood, and the five elements are witches. Inviting ancestors, spirits of the dead, faeries, Loa, Orishas, gods and goddesses, or saints to be part of your work is up to you and based on your spirituality / religion. That is witchcraft combined with spiritism / spiritualism. A moron on TikTok made a video response to me by trying to explain subatomic particles, how plants are made of atoms, and using quantum mechanics to rebuttal my statement. And that is New Age bull shit, and that is crazy.

This stance might be upsetting if you have been following influencers who use the term witch as an aesthetic or a social identity. You have to do a lot more than paint your nails black, wear a pointy hat, and sport pentagram jewelry. The most powerful witches I know would never stand out in a crowd. That is because they studied magic and became adepts at a time when witchcraft was considered evil, satanic, and was frowned upon by the general public. You can find these old school, Gen X and older, witches getting attacked on Witchtok everyday for trying to preserve this traditional approach to witchcraft. We had to go to the library to get books on the occult. We connected in chat rooms and message boards online to share secrets. You have to understand that real witchcraft is not Hollywood. It is your intention combined with carbon based materials in harmony with astrological correspondences that produce results. There is a right way and wrong way to practice witchcraft and I am going to use baking a cake as an example.

You can not say that you are going to bake a cake without using a recipe and timing the process correctly. Unless you are a trained chef, with years of experience and know formulas to experiment with, your attempt of successfully making a cake from scratch is low. You can not take a bowl and put whatever you "feel" should be in the cake with no measurements or the proper ingredients. You can not put it in the oven at whatever temperature you "feel" it should be for however long you "feel" it should bake for. Any untrained cook who tries to bake a cake like that is not going to get a cake. In the same manner witchcraft uses known and trusted correspondences to manipulate energy with astronomical observations that go back thousands of years. That means gathering the proper materials and timing the work accordingly. And I would like to add that traditional witches foraged their own herbs locally. They used the materials they had access to in the geographical region they lived. There was no Amazon that would deliver all your magical supplies with two day shipping.

Also witchcraft is not mentalism, it does not just happen in your mind. You need physical ingredients to practice witchcraft. If I wanted to make a money bowl I would get a green bowl (the color of money) and fill it with dirt and grass I dug up from a bank parking lot. People transact money at the bank and the soil holds the vibration of financial exchange. I would add ingredients that show sympathy towards wealth and prosperity like cinnamon and rice. I would put a green candle beside it and drop 21 pennies in the bowl. I would top it off by putting sticks of incense associated with luck in the bowl itself and burn them regularly. I would put the money bowl somewhere in my house where I would see it frequently. It will remind me that I am trying to draw wealth. That's casting a spell using witchcraft. If I don't have all the stuff I just mentioned it's not witchcraft. You have to cast a spell using physical things for this to work. And I would do it during a waxing or full moon on the day and hour of the Sun or Venus (both deal with wealth). And if I wanted to be thoroughly on point I would check the Nakshatras and make sure I was doing my work in a favorable Lunar Mansion. That is how I practice astrological magic.

There has never been a better time to start learning traditional witchcraft and astrological magic because we have so many apps that can calculate a chart in moments. Casting a chart and determining the best day and time to cast a spell is simple. Deciding what candles, herbs, essential oils, incense, and crystals to use for your "working" is why I wrote this book. This is actually a manual not a book and it comprises all the handouts I use in my spiritual mentorship program. I teach a free course on witchcraft and traditional magic on my YouTube channel Philip Ryan Deal. If you are interested in learning how to practice witchcraft like I do please become a subscriber. Any witch with a few months of experience will understand how to use this manual of correspondences. I will not leave you hanging, I will teach you how to put all the information together in the end.

There is a caveat to this manual and my practice. I practice

Vedic astrology and all my calculations are based sidereally on the Galactic Center. Vedic astrology, also called Jyotish (the science of light), can help you evaluate your mental conditioning and emotional patterns. At the moment of your birth, when you took your first breath, you became embodied. You are a spiritual being having a physical experience. And all the forces at play in the universe at that moment determined the experiences you are going to have in life. Your birth chart is like a life reading that determines the struggles you will encounter and how to avoid them. The relationship you have with the planets affect you everyday as they transit the Zodiac. Especially the Moon.

Understanding the Moon's phases and knowing the most auspicious time to cast a spell is witchcraft 101. This manual is the next level up. You will be learning about the Nakshatras (Lunar Mansions) and the recommended times for performing any given magical act. Everything is energy and it is that energy we are tapping into when we practice witchcraft (magical and medicinal herbalism) in harmony with celestial forces. Doing spiritual work with the support of these energies will empower your magic in ways you can't imagine. You have to try it for yourself, just like a scientist, to see the results. Witchcraft is an art and a science. We use the scientific method when approaching spell casting. First I want to touch on the Indo-European Language family and Sanskrit. I will be using Sanskrit terms and the names of the Vedic gods associated with each planet. The Nakshatra system is unique to Vedic astrology and so Sanskrit terminology must be used. It is not super complicated. And it doesn't matter what you call the planet because they have different names in every tongue and dialect according to their culture. For the Most part Western and Sidereal astrology both have the same understanding as to the nature of the signs and planets. The benefit of working with Vedic astrology is that it combines both the solar and lunar calendars harmonizing the most auspicious times for doing any particular thing from casting a spell to driving in a car.

# PROTO AND INDO-EUROPEAN LANGUAGES

The Proto-Indo-European language (PIE) is the hypothetical reconstructed ancestor of the Indo-European languages, the most widely spoken language family in the world. Sanskrit, an ancient language of India, and many European languages are descendants of this proto-language. Linguists have found numerous similarities in vocabulary, grammar, and syntax between Sanskrit and many European languages. For example, the English word "mother" is "mātṛ" in Sanskrit, "mater" in Latin and "mutter" in German, showing a clear lineage from a common ancestral language. The Proto-Indo-European language was never written down, but has been reconstructed by linguists over the last two centuries using the comparative method, which compares languages to find their common roots. Discoveries in archaeology, anthropology, and genetics have also given support to the theory of a common Indo-European origin. The Proto-Indo-European religion, from which the religious beliefs and practices of the historical and modern Indo-European ethnic groups have descended, had a pantheon of gods. The nature of these gods is reconstructed based on shared characteristics in historical Indo-European cultures and linguistic analysis.

**The Indo-European languages and Sanskrit**

The Indo-European languages are a family of several hundred related languages and dialects. There are about 445 living Indo-European languages, according to the estimate by Ethnologue, with over two-thirds (313) of them belonging to the Indo-Iranian branch. The most widely spoken Indo-European languages by native speakers are Spanish, English, Hindi, Portuguese, Bengali, Russian, Persian and Punjabi, each with over 100 million speakers, with German, French and Italian having over 50 million. The Indo-European family includes most of the languages of Europe, and many languages in Southwest Asia, Central Asia, and South Asia. It was first identified in the late 18th century, and the common ancestral Proto-Indo-European language has been reconstructed by linguists during the 19th and early 20th centuries.

Sanskrit is an ancient classical language of India, and one of the earliest attested members of the Indo-European language family. It is the primary liturgical language of Hinduism and also used in Buddhism and Jainism. Sanskrit is known for its complex grammar and incredibly rich literary tradition. The earliest known work in Sanskrit is the Rigveda, a collection of Brahmanical texts, which date to about 1500 BCE. For centuries, knowledge and learning in areas like philosophy, mathematics, astronomy, and medicine were primarily written in Sanskrit across the Indian subcontinent. Sanskrit's influence is seen in many modern Indian languages, and it is still used in ceremonial functions and religious rituals. Despite its limited use in everyday life today, Sanskrit remains an important part of the cultural and religious identity of millions of people. It is also studied worldwide for its intricate grammar, historical significance, and vast literature.

Sanskrit mantras are phrases, typically in Sanskrit, that are chanted or meditated upon for spiritual or psychological benefits. They play a significant role in many Hindu, Buddhist, and other spiritual traditions. A mantra can be as simple as a single syllable sound, like "Om", or it could be a series of phrases or sentences. Mantras are often used in meditation to focus the mind and connect with a higher power or the universe at large. They're thought to have spiritual power and are used to invoke deities, gain spiritual enlightenment, or for specific purposes like healing, protection, or success.

**To learn Sanskrit mantras, here are some steps:**

**Understanding the mantra:** Start by learning about the meaning and significance of the mantra. This helps in connecting with it on a deeper level.

**Pronunciation:** Sanskrit pronunciation can be challenging. You may want to listen to recordings or work with a teacher to get the pronunciation correct.

**Memorization:** Once you know how to pronounce the mantra, you can start memorizing it. Start with shorter mantras and gradually work up to longer ones.

**Meditation:** Incorporate the mantra into your meditation practice. This can involve silently repeating the mantra in your mind or chanting it aloud.

**Consistency:** Like any skill, mastering mantras requires practice. Be patient with yourself and try to incorporate mantra meditation into your daily routine.

**The Gayatri Mantra**

The Gayatri mantra appears in the Rig Veda, Sama Veda, and Yejur Veda (the earliest Hindu scriptures). Its origins are traced to a sage called Vishwamitra – a king who renounced his throne in order to seek spiritual awakening. Vishwamitra was the first to realize the essence of the luminous spheres of creation through the Gayatri mantra. Now, several thousand years later, his gift continues to free countless spiritual seekers. The Gayatri mantra is:

Om Bhuh Bhuvaha Swaha

Tat Savitur Varenyam

Bhargo Devasya Dhimahi

Dhiyo Yonaha Prachodayat

Meaning:

"O self-effulgent light that has given birth to all the worlds, who is worthy of worship and appears through the orbit of the sun, illuminates our intellect."

You can listen to this mantra chanted 108 times. The best time to listen to this mantra is at sunrise, noon, or sunset. This mantra will aid you in your spiritual evolution. Remember, the purpose of a mantra isn't just to repeat words, but to connect with a deeper spiritual reality. So, try to maintain a sense of mindfulness and reverence as you work with Sanskrit mantras.

**The Bhagavad Gita**

It is very important to understand Yoga and Yogic philosophy before setting out on the path to practice Vedic Astrology. Before you start your studies in astrology you must read the Bhagavad Gita which is the primary scripture to understand Hinduism. It is easy to read and easy to understand. I am giving you my recommended translation by Eknath Easwaran

**Syncretizing Wicca with Vedic astrology**

This all goes back to me being a Wiccan, because I still am one. I dedicated myself to the God and Goddess and was a solitary practitioner for almost 20 years. Shiva and Shakti are the divinities I venerate in Wicca. But did you know that there are Vodun temples in Togo Africa that have Hindu gods and goddesses painted on the walls? Yes it's ok to venerate any Divinity you want as long as you are respectful and showing up with sincere intentions, even if you do not understand why you are doing so. And as a practitioner of African diasporic practices you need to know what you are doing and be guided by a godparent to start working with initiation based traditions. So this is not a free for all. There is an order of service and a separation of the spirit groups. When you are working with Divinities of a certain pantheon do your research and know everything you can about that entity before asking for its attention.

## The Divine Masculine

I have an affinity for the masculine and I honor Lord Shiva as Pashupati, "Lord of the Animals", in his horned form. I wrote a poem as the embodiment of the Divine Masculine and I want to share it with you now.

## Your Divine Masculine

I am the Wild God

The god of ecstasy, Lord of the sacred dance

I am the Horned One, Lord of the beasts

I am the Green Man, I am the spirit of the forest

I am the Son/Sun, The light of my face brings joy to the world

And my anger scorches the surface of the earth.

I have come all this way, across the Universe, through many galaxies just to cross your path.

Through many Avatars and many incarnations I have forgotten myself.

I am the Divine Masculine.

I am the Divine child who suckles the breast of the Goddess.

I am her brother and lover

I am the Divine Prince, Lord of the Earth.

I am the Lover seeking my Beloved.

I am the Divine Warrior lusting after the blood of my enemies.

I am the Divine Father, teacher, and counselor to the gods.

I am the Divine Trickster. I bring chaos that only I can put back into order.

I forgot myself. But in your eyes I became nude and self conscious.

In your hands I released my spirit. In your mouth I released my soul.

You reawakened my soul and I remembered who I am.

I am the spirit of love. I was there in the beginning beside you. Holding your hand.

As the Mysteries of the Universe unraveled themselves I remembered my name.

My name is Love.

### Your Spiritual Path is Your Life

The last thing I would like to say before you move on to all the great homework assignments in this manual is to remember witchcraft is something you do not who you really are. And your witchcraft should look like you. Your spiritual path is your life, not something separate from day to day mundane activities. We create reality by being actively engaged in it. That means being fully present for the experience. When you get up in the morning and start your day with a cup of coffee and a prayer you are on your spiritual path. Being a spiritual person means trying everyday to elevate your consciousness to harmonize with the Divine plan... whatever that may be. The next several small chapters are suggestions for avoiding negative mental, emotional, and spiritual traps that will prevent you from accomplishing your destiny. Do not take the content of this book lightly. There is mad wisdom in these pages sourced from ancient mysteries. Read everything and do all the exercises and meditations as you go. Do not pass go or collect $200 without doing the work.

## The Scientific Method

The scientific method is a systematic approach to understanding the natural world. It involves the following steps:

**Observation**: This is the process of noticing and describing events or processes in a careful, orderly way. It can also involve identifying a problem or question that needs answering.

**Question**: After observing, a specific question is formulated. For example, "Why does this process occur?" or "What causes this event?"

**Hypothesis**: This is a proposed answer to the question based on what you know and what you observe. It's a prediction about the outcome of your research.

**Experiment**: An experiment is conducted to test the hypothesis. The results of the experiment are then recorded and analyzed.

**Analysis**: The data from the experiment is analyzed to see if it supports the hypothesis.

**Conclusion**: Based on the results of the experiment, a conclusion is drawn. If the results support the hypothesis, it may become a theory. If the results do not support the hypothesis, a new hypothesis may be proposed, and the process repeats.

**Communication**: The findings are shared with others in the scientific community for validation, further testing, or expansion of knowledge.

To practice the scientific method, you would follow these steps, starting with identifying a question or problem, formulating a hypothesis, designing and conducting experiments to test the hypothesis, analyzing the results, and then drawing a conclusion. You'd also need to communicate your findings for peer review and further testing.

So how does that apply to spellcasting? First there has to be a reason for casting a spell (observation). Determine which working is the proper solution for the reason you want to cast (hypothesis). Perform the ritual (experiment). Analyze the results. If you do not get the results you want, you have to go back to the drawing board and try again (create a new hypothesis and perform the working again). Get the advice of more experienced witches and occultists for feedback (peer review). If you go about magic in this fashion you will find that some spells you cast work at a high percentage while others do not. This is the joy of practicing witchcraft.

# LIST OF TRADITIONAL FOLK MAGIC PRACTICES

I wanted to give you a short list of the animistic and ancestral folk magic practices that are still being practiced today. What you will find is most traditional witches practice some form of Christianity mixed in with their magic. The oldest traditions being practiced in the Western Hemisphere, especially in the Caribbean, have Catholic elements to it.

**Cunning Craft**

The term "cunning craft" is not commonly used, but if you are referring to historical practices of folk magic and traditional healing, they were often associated with individuals known as "cunning folk" or "wise women/men." These practitioners were typically found in rural communities of Northwestern Europe performing various services such as spellcasting, divination, herbal medicine, and providing advice or charms for protection. However, it's important to note that these practices varied across different cultures and regions throughout history.

**Trolldom - Scandinavian Folk Magic**

Trolldom, in Norse folk magic, refers to a system of sorcery and folk beliefs practiced in ancient Scandinavia. It involves the use of charms, spells, and rituals to influence or manipulate the natural forces and spirits in order to achieve various outcomes. Trolldom practitioners, known as trollkunnig or trollkona, were believed to possess special knowledge and abilities to communicate with spirits, heal ailments, protect against malevolent forces, and influence events. Trolldom often incorporated elements of animism, shamanism, and herbalism, reflecting the close connection between humans, nature, and the spiritual realm in Norse mythology and folklore. Traditional Scandinavian magic encompasses various forms of folk magic and practices originating from the Scandinavian region, including Norway, Sweden, Denmark, Finland, and Iceland. It incorporates a blend of Norse mythology, folklore, and local beliefs.

## Traditional English Witchcraft

Traditional English Witchcraft refers to a modern form of witchcraft that draws inspiration from historical practices, folklore, and beliefs associated with witchcraft in England. It emphasizes a connection with nature, ancestral spirits, and the use of traditional magical techniques. English traditional witchcraft often incorporates elements such as herbalism, divination, spellcraft, and folk magic. It focuses on personal spiritual development, working with the cycles of nature, and honoring the spirits and deities associated with the land. It's important to note that practices and beliefs within English traditional witchcraft can vary among practitioners.

## The Grimoire Tradition

A grimoire magician is an individual who practices magic or sorcery using a grimoire as a primary tool or reference. A grimoire magician is someone who studies and applies the knowledge, spells, rituals, and techniques found within grimoires to perform magical workings. Grimoire magicians typically study and work with specific grimoires or collections of magical texts. They may follow the instructions, rituals, and spells outlined in the grimoires, incorporating elements such as invocations, conjurations, sigils, and ceremonial practices. Grimoire magicians often focus on ceremonial magic or high magic, which emphasizes formal rituals, precise procedures, and the invocation or evocation of spiritual entities such as angels, demons, or elemental forces. They may seek to acquire mystical knowledge, personal transformation, spiritual development, or the attainment of specific goals through their practice. It's worth noting that the term "grimoire magician" can be used broadly, encompassing individuals who work with a variety of grimoires from different cultural traditions or those who specialize in a particular system or school of magic associated with grimoires.

## Appalachian Folk Magic

Appalachian folk magic, also associated with the Melungeon people, refers to a system of folk beliefs, practices, and traditions that have developed within the Appalachian region of the United States. It is rooted in the cultural heritage of the people who settled in the Appalachian Mountains, including Europeans, Indigenous people, and Africans. Appalachian folk magic often involves the use of charms, herbal remedies, divination, and rituals for various purposes such as healing, protection, love, and luck. It is deeply connected to the natural world and draws upon a blend of folk wisdom, spirituality, and superstition. The Melungeon people are a fascinating ethnic group with a complex history. They are believed to be of mixed African, European, and Native American ancestry. Melungeon communities have been historically concentrated in the southern Appalachian regions of the United States, particularly Tennessee, Virginia, Kentucky, and North Carolina.

## Powwow - German Folk Magic

The term "powwow" as practiced by the Pennsylvania Dutch refers to a folk healing and magical tradition within the Pennsylvania Dutch culture. It is important to note that this usage of "powwow" is distinct from the Native American powwow gatherings. Powwow in the Pennsylvania Dutch context is a system of folk remedies, charms, and rituals that are believed to promote healing, protection, and other desired outcomes. Practitioners, known as "powwowers" or "hex doctors," employ a combination of Christian prayers, scripture verses, and other symbolic elements to address various ailments, both physical and spiritual. Powwows may use written or verbal formulas, gestures, and objects such as written charms or hex signs to perform their rituals. The practice often involves invoking divine assistance, reciting incantations, and applying remedies to the affected individuals or objects. The Pennsylvania Dutch powwow tradition has its roots in Germanic folk practices and beliefs brought by immigrants to Pennsylvania in the 17th and 18th centuries. It has evolved over time and continues to be practiced within the Pennsylvania Dutch communities as a means of healing, protection, and spiritual guidance.

## Taino Indigenous Spirituality

The Taíno indigenous people, who inhabited parts of the Caribbean islands including present-day Puerto Rico, Hispaniola, Jamaica, and Cuba, practiced a form of spirituality that was animistic and polytheistic. They believed in a variety of gods, spirits, and ancestral beings. The chief god was Yúcahu, the god of cassava (their main crop) and the sea, and his mother Atabey, who was the goddess of fresh water and fertility. There were also a host of other deities, collectively known as cemís or zemís, each with control over different aspects of the natural world. In addition to these deities, the Taíno also believed in the spiritual power of certain objects and places, and they practiced various rituals and ceremonies to honor these spirits and gods, often involving music, dance, and the use of cohoba, a hallucinogenic substance, to induce visions and connect with the spiritual realm.

## Espiritismo Cruzado

Espiritismo Cruzado, also known as Crossed Spiritism, is a syncretic spiritual and religious practice that originated in Cuba. It combines elements of Kardecist Spiritism, an Allan Kardec-inspired doctrine that emphasizes communication with spirits, with Afro-Cuban religious traditions such as Santeria (or Lucumi) and Palo Mayombe. In Espiritismo Cruzado, practitioners seek to establish communication with spirits, including ancestors, guides, and religious entities from both Kardecist Spiritism and Afro-Cuban traditions. The practice involves rituals, prayers, offerings, and mediumship sessions where mediums act as intermediaries between the physical and spiritual realms. Crossed Spiritism incorporates elements of Christian prayers, Catholic saints, African orishas, and spirit guides from various spiritual traditions. The goal is to seek healing, guidance, and spiritual development through the interaction with these spiritual entities. Espiritismo Cruzado reflects the cultural blending and syncretism that has occurred in Cuba, where diverse spiritual traditions have intersected and influenced one another. It is practiced by individuals and communities who embrace this combination of spiritual beliefs and practices.

## Palo Mayombe

Palo Mayombe, also known simply as Palo, is an Afro-Caribbean religion and spiritual practice that originated in the Congo region of Africa and was later brought to the Americas through the transatlantic slave trade. It is primarily practiced in Cuba, the Dominican Republic, and other Caribbean countries. Palo Mayombe involves the veneration of spirits, known as nfumbe or mpungo, who are believed to have the power to influence various aspects of life. These spirits are often associated with the forces of nature, ancestors, and certain objects such as sacred trees or bones. Rituals in Palo Mayombe involve offerings, sacrifices, and ceremonies that seek assistance, protection, healing, and guidance from the spirits. Palo Mayombe is characterized by its use of sacred objects and tools, including cauldrons, iron implements, and sacred sticks or "ngangas" that serve as containers for the spirits. It also incorporates elements of herbalism, divination, and ancestral reverence. While Palo Mayombe shares some similarities with other Afro-Caribbean religions like Santeria, it has its own distinct practices, cosmology, and spiritual traditions.

**Hoodoo and Rootwork**

A rootworker is an individual who practices folk magic and spiritual healing, primarily drawing from African American folk traditions. Rootwork, also known as hoodoo or conjure, is a system of magical and spiritual practices that originated in African diasporic communities in the United States. Rootworkers often work with roots, herbs, minerals, candles, and other materials to create spells, charms, potions, and ritualistic practices for various purposes such as healing, protection, love, and prosperity. Rootwork incorporates elements from African, Native American, and European magical traditions and is deeply rooted in cultural and spiritual beliefs.

**IFA - Traditional West African Religion**

Isese, in Yoruba culture, refers to the traditional religious and spiritual practices of the Yoruba people. It is a system of beliefs and rituals that is deeply rooted in the Yoruba worldview and encompasses various aspects of life, including spirituality, cosmology, ethics, and morality. Isese recognizes a supreme being known as Olodumare and involves the veneration of ancestral spirits, Orishas (deities), and other spiritual entities. It involves rituals, offerings, divination, and other practices aimed at maintaining balance, harmony, and connection with the divine and the spiritual realm. Isese plays a significant role in Yoruba society and is celebrated during festivals and ceremonies throughout the year.

The Odu Ifa refers to the sacred verses or texts of the Ifa divination system, which is an integral part of Yoruba religion and spirituality. Ifa is a divination system that originated among the Yoruba people of Nigeria and is widely practiced in West Africa and the diaspora. It involves the consultation of trained priests known as Babalawos, who use a set of divination tools and the Odu Ifa to communicate with Orunmila, the Orisha of wisdom and divination. The Odu Ifa consists of a collection of 256 Odu, which are combinations of binary patterns known as "Ese" or "Ikin." Each Odu represents a specific energy, wisdom, and guidance for individuals seeking advice or solutions to their problems. The Odu Ifa texts contain verses, stories, proverbs, and teachings that provide insight into various aspects of life, including personal challenges, relationships, health, wealth, and spiritual growth. The Odu Ifa is considered a vast body of knowledge and serves as a guide for moral conduct, decision-making, and understanding the will of the Orishas and Olodumare, the supreme being in Yoruba cosmology.

### Santeria - Lucumi

Santeria, also known as La Regla de Ocha or Luvumi, is a religious and spiritual practice that originated in Cuba and has spread to various parts of the world, particularly in the Caribbean and the Americas. It combines elements of Yoruba religion, which was brought by enslaved Africans to the Americas, with elements of Catholicism. Santeria blends the worship of orishas (deities or spirits) from the Yoruba pantheon with Catholic saints. Practitioners believe in a supreme creator, Olodumare, and honor various orishas, such as Oshun, Yemaya, and Shango, among others. Rituals, offerings, drumming, and dance are important aspects of Santeria ceremonies. The religion places a strong emphasis on personal spiritual development, healing, divination, and seeking guidance from the orishas. It has a rich mythological and ritualistic tradition and is practiced by individuals and communities who identify as Santeros or followers of Santeria.

## Haitian Vodou - 21 Divisions

In Vodou, or the 21 Divisions, practitioners venerate a pantheon of spirits or deities known as "los misterios" or "las divisiones." These spirits are believed to have specific characteristics, powers, and domains of influence. They may include African deities, Catholic saints, Indigenous spirits, and ancestral figures. Rituals and ceremonies in the 21 Divisions involve offerings, prayers, drumming, dancing, and divination. The tradition places importance on healing, protection, spiritual guidance, and personal transformation. It is often practiced within family or community settings and has variations in rituals and practices depending on the specific lineage or house. While the 21 Divisions shares some similarities with other Afro-Caribbean traditions, it has its own distinct pantheon and practices that have evolved in the Dominican Republic and other Caribbean regions.

## Hindu Folk Magic

Hindu folk magic, also known as Indian folk magic or desi magic, refers to a wide range of magical practices and beliefs that are deeply rooted in the traditional folk culture of India. It encompasses various forms of folk healing, divination, protection, and spellcasting that have been passed down through generations. Hindu folk magic often incorporates elements of animism, astrology, folk beliefs, and regional deities. It can involve the use of amulets, charms, talismans, herbs, rituals, and mantras to address everyday problems, bring good fortune, ward off evil, or fulfill specific desires. These practices vary from region to region, reflecting the diverse cultural and religious traditions within Hinduism across India.

## About Syncretism

Religious syncretism, or religious synchronism, refers to the blending or merging of different religious beliefs, practices, or traditions. It occurs when elements from two or more religious systems are combined, resulting in a new, hybrid form of religious expression. This can happen through cultural interactions, colonization, migration, or other forms of contact between different religious communities. Syncretism often leads to the creation of unique religious rituals, symbols, and beliefs that incorporate elements from multiple traditions. Most folk magic practices, including traditional witchcraft, are going to have some form of synchronism in it. That is how our magical practicing ancestors preserved the practices alive through the colonization process in Europe first, and then in West Africa.

# ABOUT CULTURAL APPROPRIATION

A few things about cultural appropriation: You cannot appropriate your own culture. I know some people that might sound moronic. But I get that question all the time. I hear, "I'm half Irish and half Puerto Rican can I practice Spiritism?" Let me tell you something, it is your birthright to practice the religion of your ancestors. If you go back far enough, we all practiced the same religion at one point in time which was Spiritism. The blood that runs through your veins, in your DNA, gives you the license to be able to call on your ancestral spirits. It does not give you the right to call on someone else's ancestors or act like a priest in a closed religion. That is cultural appropriation.

My time on TikTok has forced me to explain the difference between ethnically closed practices and initiation-based religions many times. So, I would like to talk about what is and what is not acceptable. The general rule is if you have to ask whether or not you can practice something the answer is probably no. Anyone can read any book about any cultural practices. Learning about other people's cultures and traditions is crucial for understanding the world. No one can tell you that you cannot read a book about a religion or an ethnic group or their practices. Let us look at a few religious traditions to understand the differences between closed and initiation-based practices.

Zoroastrianism is one of the oldest religions in the world. But to be a Zoroastrian means that your father and mother are both Zoroastrians by birth. Freddie Mercury was a Zoroastrian. If one of your parents is Zoroastrian and one of them is not, it means that you are not. That means only children with two Zoroastrian parents are considered in the religion. Anyone who is not born a pure Zoroastrian by ethnicity cannot convert to being a Zoroastrian. This is a closed religion based on ethnicity and one of the most extreme examples.

Let us say you want to study Judaism and the Kabbalah. Even if you become a convert to the Jewish faith you will never be Jewish. Because being Jewish means that you were born a Jew. Even though you can practice the religion you are never going to be truly Jewish. That is an example of an ethnic-based religion with foreigners as converts. Hoodoo and Rootwork is a set of folk practices that were performed by Black people in the south, predominantly in the Carolinas of the United States. When someone practices hoodoo and rootwork they are calling on their ancestral spirits. Hoodoo is African American slave magic. And if you are not Black this practice is not for you. No matter what anyone tells you, Hoodoo magical techniques do not come from any other place than West and Central Africa.

Santeria, Palo Mayombe, Vodou, and other religions that come out of the Caribbean are initiation-based religions. Anyone of any ethnicity can be initiated into them if the spirits allow it. The traditions are closed because it requires you to be initiated to practice. When you are initiated you receive a "license" to practice the religion, learn the magic, and work with the spirits. To practice the religion properly one must get Godparents, get a reading, take the first steps towards initiation, and then be crowned with their spirit. All the traditions that come out of the Caribbean have some form of initiation to officially introduce you to the spirits no matter your ethnicity. Performing rituals that are only for initiates is appropriation. There are ways to honor the "gods and goddesses" of these traditions without being disrespectful, but you should seek the advice of an elder.

A closed practice by ethnicity is something an ethnic group does in a religious ceremony and would be offensive for an outsider to perform. That goes for most all Native American traditions and rituals. A closed practice by initiation means trying to perform ceremonies that are only for initiates. You cannot wake up one morning and declare yourself a Catholic priest and perform the role of one. Well you can! But if you go down to the Catholic church on Sunday and tell everyone you will be serving Mass they will laugh in your face. All religions should be treated with the same level of respect regardless of how many people practice it. How can you avoid appropriating another person's culture then? It is simple. Work with your OWN ancestral spirits and guides. By doing so this removes any confusion about what would be and not be appropriate to practice.

You might be adopted and not know who your ancestors are through a family tree and that is OK. I recommend that everybody get a DNA test so that they can find out what their family's migration patterns are. And no, it is not OK to borrow from another tradition even if you do it "respectfully". It is disrespectful for you to feel entitled to take what is not yours just because you want to. That is spiritual colonization. And it is a slap in the face to the elders and the spirits of the tradition you have appropriated. Most of the time if you are not formally introduced to the spirits they will not be listening. At worst you will piss off a spirit and learn your lesson the hard way.

# AVOIDING SPIRITUAL PSYCHOSIS

It is sad when you watch in real time a fellow witch fall into spiritual psychosis. That means losing touch with reality. Psychosis is a mental health condition that occurs when someone loses touch with reality. This handout will show you how to recognize the symptoms and how you can bring yourself back to reality. It can involve:

Hallucinations
Delusions
Confused thoughts
Difficulty concentrating, remembering, and making plans

**Psychosis can be triggered by:**

Schizophrenia
Traumatic experiences
Stress
Physical conditions like Parkinson's disease or a brain tumor
Drug or alcohol misuse

**Symptoms of psychosis include:**

Suspiciousness, paranoid ideas, or uneasiness with others
Trouble thinking clearly and logically
Withdrawing socially and spending more time alone
Unusual or overly intense ideas, strange feelings, or a lack of feelings

Decline in self-care or personal hygiene

Psychosis is treatable, and it's possible to recover. The earlier people get help, the better the outcome. 25% of people who develop psychosis will never have another episode, and another 50% may have more than one episode but will be able to live normal lives. I want to blame the current spiritual environment for the rise in spiritual psychosis, which is just psychosis. Moving away from carbon based magic leads to this mental, emotional, and spiritual disturbance.

When you practice animistic / traditional witchcraft you are fully present and engaging directly with reality and nature. We live in a physical world, not a matrix. If you jump off a building in this world you could die. You might be able to fly in a lucid dream or in a creative visualization, but that is not what we collectively call reality. Let's talk about how you can keep your feet on the ground and not slip into fantasy land by determining that you are still in the physical world.

**Here are some approaches to help you discern reality:**

**Empirical evidence:** Rely on observable, measurable data obtained through scientific methods, such as observation, experimentation, and testing. Empirical evidence helps establish a consistent understanding of the physical world.

**Consensus:** Evaluate the collective agreement among experts and the general population on specific topics or phenomena. Consensus can offer a reliable basis for understanding reality, although it's important to consider potential biases and the possibility of misinformation.

**Logical reasoning:** Use logic and critical thinking to analyze information and draw conclusions. Assess the consistency, coherence, and compatibility of ideas with established knowledge to determine their validity.

**Personal experience:** Your direct experiences, perceptions, and senses contribute to your understanding of reality. However, be aware that personal experiences can be influenced by biases, emotions, and cognitive limitations.

**Verification and Falsifiability:** Test the validity of claims by attempting to verify or falsify them. This approach, central to the scientific method, helps refine our understanding of reality by identifying errors and inaccuracies.

**Open-mindedness and skepticism:** Be open to new ideas and information, but also maintain a healthy skepticism. Question the sources and credibility of information, and be willing to revise your beliefs in light of new evidence.

Ultimately, determining what is real requires a combination of these approaches, as well as ongoing reflection and inquiry. Keep in mind that our understanding of reality is often shaped by various factors, including our individual perspectives, cultural backgrounds, and personal experiences.

**The Physical World**, also known as the material world or the natural world, refers to the tangible, observable universe consisting of matter, energy, and the forces that interact between them. It encompasses everything from subatomic particles to celestial bodies, as well as living organisms and their environments. Our understanding of the physical world is primarily based on empirical evidence gathered through scientific observation, experimentation, and the development of theories that explain the behavior of matter and energy. This knowledge forms the basis of various scientific disciplines, such as physics, chemistry, biology, and geology, which aim to describe and predict the phenomena occurring within the physical world.

The opposite of the physical world is often considered to be the abstract, immaterial, or **Metaphysical or Spiritual realm**. This realm encompasses concepts, ideas, and phenomena that do not have a direct physical presence or tangible form. Examples include emotions, thoughts, beliefs, values, mathematics, and other theoretical constructs. These non-physical aspects of existence often play a crucial role in human experience, philosophy, and culture. They can be explored through various disciplines, such as psychology, sociology, and the humanities, as well as through spiritual and philosophical inquiry.

# STARTING YOUR PERSONAL JOURNAL / GRIMOIRE

A personal journal is a valuable tool for self-reflection, self-improvement, and self-expression. This guide will help you begin and maintain a journaling practice. Your journal can double as your Book of Shadows or magical grimoire. My preferred style of record keeping is called "bullet journaling". If you go to YouTube and search for it you will get a lot of tutorials on how to use the method.

**Choose Your Journaling Method:** Physical journal: Select a notebook or journal that appeals to you in terms of size, design, and paper quality. Digital journal: Use a word processor, an app, or an online platform dedicated to journaling (I use the Day One app).

**Set Up Your Journal:** Personalize the cover or first page with your name, contact information, and any inspirational quotes or images. Number the pages (if not pre-numbered) to track your progress and make referencing easier.

**Establish a Routine:** Set aside a specific time each day or week for journaling. Create a comfortable and quiet space where you can focus on your writing. Commit to a regular schedule, but be flexible and adjust it according to your needs.

**Choose a Writing Style:** Stream of consciousness: Write freely without worrying about grammar, spelling, or punctuation. Structured entries: Use headings, bullet points, or templates to organize your thoughts. Mixed style: Combine various writing styles and formats according to your preferences.

**Create Journaling Prompts and Topics:**

Daily events: Record significant or mundane events and your feelings about them.
Gratitude: Write down things you're grateful for to cultivate a positive mindset.
Goals and dreams: Set short-term and long-term goals, and track your progress.
Self-reflection: Explore your thoughts, emotions, and personal growth.
Creative expression: Include artwork, poetry, or short stories.

**Techniques for Effective Journaling:**

Be honest: Treat your journal as a safe space for expressing your true feelings without judgment.
Be specific: Include details and examples to make your entries more vivid and memorable.
Use all your senses: Describe experiences using sight, sound, smell, taste, and touch.
Ask questions: Explore your thoughts and emotions by asking open-ended questions.

**Reviewing and Reflecting:** Periodically review your journal entries to identify patterns, growth, and areas for improvement. Use your insights to set new goals, make decisions, or gain a deeper understanding of yourself.

**Privacy and Security:** Keep your physical journal in a secure location or use a lockable diary. For digital journals, use strong passwords and enable encryption features if available.

**Embrace the Journey:** Be patient and persistent as you develop your journaling practice. Don't be discouraged by missed days or writer's block; the key is to keep going and enjoy the process of self-discovery.

Remember that your journal is a personal and evolving record of your life. Find what works best for you, and embrace the benefits of this rewarding practice.

## Creating a Daily Spiritual Routine

Creating a spiritual daily program can be a wonderful way to cultivate inner peace and personal growth. It is my belief a little spiritual work done daily greatly increases your abilities. As opposed to practicing magic without a schedule sporadically here and there. Just choose one of these suggestions and try it everyday for a week. Mix it up and create a schedule combining these suggestions. Journal about the results. Here are some suggestions to help you get started:

**Morning Meditation:** Begin your day with a few minutes of meditation or mindfulness practice. This can help center your mind, increase self-awareness, and set a positive tone for the day.

**Gratitude Practice:** Take a moment each morning to express gratitude for the blessings in your life. Consider keeping a gratitude journal or simply reflecting on what you are thankful for.

**Reading Inspirational Material:** Set aside time each day to read spiritual or inspirational books, articles, or quotes. This can provide you with new insights, wisdom, and inspiration for your spiritual journey.

**Daily Affirmations:** Create positive affirmations that align with your spiritual goals and values. Repeat these affirmations throughout the day to reinforce positive beliefs and intentions.

**Mindful Eating:** Practice mindful eating by savoring each bite, expressing gratitude for the nourishment, and being present in the moment. This can help cultivate a deeper connection with your food and enhance your awareness of the present moment.

**Connection with Nature:** Spend time outdoors, connecting with the natural world. Whether it's a walk in the park, gardening, or simply sitting in nature, immersing yourself in the beauty of the earth can be deeply grounding and spiritually uplifting.

**Service to Others:** Engage in acts of kindness and service to others. Whether it's volunteering, supporting a charitable cause, or simply offering a helping hand to someone in need, acts of service can foster a sense of compassion and connection with others.

**Evening Reflection:** Take a few moments before bed to reflect on your day. Consider journaling about your experiences, insights, and any areas for personal growth. Express gratitude for the lessons learned and set intentions for the following day.

Remember, creating a spiritual daily program is a personal journey, so feel free to modify these suggestions to suit your own beliefs and preferences.

# SIMPLE BODY SCAN MEDITATION

The body scan is the most basic, but most powerful meditation technique you can master because it puts you in contact with your energy and nervous system. Use this method to check in with yourself throughout the day. Try to body scan yourself in the morning while you have coffee, at work in the late afternoon, and at night as you are starting to unwind. Journal about how you notice the fluctuations of your energy each day. This also encourages mindfulness.

**Start in a comfortable position:** Find a quiet, comfortable place where you can sit or lie down. Close your eyes and take a few deep breaths.

**Focus on your breath:** Pay attention to your breathing, notice the inhalation and exhalation, how your chest rises and falls. This anchors your mind in the present moment.

**Start the scan:** Begin the body scan at the top of your head. Notice any sensations, tension, or relaxation there. Don't try to change anything, just be aware of it.

**Move through your body:** Gradually move your attention down through your body. From your head to your neck, shoulders, arms, hands, chest, abdomen, back, hips, legs, and finally to your feet.

**Observe and accept:** As you scan each part of your body,

observe any sensations you feel, including pain, discomfort, warmth, coolness, or anything else. Try to accept these feelings without judgment.

**Breath into tension:** If you find any areas of tension, imagine breathing into them and releasing the tension on the exhale.

**Complete the scan:** Once you've reached your feet, spend a moment recognizing your body as a whole.

**Return to your day:** Slowly bring your awareness back to the room, move your fingers and toes, stretch a little, and when you feel ready, open your eyes. Remember, the purpose of this meditation is to build awareness and acceptance of your body, not to judge or change your sensations.

# HOW TO GET RID OF NEGATIVE ENERGY

**Practice Mindfulness:** Focus on the present moment and become aware of your thoughts and emotions. Acknowledge any negative feelings without judgment, and then let them go.

**Breathing Exercises:** Find a quiet space and sit comfortably. Take slow, deep breaths, inhaling through your nose and exhaling through your mouth. Focus on your breath and visualize negative energy leaving your body as you exhale.

**Meditation:** Set aside time each day for meditation, which can help you release negative energy and cultivate a sense of inner peace. Guided meditation, mindfulness meditation, or loving-kindness meditation are all effective techniques.

**Physical Activity:** Engage in regular physical exercise, such as jogging, yoga, or dance, to help release negative energy and boost your mood.

**Declutter Your Space:** Remove unnecessary items from your living and workspaces to create a more organized and harmonious environment. Donate or discard items that no longer serve a purpose or hold negative memories.

**Use Aromatherapy and Herbs:** Diffuse essential oils like lavender, garden / green sage, or citrus scents to cleanse the atmosphere and promote positive energy. You can also smoke clean using the proper dried herb bundles, especially cedar.

**Practice Gratitude:** Keep a gratitude journal or make a mental list of things you're grateful for to shift your focus from negative to positive aspects of your life.

**Surround Yourself with Positive People:** Spend time with individuals who uplift and support you, and distance yourself from toxic or energy-draining relationships.

**Use Positive Affirmations:** Repeat positive affirmations to yourself, such as "I am capable," "I am worthy," or "I choose happiness," to counteract negative thoughts and beliefs.

**Seek Professional Help:** If negative energy is significantly impacting your mental health, consider seeking guidance from a professional therapist or counselor. Remember that getting rid of negative energy is an ongoing process. Be patient with yourself, and practice these techniques consistently to cultivate a more positive and balanced life.

# HOW TO STOP NEGATIVE SELF-TALK

**Develop Self-Awareness:** Pay attention to your thoughts and identify when you're engaging in negative self-talk. Recognize common patterns and triggers, such as specific situations or emotions.

**Interrupt the Negative Thought Cycle:** When you notice negative self-talk, pause and take a deep breath. Visualize a stop sign or say "stop" to yourself as a reminder to break the cycle.

**Challenge Negative Thoughts:** Ask yourself if the negative thought is true, helpful, or based on evidence. Consider alternative explanations or perspectives that are not self-critical.

**Replace Negative Thoughts with Positive Affirmations:** Develop a list of positive affirmations that counteract your common negative thoughts. Repeat these affirmations to yourself whenever you catch yourself engaging in negative self-talk.

**Practice Mindfulness and Meditation:** Incorporate mindfulness and meditation into your daily routine to become more aware of your thoughts and emotions. These practices can help you calmly acknowledge and release negative self-talk.

**Cultivate Gratitude:** Focus on the positive aspects of your life by keeping a gratitude journal or reflecting on what you're grateful for each day. This practice can help shift your mindset from self-criticism to appreciation.

**Surround Yourself with Positivity:** Spend time with supportive and uplifting people who encourage positive thinking. Limit exposure to negative influences, such as toxic relationships or excessive media consumption.

**Set Realistic Expectations:** Recognize that nobody is perfect and that making mistakes is a natural part of growth. Adjust your expectations to be more compassionate and understanding towards yourself.

**Celebrate Your Accomplishments:** Acknowledge and celebrate your achievements, no matter how small they may seem. This practice can help boost your self-esteem and counteract negative self-talk.

**Seek Professional Help:** If negative self-talk is significantly affecting your mental health and well-being, consider seeking the support of a therapist or counselor. Remember that stopping negative self-talk takes time and consistent effort. Be patient with yourself and practice these techniques regularly to cultivate a more positive and self-compassionate mindset.

# CREATING HEALTHY BOUNDARIES

Creating healthy boundaries with other people is crucial for maintaining your well-being and fostering healthy relationships. Here are some suggestions:

**Self-awareness:** Understand your own needs, values, and limits. This self-awareness will help you define and communicate your boundaries effectively.

**Clearly communicate:** Clearly express your needs, limits, and expectations to others. Be respectful, assertive, and use "I" statements to convey your boundaries without blaming or criticizing.

**Learn to say no:** Don't feel obligated to say yes to every request. Practice saying no when something doesn't align with your needs or values. Remember, saying no is a form of self-care.

**Prioritize self-care:** Make self-care a priority in your life. Set aside time for activities that recharge and nourish you. This will help you maintain a healthy balance and prevent burnout.

**Recognize red flags:** Pay attention to signs of unhealthy behavior or boundary violations from others. Trust your instincts and be prepared to protect your boundaries if necessary.

**Practice self-compassion:** Be kind to yourself when setting and enforcing boundaries. It's normal to feel guilty or anxious initially, but remember that you have the right to prioritize your well-being.

**Seek support:** Surround yourself with people who respect your boundaries and offer support. Consider discussing boundary-setting with a trusted friend, therapist, or support group.

Remember, creating and maintaining healthy boundaries is an ongoing process. It may take time and practice, but it is essential for your overall well-being and cultivating positive relationships.

# OVERCOMING CODEPENDENCY

Codependency is a behavioral condition in a relationship where one person enables another person's addiction, poor mental health, immaturity, irresponsibility, or under-achievement. It often involves placing a lower priority on one's own needs, while being excessively preoccupied with the needs of others. It can lead to a dysfunctional, one-sided relationship.

A codependent person is someone who develops patterns of behavior where they overly focus on caring for, rescuing, or controlling others, often at the expense of their own needs and well-being. They may have a strong desire to please others and a fear of rejection or abandonment. Codependency often stems from early life experiences, and can lead to problematic relationships in adulthood. Here are suggestions for starting to change codependent thinking.

**Therapy and Counseling:** Speaking with a mental health professional can provide insight into codependent behaviors and help develop healthier patterns.

**Self-Care:** Prioritize your needs and well-being, regularly engage in activities that you enjoy.

**Establish Boundaries:** Learn to say no and set limits in your relationships, which can help maintain a healthy balance between your needs and the needs of others.

**Self-Awareness:** Recognize your codependent behaviors and understand why they occur. This is the first step towards changing these behaviors.

**Support Groups:** Joining a group like Codependents Anonymous can provide a supportive space to share experiences and learn from others who are facing similar issues.

**Self-Esteem Building:** Practice positive self-talk and engage in activities that make you feel good about yourself.

**Develop Independence:** Cultivate your own interests, hobbies, and friendships outside of your primary relationships.

**Practice Assertiveness:** Learn to express your own feelings, needs, and wants in a direct, respectful manner.

**Mindfulness and Relaxation Techniques:** Activities like yoga, meditation, or deep breathing can help reduce anxiety and increase awareness of your thoughts and feelings.

**Education:** Read books and articles about codependency to better understand the condition and how to overcome it.

Remember, it's important to seek professional help if you're struggling with codependency. It can take time to change these patterns, but with the right support, it's definitely achievable. Here's a simple mindfulness meditation you can try in the meantime:

**Find a quiet, comfortable space:** Sit or lie down, whatever is more comfortable for you. Close your eyes and take a few deep breaths.

**Body scan:** Scan your body from head to toe, releasing tension as you go.

**Focus on your breathing:** Bring your attention to your breath, following it as it goes in and out. This will help anchor your mind in the present moment.

**Practice self-love:** Visualize your heart filling with love and kindness. As you inhale, imagine this love entering your body, and as you exhale, imagine it spreading throughout your body.

**Affirmations:** Repeat affirmations that promote independence and self-sufficiency. You might say in your mind, "I am enough on my own," or "I am capable and strong."

**Visualize independence:** Imagine yourself standing strong and independent. Feel the emotions associated with this visualization.

**Gentle return:** When your mind wanders, gently bring it back to your breath. Don't judge or criticize yourself.

**End the session:** Slowly bring your awareness back to your surroundings. Open your eyes when you feel ready.

Remember, overcoming codependency takes time and practice. It might be beneficial to seek professional help, such as therapy or counseling, alongside your meditation practice.

# CREATING A SELF-ALTAR

Creating a self-altar can be a powerful way of honoring your individuality and personal journey. This shrine represents you and your energy however that manifests itself in reality. In IFA it is called the Ori shrine. The house that holds your Divine consciousness. The "Atma" or "Self" in Vedic philosophy is who you really are. When you create an altar for the part of you that is intimately connected to the Divine, you strengthen that relationship between the two over time.

**Here are some steps you can follow:**

**Choose a Space:** It can be a small table, a shelf, or even a windowsill. Choose a place that feels special to you and where you'll be able to sit peacefully. This is an altar you can have in your bedroom even beside your bed.

**Cleanse the Area:** Clean the physical space, then consider cleansing it energetically as well. This might be done through smudging with cedar or tobacco, ringing a bell or singing bowl, and setting an intention of calmness and purity. Not in the moral sense in the sense that you want to be physically clean, vibrant in spirit, and healthy.

**Choose Items:** Select objects that represent you, your growth, and your aspirations. This may include photos of yourself at different stages of life, mementos, symbols of your achievements, or items representing your goals.

**Include Elements:** Consider including representations of the elements earth, air, fire, and water to bring balance and harmony into your energy field. This could be as simple as a stone for earth, a feather for air, a candle for fire, and a bowl of water. There should always be at least water and a tea light on your shrine at all times. Give yourself a fresh glass of water every few days to refresh your own head.

**Personal Symbols:** You might want to include symbols of your spiritual or religious beliefs, if you have any. These could include statues, symbols, crystals, or candles.

**Maintain Your Altar:** Keep your altar clean and spend time there regularly. It's not just about setting it up, but also about using it as a space for reflection, meditation, or prayer.

Remember, the purpose of this altar is to honor and celebrate you, so it should reflect what's important to you. If your altar starts looking a mess then you need to stop and ask yourself whether you are showing yourself care or are you neglecting your own needs emotionally, mentally, physically, and spiritually.

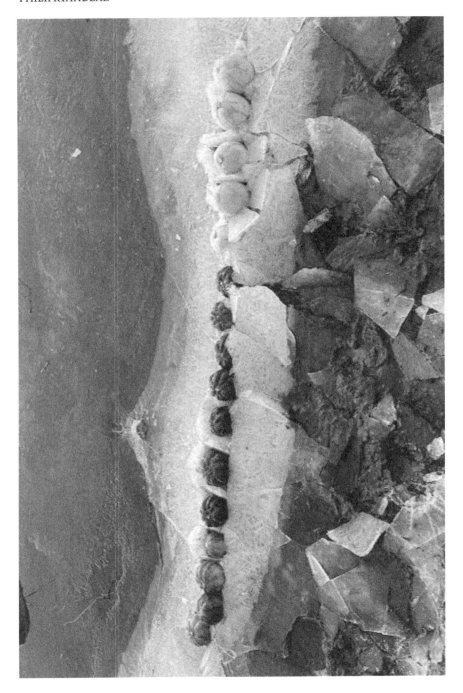

# ANIMISTIC WITCHCRAFT

Animism is a belief system or worldview that attributes spirits or souls to natural phenomena, such as animals, plants, rocks, rivers, and other elements of the natural world. In animistic beliefs, these spirits are considered to be conscious and to possess their own will and agency. Animism is often associated with indigenous cultures and is one of the oldest known belief systems. It views the world as interconnected and emphasizes the importance of living in harmony with nature and respecting the spirits that inhabit it. Here are some ways you can start exploring and practicing animism:

**Connect with nature:** Spend time in natural surroundings, such as forests, mountains, or bodies of water. Observe and appreciate the beauty and interconnectedness of the natural world.

**Cultivate a relationship with local spirits:** Research the indigenous or local belief systems of your area and learn about the spirits that are traditionally acknowledged there. Develop a respectful and reciprocal relationship with them through offerings, prayers, or rituals.

**Engage in nature-based rituals:** Create your own rituals that honor and celebrate the cycles of nature. This could involve marking solstices, equinoxes, or other significant natural events.

**Practice mindfulness:** Cultivate a sense of presence and attentiveness to the world around you. Observe the subtle details of nature, listen to the sounds, and feel the textures. This can deepen your connection to the spirits and energies within the natural world.

**Study animistic beliefs and traditions:** Read books, articles, or scholarly works on animism to gain a deeper understanding of its principles, practices, and cultural variations. Learning from different cultures can enrich your own practice.

**Create an altar or sacred space:** Set up a dedicated space in your home or outdoors where you can connect with the spirits. Decorate it with items from nature, such as stones, feathers, or plants, and use it as a focal point for your rituals and prayers.

Remember, animism is a deeply personal and individual practice. Feel free to adapt and tailor these suggestions to align with your own beliefs and experiences.

**The Five Elements**

In Vedic philosophy, the five Bhutas or Mahabhutas represent the five fundamental elements of the universe. They are believed to be the basic components of all physical matter, including the human body. Here are the five Bhutas:

**Prithvi (Earth):** Prithvi symbolizes the solid state of matter and represents stability, permanence, and rigidity. It represents the body, physicality, and the sense of smell.

**Ap (Water):** Ap represents the liquid state of matter and is associated with cohesiveness. It signifies change, fluidity, taste, and the principle of attraction.

**Tejas or Agni (Fire):** Tejas represents the power to transform, or the energy that drives the change. It is associated with heat, light, perception, and the sense of sight.

**Vayu (Air):** Vayu symbolizes the gaseous state of matter and represents the principle of movement. It is associated with the sense of touch and signifies motion, flexibility, and subtlety.

**Akasha (Ether/Space):** Akasha represents the space that the other elements fill. It is associated with the sense of hearing, and stands for the concepts of openness, emptiness, and connection.

These elements are believed to be present in everything in the universe in various proportions. The concept of the five Bhutas is fundamental in Ayurveda, where they are associated with the body's constitution (doshas), and in Yoga and Meditation, where they relate to energetic imbalances within the body and mind.

**Connecting with Earth**

Connecting with the **Earth's Energy**, also known as grounding or earthing, can be a great way to balance your energies and promote physical and emotional well-being. Here are some suggestions:

**Spend Time in Nature:** Take a walk in the park, hike in the woods, or just sit in your garden. The simple act of being outdoors can help you connect with Earth's energy.

**Barefoot Walking:** Walking barefoot on natural surfaces like grass, sand, or soil is a direct way to connect with the Earth's energy. This practice is often known as "earthing" or "grounding."

**Gardening and Foraging:** Working with plants and soil can be a therapeutic way to connect with the Earth. Gardening encourages you to physically touch and interact with the Earth.

**Meditation:** Practice grounding meditations which focus on connecting with the Earth's energy. Visualize roots growing from your feet into the Earth, grounding you and connecting you to its energies.

**Yoga:** Certain yoga poses like Mountain Pose (Tadasana), Tree Pose (Vrksasana), or any poses that connect your body directly to the floor can help you feel more grounded.

**Eat Earthy Foods:** Consuming foods that come directly from the Earth, like root vegetables, can help you feel more connected to the Earth's energy.

**Spending Time with Animals:** Animals are naturally connected to the Earth's energy. Spending time with them, particularly outdoors, can help us tap into that energy.

**Crystals and Rocks:** Certain stones and crystals, like hematite, smoky quartz, or black tourmaline, are believed to have grounding properties. Holding these or having them nearby can help connect with Earth energy.

**Disconnect from Technology:** Spend some time each day without your phone, computer, or other electronics. This can help you feel more present and connected to your surroundings. Remember, the key to connecting with Earth's energy is to be present, mindful, and open to the energies around you. It's about allowing yourself to feel a part of the natural world.

## Connecting with Air

Connecting with the **Energy of Air** can help improve your communication, intellect, and can enhance your ability to adapt to new situations. Here are some ways to connect with air energy:

**Spend Time Outdoors:** Simply spending time outside, feeling the wind on your skin, can help you connect with air energy.

**Practice Deep Breathing:** Deep, mindful breathing exercises can help you connect with the energy of air. Try pranayama breathing techniques from yoga.

**Fly a Kite:** This is a fun and playful way to connect with air energy.

**Meditate with Visualization:** During your meditation, visualize the air around you, moving through you, and carrying away negative energy.

**Aromatherapy:** Essential oils like lavender, peppermint, and eucalyptus are associated with the air element. Use them in a diffuser and inhale their scents deeply.

**Travel:** Air is associated with freedom and adventure. Traveling, especially to new places, can help you connect with air energy.

**Air-related Crystals:** Certain crystals, like clear quartz, sodalite, and amethyst, are associated with air energy. Hold them, meditate with them, or carry them with you.

**Listen to Wind Instruments:** Listening to music, especially wind instruments like the flute or saxophone, can help you connect with air energy.

**Keep Windows Open:** Let fresh air circulate in your living and working spaces. This not only refreshes the atmosphere but also helps connect with the element of air.

**Feather Observation:** Watch birds fly or simply observe a feather. Birds and feathers have strong symbolic ties to the air element. Remember, the goal is to be mindful and present during these activities, opening yourself to the energy of air and allowing it to inspire and energize you.

## Connecting with Fire

Connecting with the **Energy of Fire** can help ignite your inner strength, passion, and creativity. Here are some ways to connect with fire energy:

**Light a Candle:** Spend some time gazing into the flame of a candle. Notice its warmth, its movement, and its colors. This can also be a form of meditation.

**Enjoy a Bonfire or Fireplace:** If you have the opportunity, sitting near a bonfire or fireplace can be a very direct way to connect with fire energy.

**Sun Grazing:** Spend time outside under the sun, especially during sunrise or sunset. Feel its warmth and energy.

**Fire Meditation:** Visualize a fire within you, burning brightly. Feel its warmth and power, and let it fill you with energy and passion.

**Practice Fire-related Yoga:** Certain yoga poses, like Sun Salutations, are related to the element of fire and can help you connect with its energy.

**Eat Spicy Food:** The heat from spicy food can help you connect with fire energy. Be sure to eat mindfully and enjoy the sensation of heat.

**Use Fire Crystals:** Certain crystals, like carnelian, garnet, or fire opal, are associated with fire energy. Meditate with these stones or carry them with you.

**Engage in Passionate Activities:** Anything that stokes your passion and makes you feel alive can help you connect with fire energy. This could be a hobby, a creative pursuit, or even an intense workout.

**Fire Breathing:** This is a type of breath work that involves quick, forceful breaths, and can help you connect with fire energy. Be sure to learn this from a trained practitioner. Remember, fire is a powerful element, and it's important to approach it with respect and caution. Always ensure your safety when dealing with actual fire.

**Connecting with Water**

Connecting with **Water Energy** can help bring emotional healing, peace, and tranquility. Here are a few suggestions on how to connect with water energy:

**Spend Time Near Water:** Visit a body of water such as a beach, lake, river, or even a local fountain or pond. Take time to watch the water, listen to its sounds, and if possible, touch or immerse yourself in it.

**Take a Bath or Shower:** A bath or shower can be a very soothing way to connect with water. You can enhance this by adding sea salts or essential oils, or visualizing the water washing away stress and negativity.

**Drink Water Mindfully:** When drinking water, take a moment to appreciate it. You can even try charging your water with positive intentions or gratitude before drinking it.

**Meditate with Water:** You can meditate near a body of water, or visualize being near or in water during your meditation. There are also guided meditations available that focus on water.

**Use a Water Feature:** Having a water feature in your home, like a small fountain, can bring the energy of water into your space.

**Practice Aquatic Exercises:** Swimming, water aerobics, or even gentle movements in water can help you connect with water energy.

**Use Crystals Associated with Water:** Certain crystals are associated with water energy, like aquamarine, moonstone, or lapis lazuli. Consider meditating with these stones or carrying them with you.

**Rain and Storm Observance:** Watch and listen to the rain during a storm or walk in the rain. The energy of a storm is powerful water energy. Remember, the goal is to be fully present and mindful during these activities, allowing yourself to connect with, appreciate, and draw energy from the water.

## The Chakras and their Correspondences

The chakras are energy centers within the human body according to various spiritual and esoteric traditions. There are seven main chakras, each associated with a specific location, color, astrological sympathy, and mantra. The chakras are often associated with specific glands or organs in the body. Here are general correspondences between the seven main chakras and their associated glands. This is important because focusing on how your body is feeling is very important to be mindful.

**Root Chakra - Muladhara:** Located at the base of the spine, associated with stability and grounding. Its color is red. It is associated with Saturn, Aquarius, and Capricorn. It's seed sound is LAM.

**Adrenal Glands** - These glands are responsible for producing hormones that regulate stress response and the body's metabolism.

**Sacral Chakra - Svadhisthana:** Located in the lower abdomen, associated with creativity and emotions. Its color is bright orange. It is associated with Jupiter, Pisces, and Sagittarius. Its seed sound is VUM.

**Gonads/Reproductive Glands** - In women, this refers to the ovaries, and in men, it refers to the testes. These glands are associated with reproductive functions and hormonal balance.

**Solar Plexus Chakra - Manipura:** Located in the upper abdomen, associated with personal power and confidence. Its color is bright yellow. It is associated with Mars, Aries, and Scorpio. Its seed sound is RAM.

**Pancreas** - The pancreas plays a crucial role in regulating blood sugar levels by producing insulin and glucagon.

**Heart Chakra - Anahata:** Located in the center of the chest, associated with love and compassion. Its color is green. It is associated with Venus, Taurus, and Libra. Its seed sound is YUM.

**Thymus Gland** - The thymus gland is responsible for the development and maturation of certain immune cells, playing a vital role in immune system function.

**Throat Chakra - Vishuddha:** Located at the throat, associated with communication and self-expression. Its color is blue. It is associated with Mercury, Gemini, and Virgo. Its seed sound is HUM.

**Thyroid and Parathyroid Glands** - The thyroid gland produces hormones that regulate metabolism, while the parathyroid glands help regulate calcium levels in the body.

**Third Eye Chakra - Ajna:** Located between the eyebrows, associated with intuition and insight. Its color is violet. It is associated with the Sun, the Moon, Leo, and Cancer. Its seed sound is OM.

**Pituitary Gland** - Often referred to as the "master gland," the pituitary gland produces and regulates several hormones that control various bodily functions.

**Crown Chakra - Sahasrara:** Located at the top of the head, associated with spiritual connection and enlightenment. Its color is white. It is not associated with anything in the physical world and has no seed sound.

**Pineal Gland** - The pineal gland is associated with the production of melatonin, which helps regulate sleep-wake cycles and other biological rhythms.

These chakras are believed to be interconnected and influence various aspects of our physical, emotional, and spiritual well-being. Balancing and harmonizing the chakras is often a focus in practices like meditation, yoga, and energy healing.

# ASTROLOGICAL WITCHCRAFT

A lot of new witches dread the idea of having to calculate astrology for magical workings. In the old days we used a Farmer's Almanac. Now you can download apps on your smartphone that will generate a chart for you in seconds. I am going to recommend to you the apps I use to follow the Moon phases and planetary transits. I am going to suggest the Deluxe Moon app and Astro Gold app to do your calculations. Remember you must manually change the settings from Tropical to Sidereal calculations to practice like me. I use the Usha Shasi ayanamsa in the Astro Gold app.

To practice Astrological Magic is very simple. Choose the spiritual experience you want to have and make it happen. Use the following guidelines to build your practice. Try something easy like making a spiritual bath. Take a bath on the proper planetary day and hour using the proper essential oils and herbs associated with the planet you want to work with. Burn the incense and use crystals associated with the zodiac sign you are in. This is your first assignment. After you have made yourself a bath, you will understand the simplicity of aligning with astrological energy. There is no reason to be overly stressed about all these correspondences. Whenever you want to do a working use this manual to double check your timing to try to "catch the wave" of celestial forces flowing through the world.

**My Ayanamsa / Calculation of the Zodiac**

The Galactic Center is the rotational center of the Milky Way galaxy. It's located in the direction of the constellations Sagittarius, Ophiuchus, and Scorpius where the Milky Way appears brightest. Observationally, it's very hard to determine the precise location of the Galactic Center due to dust and gas blocking our view. However, astronomers have determined that the Galactic Center is approximately 26,000 light-years away from Earth. At the center of our galaxy, there's a supermassive black hole known as Sagittarius A*, which plays a significant role in the movement of stars within the Milky Way. Our Sun revolves around the supermassive black hole, and our earth revolves around the Sun. Since the Galactic Center is... the center... I calculate all of my astrology off it. My Ayanamsha, method of calculating, is the Galactic Center Middle of the Mula Nakshatra for those who wish to practice as I do. There are many other ways to calculate sidereal astrology such as the Fagan-Allen Ayanamsa which is based on Chaldean and Babylonian tablets. I will leave that research up to you to decide which one works best for you. And yes, you can use this book using Western Tropical Astrology also. Whatever ayanamsa you choose to use, these correspondences will be correct. That is because these lists are based on unanimous opinions of professional witches for the most part.

**The Three Gunas**

In Vedic philosophy, the three Gunas are fundamental attributes that represent the natural laws of the universe and create, preserve, and destroy all things in existence. They also play an important role in magic because they categorize the nature / quality of any given thing. These three Gunas are:

**Sattva (Purity):** Sattva guna is associated with purity, knowledge, and harmony. It is the quality of goodness, positivity, truth, wholesomeness, serenity, balance, and peace. A predominance of Sattva is said to lead to wisdom and is often associated with spiritual practices.

**Rajas (Activity):** Rajas guna represents activity, desire, restlessness, and passion. It is the force of movement, change, and dynamism. Rajas are associated with a thirst for life, action, change, and progress. It is not inherently negative, but when out of balance, it can lead to restlessness, desire for power, and overly ambitious behavior.

**Tamas (Inertia):** Tamas guna is associated with inertia, darkness, ignorance, and lethargy. It is the force that leads to ignorance and is associated with matter and the physical world. Tamas can lead to feelings of laziness, depression, confusion, and disorientation when it dominates.

According to Vedic philosophy, all beings, both living and nonliving, are made up of a combination of these three Gunas. The balance of these qualities within an individual can influence their behavior, consciousness, and spiritual growth. The ultimate goal of human life, according to this philosophy, is to transcend these Gunas to realize the true self.

### Days and Planets

The practice of associating days of the week with planets dates back to ancient civilizations. This association is rooted in astrological traditions and the understanding of celestial bodies at the time. The seven-day week, widely adopted across many cultures, corresponds to the seven classical planets visible to the naked eye: the Sun, Moon, Mars, Mercury, Jupiter, Venus, and Saturn.

**Sunday:** This day is associated with the Sun. In Old English, Sunday was known as 'Sunnandæg,' which translates to 'Sun's day.'

**Monday:** Monday is associated with the Moon. In Old English, this day was known as 'Monandæg,' meaning 'Moon's day.'

**Tuesday:** Tuesday is associated with Mars. In Old English, it was known as 'Tiwesdæg,' named after Tiw (or Tyr), the Germanic god of war, who was associated with the Roman god Mars.

**Wednesday:** This day is associated with Mercury. It was known as 'Wodnesdæg' in Old English, named after Woden (or Odin), who was often equated with the Roman god Mercury.

**Thursday:** Thursday is associated with Jupiter. In Old English, it was known as 'Þūnresdæg,' named after Thunor (or Thor), who was associated with the Roman god Jupiter.

**Friday:** Friday is associated with Venus. It was known as 'Frigedæg' in Old English, named after Frig, the Germanic goddess of love, who was often equated with the Roman goddess Venus.

**Saturday:** Saturday is associated with Saturn. It is the only English weekday that retains its Roman origin in English, named after the Roman god Saturn.

This system originated in Hellenistic Egypt, later adopted by the Roman Empire, and then spread throughout the rest of Europe. This is why many European languages have similar names for the days of the week.

# THE NAVAGRAHA / PLANETS AND THEIR QUALITIES

**Surya / The Sun**

Lord Surya (also known as Aditya) is the Hindu god of the Sun. He is considered the creator of the universe and the source of all life. He is the supreme soul who brings light and warmth to the world. Each day he travels across the sky in his golden chariot pulled by seven horses and driven by red Aruna, a personification of Dawn. Surya first appears in literature in the Rigveda, oldest of the Vedas sacred texts and composed between 1500 and 1000 BCE. Surya and the Adityas, the collective name for the solar deities, were especially popular in the Vedic period, the sun-god being considered at that time one of the three most important gods. Later, Surya was replaced in importance by such deities as Shiva and Vishnu. He is also about forgiveness, charity, and represents the most idealistic parts of ourselves.

The Sun represents the Self. The Atma, your pure conscious awareness. He is the King of the Kingdom. He rules over this solar system. He is considered a malefic planet because he asks for a self-sacrificing attitude with service towards others. At best the Sun can be warm, forgiving, and paternalistic. At worst he can be scorching, cruel, and authoritarian. The rays of light we receive from the Sun supports and creates all life on Earth. So the Sun in good dignity can create and sustain us in the journey towards liberation. If he is not doing well this aspect of our life will suffer. The Sun, You, are the King of your Kingdom. How do you rule your kingdom? How do you rule your world? Is your kingdom under control or under siege? Your ability to know yourself, and trust yourself, will determine your ability to cope with the stress related to this house. So you must spend a few minutes a day in reflection over your life to keep yourself in perspective.

**Here are some qualities associated with the Sun:**

**Physical and Mental Strength:** The Sun denotes energy, vitality, and health. It provides physical strength and mental determination.

**Leadership and Authority:** The Sun is associated with power, authority, and leadership. It signifies individuals who have the potential to lead and influence others.

**Courage and Confidence:** The Sun symbolizes courage, confidence, and a strong willpower. It gives individuals the ability to face challenges head-on.

**Father and Government:** In a horoscope, the Sun represents the father or father figure. It also represents government and high-ranking officials.

**Career and Profession:** The Sun is often associated with career and profession. It could determine a person's ambition and professional success.

**Ego and Pride:** On the negative side, the Sun can represent ego, pride, and arrogance. It could lead to a sense of entitlement or a superiority complex.

**Heart and Eyes:** In terms of body parts, the Sun represents the heart and the eyes in Vedic astrology.

The placement of the Sun in an individual's birth chart can significantly influence their character, profession, health, relationships, and life path.

## Chandra / The Moon

Chandra, the Moon, is lord of plants and vegetation. Chandra is portrayed as a fair and young man, with two hands holding a club and a lotus. He rides his chariot across the sky every night, pulled by an antelope. He is the father of Budha (the planet Mercury). He is married to 27 daughters of Lord Daksha, after whom the Nakshatras are named. The Moon is praised as lord of the wise men and remover of all sins. He also helps to remove the afflictions caused by ancestors. He is called the fulfiller of wishes and dreams. Worshiping Chandra is said to bring relief from all sorrows and helps in increasing mental and emotional strength.

The Moon is easily influenced by the energies of other planets. The Moon represents your mind and reflects the Sun's light just as your mind reflects the light of your consciousness. In Vedic astrology waxing and full moons are most preferred and auspicious whereas the waning Moon is considered to be malefic. The ancients feared the dark moon because it meant a time of darkness and dangers. Today we fear the Moon because we associate it with our subconscious mind. It's very important that you keep a dream journal. Keep it beside your bed and when you wake up in the morning before you do anything else write down what you can remember.

**Here are the qualities associated with the Moon in Vedic Astrology:**

**Mind and Emotions:** The Moon is considered the ruler of the mind. It represents emotions, feelings, sensitivity, and mood. The Moon's placement can indicate a person's emotional well-being and how they react to situations.

**Mother and Nurturing:** In a birth chart, the Moon represents the mother or mother figure and the relationship with her. It is associated with nurturing, care, and comfort.

**Intuition and Imagination:** The Moon is also connected with intuition, imagination, and psychic abilities. It can indicate a person's creative potential.

**Memory and Past:** The Moon governs memory and past experiences. It can show our subconscious mind and habits formed from the past.

**Home and Domestic Life:** The Moon has a strong influence on home, domestic life, and family matters. It can indicate a person's need for security and stability.

**Changeability and Adaptability:** As the fastest moving planet, the Moon represents changes, fluctuations, and adaptability. It can show how a person responds to changes in life.

**Body Parts:** In terms of body parts, the Moon represents the stomach, breasts, bodily fluids, and the left eye in women and the right eye in men.

The Moon's placement in a person's birth chart can provide insights into their emotional nature, mental traits, and aspects of their personal life.

### Mangala / Mars

According to Vedic astrology, Mars is a fierce planet and the commander among the Navagraha. Mars is a highly energetic planet that can symbolize the emotional aspects of a person. Mars is the warrior planet as well as the most virile. Mangala in Vedic astrology rules over our energy, potency, and motivation. Well placed he gives you the power you need to overcome life's challenges. If not well placed he is agitated, frustrated, and lashes out like a bull in a china shop. Mars brings the fire into any area of life and any relationships. If your Mars is well placed you should have a feeling of self confidence, exuberance, and a strong moral compass. If you are not experiencing these feelings you need to ask yourself why. What is it in my life that is suppressing my natural abilities as a leader?

**Here are the qualities associated with Mars in Vedic Astrology:**

**Energy and Courage:** Mars is the planet of energy, action, and desire. It symbolizes courage, bravery, and the drive to achieve one's goals.

**Aggression and Anger:** On the negative side, Mars can represent aggression, anger, and conflict. It can sometimes indicate a hot-tempered or argumentative nature.

**Independence and Determination:** Mars is associated with independence, determination, and a strong will. It can indicate a person's ability to stand on their own and their determination to succeed.

**Physical Strength and Athletics:** Mars is also connected to physical strength, athleticism, and martial arts. It's often associated with soldiers, warriors, and athletes.

**Leadership and Pioneer Spirit:** Mars represents leadership abilities and a pioneering spirit. It can indicate a person's ability to lead others or to forge new paths.

**Technical and Mechanical Skills:** Mars rules over technical and mechanical skills. It is often associated with engineers, surgeons, and other professions that require precision and skill.

**Real Estate and Property:** Mars governs land and property. It can indicate a person's fortunes related to real estate and property.

**Body Parts:** In terms of body parts, Mars represents the muscular system, the head, and the reproductive organs.

Mars' placement in a person's birth chart can provide insights into their energy levels, ambitions, anger issues, and aspects of their personal and professional life.

### Budha / Mercury

Budha is the god of intelligence, communication, fine arts, humor and wit. He is also the god of merchandise and protector of merchants. The planet governs the nervous system. Worshiping Budha on Wednesday is an effective way to get his blessings. Budha is the son of Chandra, the moon God. He rides an Eagle or a Chariot drawn by Lions. Budha is treated as a bestower of happiness and intelligence. He is referred to as the Lord who can cure all kinds of diseases. It is also believed that reciting or hearing the chants makes any person victorious. Mercury is the planet that rules over communication. He influences thoughts, writing, and travel. He is our rational mind and gives us intelligence and adaptability in interpersonal relationships. Mercury can take on the characteristics of planets that he is close to in a chart. People with a strong Mercury always look younger than they actually are.

### Here are some qualities associated with Mercury in Vedic Astrology:

**Communication and Expression:** Mercury is the planet of communication. It governs all forms of expression, be it spoken, written, or even non-verbal communication.

**Intellect and Learning:** Mercury represents intellect, learning, and education. It governs analytical thinking, logical reasoning, and problem-solving abilities.

**Business and Trade:** Mercury is often associated with business, trade, and commerce. It represents negotiation skills and the ability to make profitable deals.

**Technology and Information:** Mercury governs technology, information, and data. It signifies a person's ability to handle and process information.

**Youthfulness and Playfulness:** Mercury is also associated with youthfulness, playfulness, and a sense of curiosity. It can indicate a person's ability to adapt and learn new things.

**Travel and Transportation:** Mercury governs short-distance travel and transportation. It can indicate a person's propensity to travel or relocate.

**Body Parts:** In terms of body parts, Mercury represents the nervous system, the skin, and the hands.

**Dualism:** Mercury is a dual planet, and thus it often represents duality in a person's nature. It can indicate a person's ability to see both sides of an issue.

The placement of Mercury in an individual's birth chart can significantly influence their communication style, intellect, career, and travel opportunities.

### Sukra / Venus

Venus is named Shukra in Vedic astrology and is the planet of harmony, balance, and compromise. Venus is considered one of the two gurus, the other being Jupiter. It is sensual, erotic, romantic, and gives good health and wealth to you if well placed. If poorly placed his influence can result in over indulgence and being overly dependent on others. Venus represents all the good things in life. Venus in general is considered to be the most benevolent of all the planets. The word Sukra in Sanskrit means lucid, clear and bright. As such Sukra is the brightest planet. Venus has feminine energy. Areas of life attributed to Venus are material pleasure, affection to family members, intimacy, luxury, comfort, sensual satisfaction, passions, vitality, artistic talents and fine arts. Venus is an embodiment of love and beauty. Sukra is the guru of Asuras, the demons, and is also referred to as Shukracharya. If Sukra is strongly placed, he can provide wealth, luxuries, worldly pleasures, good luck, peace of mind, a strong intellect, and a very good love life.

**Here are some qualities associated with Venus in Vedic Astrology:**

**Love and Relationships:** Venus is the planet of love, romance, and relationships. It governs the matters of the heart and indicates the quality of relationships, marriage, and partnerships.

**Beauty and Aesthetics:** Venus represents beauty, charm, and aesthetics. It is often associated with an appreciation for beauty, fashion, and the arts.

**Luxury and Comfort:** Venus is the planet of luxury, comfort, and indulgence. It signifies a love for the finer things in life and a desire for comfort and ease.

**Creativity and Art:** Venus governs creativity, art, and music. It indicates artistic talents and creative abilities.

**Wealth and Prosperity:** Venus also signifies wealth and prosperity. It can indicate a person's financial status and their approach to money and possessions.

**Sensuality and Pleasure:** Venus is associated with sensuality, pleasure, and enjoyment. It governs physical attraction and sexual desire.

**Diplomacy and Harmonious Relations:** Venus represents diplomacy and the ability to create harmonious relationships. It indicates a person's social skills and their ability to cooperate with others.

**Body Parts:** In terms of body parts, Venus represents the kidneys, throat, chin, cheeks, and the reproductive system.

The placement of Venus in a person's birth chart can provide insights into their relationships, financial status, creative abilities, and aspects of their personal life.

### Guru / Jupiter

Jupiter is named Guru in Vedic astrology and is the personification of the wise sage. He is the philosopher concerned with our spiritual development. He represents expansion, creativity, religion, ritual, compassion, good fortune, and luck. Jupiter's gifts are Divine grace. Jupiter is one of the two gurus in Vedic astrology, the other being Venus. His energy is masculine and is considered as one of the most benefic planets. Jupiter represents eternal intelligence and the Divine spirit. He is filled with joy, fun loving, and ready to share. Strong Jupiter gives robust health, joyful nature, creates inclination towards administration, management, education, religion, astronomy, astrology.

**Here are some qualities associated with Jupiter in Vedic Astrology:**

**Wisdom and Knowledge:** Jupiter is often associated with wisdom, knowledge, and intellect. It represents a person's ability to learn and grow, both in terms of worldly knowledge and spiritual understanding.

**Wealth and Prosperity:** Jupiter is also known as the planet of wealth and prosperity. It signifies good fortune and abundance in a person's life.

**Spirituality and Religion:** Jupiter represents spirituality, religion, and philosophy. It is associated with a person's moral and ethical stance, their religious beliefs, and their spiritual growth.

**Optimism and Generosity:** Jupiter is known for its optimistic and generous nature. It often indicates a person's positive outlook on life, their generosity, and their sense of humor.

**Teachers and Mentors:** Jupiter is often associated with teachers, mentors, and guides. It represents a person's ability to guide others, as well as their own openness to learning from others.

**Children and Progeny:** Jupiter also governs children and progeny. It can indicate the likelihood of having children and the relationship with children.

**Honors and Recognition:** Jupiter can signify a person's status in society, their reputation, and any honors or recognition they may receive.

**Body Parts:** In terms of body parts, Jupiter represents the liver, the thighs, and the fat within the body.

The placement of Jupiter in a person's birth chart can provide insights into their wisdom, prosperity, spiritual inclination, and other aspects of their life.

### Shani / Saturn

Saturn is named Shani in Vedic astrology and is the planet of hard work and restrictions. He is Old Father Time. In contrast to Jupiter, Saturn is stern, serious, and despondent. When Saturn is well placed he can help you with determination, patience, and the ability to organize your life. Saturn is a very slow moving planet. Saturn gains strength, power, and momentum as we grow older. Saturn is a powerful planet that has a power to obstruct, destroy, and depress. Saturn represents austerity, longevity, old age, concentration and meditation, discipline, and suffering. He is the significator of old age, death, and disease.

**Here are some qualities associated with Saturn in Vedic Astrology:**

**Discipline and Restriction:** Saturn is known for its disciplining and limiting effects. It represents hard work, discipline, and perseverance. It can also indicate areas where a person may face limitations or restrictions.

**Karma and Justice:** Saturn is associated with karma and justice. It is believed to bring the results of past actions, both good and bad, in a person's life.

**Hardships and Challenges:** Saturn is often associated with hardships, challenges, and delays. It signifies the struggles and difficulties that a person may face in their life.

**Longevity and Time:** Saturn represents longevity and time. It can indicate the length of a person's life and is also associated with old age.

**Responsibility and Duty:** Saturn signifies responsibility, duty, and commitment. It can indicate a person's sense of responsibility and their commitment towards their duties.

**Patience and Endurance:** Saturn represents patience and endurance. It signifies a person's ability to endure hardships and their patience in dealing with difficult situations.

**Detachment and Solitude:** Saturn is also associated with detachment and solitude. It can indicate a person's tendency towards introspection and solitude.

**Body Parts:** In terms of body parts, Saturn represents the bones, teeth, knees, and the skin.

The placement of Saturn in a person's birth chart can provide insights into their discipline, karma, challenges, and other aspects of their life. Saturn's influence is often considered to bring significant growth and evolution through challenges.

### Rahu, the North Node of the Moon

Rahu and Ketu set the stage for your life. Rahu is where you are headed and Ketu is where you've been. Wherever Rahu lands in your chart reveals what area of your life you have the least experience in. That means seeking outside assistance from therapists and life coaches can be helpful to give you guidance. Rahu represents craving and desires. It is why we incarnate, or better yet represent the experiences we want to have. Rahu teaches you what you need to let go of. Rahu manipulates facts and could be considered a magician. It's all smoke and mirrors in this area of life. Rahu also can make you feel like an outcast since he rails against traditional norms. Rahu governs one's ego, anger, lust, and addictions. It also governs many awry activities of life. Rahu is often related with the unconscious desires, dissatisfactions, fears, obsessions, ambitions, illusion, hallucination, trance, and unresolved issues from previous lives. Many scriptures describe Rahu having just a head without torso and limbs. He is often portrayed as riding a dark Lion.

**Here are some qualities associated with Rahu in Vedic Astrology:**

**Illusion and Confusion:** Rahu is often associated with illusion, confusion, and deception. It represents the areas of life where we may be deceived or where we may not see the full truth.

**Material Desires:** Rahu represents material desires and worldly ambitions. It is often associated with a strong desire for worldly success, material gains, and luxuries.

**Unexpected Events:** Rahu is known for bringing sudden changes and unexpected events. It can disrupt plans and bring about unexpected results.

**Foreign and Unfamiliar:** Rahu governs things that are foreign or unfamiliar. It can indicate a person's relationship with foreign lands, people from different backgrounds, or anything that is outside their comfort zone.

**Innovation and Rebellion:** Rahu can signify innovation, rebellion, and a break from tradition. It can indicate a person's tendency to challenge norms and break away from traditional ways of thinking.

**Obsession and Addiction:** Rahu can drive obsession and addiction. It can indicate the areas of life where a person may become overly attached or obsessive.

**Body Parts:** In terms of body parts, Rahu represents the head of the celestial snake. It governs the brain, neurological system, and mental disorders.

The placement of Rahu in a person's birth chart can provide insights into their ambitions, sudden changes in their life, and other aspects related to the unknown. It can bring about significant growth and evolution, but often through unexpected or challenging circumstances.

### Ketu, the South Node of the Moon

The South Node of the Moon, Ketu, represents your psychic forces. It is the subconscious behaviors and compulsions we deal with. These traits come to us from previous lives. Ketu is also a planet of rebirth and regeneration. Ketu shows you where you can turn kama (desire) into good karma (action). You have to treat this area of your life as if it were sacred. It is closely associated with God and the Divine. What a house to have it in though. For this house Ketu represents burning desire over countless lifetimes. It's your lust for life. Wherever Ketu shows up there is always want. It's a part of your life that always feels unfinished. There is always something to do in this house. This is where things get complex. To be able to have access to the subconscious mind means digging deep. It requires meditation. It requires a lot of self awareness because these impulses and triggers are connected to our nervous system. They are almost hardwired into the brain. Years and years of acting without conscious awareness of these drives only reinforces the programing.

So in my opinion these subconscious forces are manifest in the body. Or at least to access them requires the study of the body and Yoga. But the work involved is not pretty. It's gut wrenching actually. The mental states have driven some people mad. Almost a fate worse than death. I know. You also inherit the past traumas of your ancestors here, it's embedded in the DNA. According to vedic astrology, if Ketu is well placed, it can bestow wisdom, spiritual tendencies, asceticism, non attachment towards worldly desires and ambitions. Ketu also gives psychic abilities to its natives and makes them experts in the art of healing. However, if Ketu is placed weakly it can give boundless worries, weak eyesight and poor concentration power.

**Here are some qualities associated with Ketu in Vedic Astrology:**

**Spirituality and Enlightenment:** Ketu is often associated with spirituality and the pursuit of enlightenment. It represents our spiritual path and can indicate a strong inclination towards introspection and spiritual practices.

**Detachment and Loss:** Ketu signifies detachment, loss, and the letting go of material possessions. It can indicate areas in life where one needs to let go and move on.

**Past Life Karma:** Ketu is believed to represent past life karma. It signifies the lessons and experiences from past lives that influence the current life.

**Unseen and Mysterious:** Ketu is associated with the unseen, hidden, and mysterious aspects of life. It can indicate hidden enemies, diseases, and challenges.

**Mastery and Wisdom:** Ketu can signify mastery and wisdom that come with experience. It can indicate areas of life where one has a lot of wisdom and knowledge.

**Unexpected Changes:** Like Rahu, Ketu is also known to bring sudden and unexpected changes in life. It can disrupt the status quo and force one to adapt to new circumstances.

**Body Parts:** In terms of body parts, Ketu represents the tail of the celestial snake. It is connected to the body parts below the navel such as legs, knees, and feet.

The placement of Ketu in a person's birth chart can provide insights into their spiritual path, past life karma, areas of mastery, and other aspects related to the unseen and mysterious. Though often associated with challenges, Ketu's influence can also lead to significant spiritual growth and wisdom.

## Uranus / The Planet of Individuality

Uranus represents our longing to express our own individuality in the world. To be acknowledged and recognized. It is the first planet that moves us to meditate on deeper levels of self. Who am I really? Why did I incarnate? Am I fulfilling my destiny? What will be my legacy? This planet reveals, in the house it finds itself in, who it is we are striving to become. Uranus classically represents everything good. The nature of Uranus is surprising and shocking. It's the avant-garde planet. It consistently relates to the unexpected, innovative, and unconventional. In this house you will be able to uniquely express yourself to the amazement of yourself and to others. Uranus is concerned with all things new and is the ultimate free spirit. This planet brings a huge level of unpredictability to this house. Having Uranus in this house indicates you will approach its affairs unconventionally. Uranus brings you a constant sense of adventure and the desire to experience this house from many perspectives. In Western Astrology, Uranus is considered a modern planet and is associated with change, innovation, and unpredictability. It is not traditionally used in Vedic Astrology.

**Here are some qualities associated with Uranus in Astrology:**

**Change and Revolution:** Uranus is often associated with sudden changes, revolution, and upheaval. It represents the areas of life where we may experience abrupt shifts and changes.

**Innovation and Technology:** Uranus is the planet of innovation, invention, and technology. It can signify a person's ability to think out of the box and can indicate their relationship with technology and innovative ideas.

**Freedom and Individuality:** Uranus represents freedom and individuality. It can indicate a person's desire for freedom and their individualistic approach to life.

**Rebellion and Disruption:** Uranus is known for its rebellious energy. It can indicate a person's tendency to challenge norms, rebel against tradition, and disrupt the status quo.

**Unexpected Events:** Uranus is associated with unexpected events and surprises. It can bring sudden opportunities or challenges in a person's life.

**Progress and Future:** Uranus is often associated with progress and the future. It can indicate a person's attitude towards progress and their vision for the future.

**Awakening and Enlightenment:** Uranus can also signify spiritual awakening and enlightenment. It can indicate a sudden awakening or realization in a person's life.

The placement of Uranus in a person's birth chart can provide insights into their attitude towards change, innovation, freedom, and other aspects related to progress and the future. Uranus' influence often brings about significant shifts and changes, leading to growth and evolution.

### Neptune / The Planet of Deep Longing

Neptune brings us the desire to connect with something greater than ourselves. You will have deep longings for the affairs going on in this house. Neptune is like Ketu, but not the same. Sometimes we have the fantasy that if we "do things a certain way" we will get what we want. Or somehow by obtaining your desires in that house you will feel complete. Neptune has a mystical and transcendental quality to it that is intimately connected to the spirit world. Neptune has been referred to as an "insidious malefic." It has the ability to make you live in a fantasy land in this house. The good and the bad aspects of the house can become conflated with each other, almost to the point of being indistinguishable. Neptune is the static that prevents you from distinguishing your own voice from the psychic forces around you. Neptune weakens the strength of the planets he surrounds also. In comparison with the adventurous nature of Uranus, Neptune dramatizes loss, scandals, and just makes you shallow in this area of life. Uranus is very independent while Neptune is very dependent. So you have to be careful about keeping your feet on the ground even if your head is in the clouds. Because Neptune can bring delusions of grandeur, and the inability to distinguish reality from fiction. Either way your fantasies, based in reality or not, will get played out in this house. In Western Astrology, Neptune is considered the planet of dreams, spirituality, and illusion. It is a modern planet and is not traditionally used in Vedic Astrology.

**Here are the qualities associated with Neptune in Astrology:**

**Spirituality:** Neptune represents the spiritual self, the unconscious mind, and the realm of dreams. It is associated with intuition, mysticism, and spiritual enlightenment.

**Illusion and Fantasy:** One of the most common associations of Neptune is with illusion, dreams, and fantasy. This can manifest as creativity and imagination, but it can also lead to confusion, deception, or a tendency to escape reality.

**Compassion and Empathy:** Neptune is also associated with compassion, empathy, and selfless love. It governs our sense of unity with others and the universe.

**Creativity and Arts:** Neptune is the ruler of arts and music, representing creativity and inspiration. It is often prominent in the charts of artists, musicians, and creative individuals.

**Sensitivity:** Neptune is associated with sensitivity, both emotional and physical. It can indicate a heightened sensitivity to one's environment and to the feelings and needs of others.

**Dissolution and Surrender:** Neptune is also the planet of dissolution, surrender, and letting go. It can indicate where we need to let go of our ego-based desires and surrender to a higher power or greater flow.

**Addictions and Escapism:** On the negative side, Neptune can also be associated with confusion, deception, delusion, and a tendency to escape reality through addictions or other forms of escapism.

The placement of Neptune in a person's birth chart can provide insights into their spiritual path, creative abilities, areas of sensitivity, and potential areas of illusion or confusion. Neptune's influence often brings about a deepening of spiritual and creative insights, but can also lead to periods of confusion or disillusionment.

## Pluto / The Ego Destroyer

Pluto is the ego destroyer. Pluto is the planet of breakthroughs. It has the need to destroy ego centric ideas about "I" and "Mine" in the house that it lands in. Pluto reminds us when we try to force, or make things go our way, we only bring suffering to ourselves. Pluto can make you an extremist. You have to guard against extremism in regards to this house. This planet can make you feel cut off and isolated from others. This planet is an "all or nothing" planet. Positively it can give you ambition and a desire to succeed in whatever your pursuits. Negatively it can cause a lot of damage to yourself and everyone around you. There are misfit and antisocial behaviors associated with Pluto. Even one that makes you hypercritical and reclusive. There is a saying that if you "don't handle your issues, your issues will handle you." And that is exactly the case with Pluto. It is a transcendental planet and strongly connected to the collective unconscious. If Pluto brings you pain it is probably because you are receiving an initiation into higher levels of consciousness. It is both beautiful and terrifying at the same time. In astrology, Pluto is considered a modern planet and symbolizes transformation, power, rebirth, and the subconscious. The planet is not traditionally recognized in Vedic astrology but is widely used in Western astrology.

**Here are some qualities associated with Pluto:**

**Transformation and Rebirth:** Pluto is most known for its association with transformation, upheaval, and rebirth. It's connected with the cycle of death and rebirth and represents significant life-changing events and personal transformations.

**Power and Control:** Pluto symbolizes power, domination, control, and manipulation. It can indicate a person's desire for control and their relationship with power dynamics.

**Subconscious and Shadow Self:** Pluto represents the subconscious mind and the shadow self. It brings to light the hidden, suppressed, and unconscious aspects of oneself.

**Intensity and Passion:** Pluto is associated with intensity and passion. It can signify a person's deep passions and intense emotional experiences.

**Regeneration and Healing:** Pluto is also linked with regeneration and healing, especially emotional and psychological healing. It represents the ability to recover, heal, and transform after challenging experiences.

**Secrets and Investigations:** Pluto is connected with secrets, mysteries, and investigations. It can indicate a person's interest in uncovering secrets or their ability to get to the bottom of things.

**Obsession and Compulsion:** On a negative side, Pluto can also be associated with obsession, compulsion, and destructive behaviors. It can represent areas of life where one might experience obsession or compulsion.

The placement of Pluto in a person's birth chart can give insights into their deep-seated fears, transformations, power dynamics, and healing abilities. It can also shed light on potential areas of obsession, compulsion, and intense emotional experiences.

## The Rashis / Signs

**Aries** is ruled by Mars and its characteristics are independent, practical, courageous, structured, self centered, and sometimes extreme. Aries is cardinal, active, and a Fire sign. The strength of this sign depends on the placement of Mars and whether he is doing well or poorly.

**Taurus** is ruled by Venus and its characteristics are affectionate, sensual, visual, art-loving, and stubborn. Taurus is fixed, passive, and an Earth sign. The strength of this sign depends on the placement of Venus and whether he is doing well or poorly.

**Gemini** is ruled by Mercury and its characteristics are ingenious, quick-witted, flirtatious, versatile, inconsistent, and communicative. Gemini is mutable, active, and an Air sign. The strength of this sign depends on the placement of Mercury and whether he is doing well or poorly.

**Cancer** is ruled by the Moon and its characteristics are sensitive, intuitive, nurturing, receptive, adaptable, and artistic. It is cardinal, passive, and a Water sign. The strength of this sign depends on the placement of the Moon and whether he is doing well or poorly.

**Leo** is ruled by the Sun and its characteristics are magnetic, ambitious, loyal, entertaining, forgiving, and warm-hearted. Leo is fixed, conservative, active, and a Fire sign. The strength of this sign depends on the placement of the Sun and whether he is doing well or poorly.

**Virgo** is ruled by Mercury and its characteristics are methodical, clean, discriminating, analytical, shy, and sometimes self-critical. Virgo is mutable, passive, and an Earth sign. The strength of this sign depends on the placement of Mercury and whether he is doing well or poorly.

**Libra** is ruled by Venus and its characteristics are pleasing, harmonious, artistic, diplomatic, influential, and refined. Libra is cardinal, active, and an Air sign. The strength of this sign depends on the placement of Venus and whether he is doing well or poorly.

**Scorpio** is ruled by Mars and its characteristics are sarcastic, vindictive, opinionated, adversarial, mystical, sexual, and strategic. Scorpio is fixed, is passive, and a Water sign. The strength of this sign depends on the placement of Mars and whether he is doing well or poorly.

**Sagittarius** is ruled by Jupiter and its characteristics are philosophical, idealistic, honest, educated, passionate, playful, and sometimes impulsive. Sagittarius is mutable, active, and is a Fire sign. The strength of this sign depends on the placement of Jupiter and whether he is doing well or poorly.

**Capricorn** is ruled by Saturn and its characteristics are conservative, industrious, methodical, persevering, self-willed, aloof, and sometimes controlling. Capricorn is cardinal, passive, and an Earth sign. The strength of this sign depends on the placement of Saturn and whether he is doing well or poorly.

**Aquarius** is ruled by Saturn and its characteristics

are scientific, visionary, intellectual, humane, democratic, eccentric, and sometimes misunderstood. Aquarius is fixed, active, and an Air sign. The strength of this sign depends on the placement of Saturn and whether he is doing well or poorly.

**Pisces** is ruled by Jupiter and its characteristics are empathetic, truthful, psychic, religious, just, reserved, and dignified. Pisces is mutable, passive, and a Water sign. The strength of this sign depends on the placement of Jupiter and whether he is doing well or poorly.

### Phases of the Moon

The phases of the moon are determined by the relative positions of the moon, the sun, and the earth in the solar system. As the moon orbits the earth, different portions of its surface are illuminated by the sun, creating the various phases. Here are the main phases of the moon and the best workings to perform:

**New Moon:** This is the first phase of the lunar cycle. The moon is located between the sun and the earth, and so the side of the moon facing the earth is in shadow. As a result, the moon is not visible from earth.

**Waxing Crescent:** After the new moon, the moon moves slightly eastward in its orbit, causing a small, crescent-shaped section of the moon to be illuminated by the sun's light. This is visible from earth just after sunset.

**First Quarter:** After about a week, the moon has completed one quarter of its orbit around the earth. Half of the moon's surface is illuminated and visible from earth. This phase is also known as the half moon.

**Waxing Gibbous:** As the moon continues moving eastward,

more than half of its surface is illuminated. This phase is known as waxing gibbous, waxing meaning growing.

**Full Moon:** Approximately two weeks after the new moon phase, the moon is on the opposite side of the earth from the sun, and its entire surface is illuminated, making it fully visible from earth.

**Waning Gibbous:** After the full moon, the moon starts to move into the shadow of the earth, and less than half of its surface is illuminated. This phase is known as waning gibbous, waning meaning shrinking.

**Third Quarter:** Similar to the first quarter, but the illuminated half of the moon is now shrinking. This phase is also referred to as the last quarter or half moon.

**Waning Crescent:** In this phase, only a small, crescent-shaped section of the moon is illuminated and visible from earth, just before sunrise.

The cycle then repeats, with the moon returning to the new moon phase. The full cycle lasts approximately 29.5 days, which is known as a lunar month. Witches often observe lunar cycles for their rituals and the full moons in particular are very important. This is a time for meditation, spellwork, divination, healing, and recharging magical items. It's important to note that practices can vary widely, as witchcraft is a highly individualistic religion, and people tailor their rituals to their personal beliefs and needs.

# THE NAKSHATRAS / LUNAR MANSIONS

Nakshatras are lunar mansions in Hindu astrology. There are 27 Nakshatras in total, each related to a certain portion of the celestial sphere. They are used for various purposes, including determining the characteristics of an individual based on the nakshatra of their natal moon, and for finding auspicious times for events or actions. The Nakshatras are organized along the ecliptic - the apparent path that the Sun takes across the sky over the course of a year. The ecliptic is divided into 27 equal parts, each corresponding to one Nakshatra. Each Nakshatra covers approximately 13 degrees and 20 minutes of the ecliptic.

Each Nakshatra is further divided into four quarters or "padas". These quarters are used in the system of Vedic astrology to determine the lunar zodiac for astrological calculations, and they're critical in determining the dasha (planetary period) system of timing events. The Nakshatras are also associated with one of the nine planets in Vedic astrology, and they're ruled by different deities, have various attributes, and are associated with specific symbols and qualities. These attributes are used for interpretation in horoscope readings. So, Nakshatras play a crucial role in understanding an individual's life path, determining auspicious timings, and suggesting remedies for problems.

The sequence of ruling planets follows a specific order: Ketu,

Venus, Sun, Moon, Mars, Rahu, Jupiter, Saturn, Mercury. This order repeats itself three times to cover all 27 Nakshatras. In Vedic astrology, Nakshatras are considered extremely important for several reasons:

**Birth Star:** The Nakshatra in which the Moon is located at the time of birth is called the individual's birth star. This is used to make various astrological predictions about the person's nature, behavior, career, health, etc.

**Timing of Events (Muhurta):** Nakshatras are used to determine auspicious times (Muhurta) for various events like marriages, starting a business, buying a house, etc. Each Nakshatra has certain characteristics that make it good or bad for certain types of activities.

**Compatibility Matching:** In marriage matching (Kundali matching), the Nakshatras of the prospective bride and groom are compared and matched for compatibility.

**Dasha System:** The Vimshottari Dasha system, which is used to predict the timing of significant life events, is based on the Nakshatra that the Moon was in at the time of birth.

**Remedial Measures:** Nakshatras are also used to suggest remedial measures to alleviate negative astrological influences.

In Vedic astrology, each of the 27 Nakshatras is ruled by a planet. Here's the list of Nakshatras along with their ruling Planet, Guna (quality), and the best activities to do workings on.

**1. Ashwini:** 0°00' - 13°20' Aries
Planet - Ketu
Guna - Tamas

**Recommended Workings:** Healing, good for practicing magic that gets results quickly, better health, more wealth, conquering enemies, stating new studies, setting up an altar, transportation.

**2. Bharani:** 13°20' - 26°40' Aries
Planet - Venus
Guna - Rajas

**Recommended Workings:** Good for destructive magic, driving out evil spirits, exorcism, spiritual warfare.

**3. Krittika:** 26°40' Aries - 10°00' Taurus
Planet - Sun
Guna - Rajas

**Recommended Workings:** Winning an augment, winning a competition, money retrieval, avoid driving vehicles, try not to travel.

**4. Rohini:** 10°00' - 23°20' Taurus
Planet - Moon
Guna - Rajas

**Recommended Workings:** Starting new projects, good for building finances, love, marriage, fertility, self-improvement, increase health.

**5. Mrigashirsha:** 23°20' Taurus - 6°40' Gemini
Planet - Mars
Guna - Tamas

**Recommended Workings:** Love magic, new friends and partnerships, travel spells, housewarming spells.

**6. Ardra:** 6°40' - 20°00' Gemini
Planet - Rahu
Guna - Tamas

**Recommended Workings:** Good for aggressive magic, restricting and limiting others, restraining spells, legal prosecution, working with toxic materials and poisonous plants. Also spells to focus on learning new skills.

**7. Punarvasu:** 20°00' Gemini - 3°20' Cancer
Planet - Jupiter
Guna - Satwa

**Recommended Workings:** Spells for new beginnings, remedial action against unfavorable conditions, health, very auspicious time for getting married.

**8. Pushya:** 3°20' - 16°40' Cancer
Planet - Saturn
Guna - Tamas

**Recommended Workings:** Some consider this the best Nakshatra, good for all nourishing spells and charms except for marriage, traditionally Ayurvedic herbs are harvested, assaults from enemies are weak, and auspicious for travel.

**9. Ashlesha:** 16°40' - 30°00' Cancer
Planet - Mercury
Guna - Tamas

**Recommended Workings:** Cord cutting, burning bridges, entering competition, cleaning house of the people, places, and things that are not serving you. Auspicious for good luck spells and money magic, gambling.

**10. Magha:** 0°00' - 13°20' Leo
Planet - Ketu
Guna- Tamas

**Recommended Workings:** Dangerous workings are supported, activities using water are favorable, a good time to honor the dead.

### 11. Purva Phalguni: 13°20' - 26°40' Leo
Planet - Venus
Guna - Rajas

**Recommended Workings:** Justice magic, baneful workings, destructive magic. Entrapment of your enemies, Even though these actions are negative they will produce positive results.

### 12. Uttara Phalguni: 26°40' Leo - 10°00' Virgo
Planet - Sun
Guna - Rajas

**Recommended Workings:** Creating packs, making vows, swearing of magical oaths, construction and renovations on the home, performing rituals.

### 13. Hasta: 10°00' - 23°20' Virgo
Planet - Moon
Guna - Rajas

**Recommended Workings:** Time for getting a grip, positive intentions starting now will have lasting effects, making important decisions, connect with important players in your life they should be open to influence and responsive.

### 14. Chitra: 23°20' Virgo - 6°40' Libra
Planet - Mars
Guna - Tamas

**Recommended Workings:** Health improvement, taking care of your self image, glamor magic, spells to improve your appearance, auspicious for performing ritual

### 15. Swati: 6°40' - 20°00' Libra
Planet - Rahu
Guna - Tamas

**Recommended Workings:** Good time to do anything but travel, consecrate new ritual tools and equipment.

**16. Vishakha:** 20°00' Libra - 3°20' Scorpio
Planet - Jupiter
Guna - Satwa

**Recommended Workings:** Healing magic, herbs and medicines used now will be more effective,

**17. Anuradha:** 3°20' - 16°40' Scorpio
Planet - Saturn
Guna - Tamas

**Recommended Workings:** Love magic, good for all positive workings, home and hearth magic, swearing oaths and taking vows, travel is auspicious.

**18. Jyeshtha:** 16°40' - 30°00' Scorpio
Planet - Mercury
Guna - Satwa

**Recommended Workings:** Confrontation magic, attacking opponents, settling legal matters, collecting on creditors, working with metals is auspicious.

19. Mula: 0°00' - 13°20' Sagittarius
Planet - Ketu
Guna - Tamas

**Recommended Workings:** Breaking pacts or agreements, good for travel, engaging in conflict.

**20. Purva Ashadha:** 13°20' - 26°40' Sagittarius
Planet - Venus
Guna - Rajas

**Recommended Workings:** Liberation magic, helping another out with magic, court cases, traveling is not recommended.

21. Uttara Ashadha: 26°40' Sagittarius - 10°00' Capricorn
Planet - Sun
Guna - Rajas

**Recommended Workings:** Good for love magic, good for marriages, redecorating, glamor magic, starting working now will bear good fruits later.

**22. Shravana:** 10°00' - 23°20' Capricorn
Planet - Moon
Guna - Rajas

**Recommended Workings:** Positive magic is supported, medical and remedial actions are more effective now.

**23. Dhanishta:** 23°20' Capricorn - 6°40' Aquarius
Planet - Mars
Guna- Tamas

**Recommended Workings:** Aggressive and proactive magic, getting new transportation, good or travel.

**24. Shatabhisha:** 6°40' - 20°00' Aquarius
Planet - Rahu
Guna - Tamas

**Recommended Workings:** Negotiations, legal contracts, be financially aggressive, money magic, business magic.

**25. Purva Bhadrapada:** 20°00' Aquarius - 3°20' Pisces
Planet - Jupiter
Guna - Satwa

**Recommended Workings:** The best time to take big risks

even dangerous ones, negotiations, casting spells that can't be predicted.

**26. Uttara Bhadrapada:** 3°20' - 16°40' Pisces
Planet - Saturn
Guna - Tamas

**Recommended Workings:** Making promises and commitments, favorable for marriage, love magic, all positive workings should be successful

**27. Revati:** 16°40' - 30°00' Pisces
Planet - Mercury
Guna- Satwa

**Recommended Workings:** Any working started in a positive nature will yield results, make big ticket purchases, best time to exchange vows.

# PUTTING IT ALL TOGETHER

So now that you have all these correspondences what are you going to do with them? Here is the method I would you to decide how to cast a spell with astrological magic:

**Pick a Spell:** Decide what your intention is and how you want to express that in ritual.

**Pick a Moon Phase:** Is it best to cast during a waxing, full, or waning moon?

**Pick a Nakshatra:** Find the Lunar mansion whose energy best corresponds to the intention. At least check to see if there would be any blocks.

**Pick a Planet:** Choose the planetary energy you are trying to harmonize with and would be most suited for the working. You will cast the spell on the proper day and hour associated with the planet. Use the Moon phase app on your phone to find the right time.

**Gather materials:** Get whatever color candles you need, food and drink offerings if you are working with spirits. Gather your herbs, oils, potions, and lotions. Decide how you want to perform the ritual and execute your spell.

**Perform ritual at designated time and location:** You are trying to catch a celestial wave and life isn't perfect. You might not get all the correspondence and timing that is perfect, but that's ok. As we discussed earlier, trying to cast a spell without using auspicious timing can produce no results or bad results.

There is never a bad time to harmonize with the Universe: Magic that is for your mental, emotional, behavioral, physical, and spiritual self is always a good thing and can be done anytime. Offensive and protection magic is a good thing to do regularly. But if you are going to retaliate or cast a magical attack make sure it is on a day the Universe is here for it.

Next I am giving you my full planetary invocation ritual. It's a lovely meditation and I have never seen anything like it in print. Perhaps it will be the first.

# FULL PLANETARY INVOCATION RITUAL

This is a full-length planetary invocation to be performed as a meditation. Feel free to change or modify any text to suit your personal belief system. The associations in this invocation use Vedic astrological correspondences.

The order of service goes something like this.

Stand in the location you have cleared for spiritual work. Use our method for getting rid of negative energy.

Facing East, you will start the meditation imagining that you are no longer in your room but on the top of a mountain peak staring into empty space.

Imagine the stars above you becoming visible filling the night sky. Start imagining that the Sun is rising on the Eastern horizon. After saying your introductory prayers, speak the invocation to the Sun.

Turn an 8th to face Southeast and invoke Venus. Continue to turn and invoke each planet associated with its direction:

**Sun** - East

**Venus** - Southeast

**Mars** - South

**North and South Nodes of the Moon** - Southwest

**Saturn** - West

**Moon** - Northwest

**Mercury** - North

**Jupiter** - Northeast

**Turning back to the East and saying the prayers for a Good Destiny and a Long Healthy Life.**

Finish the invocation by calling the signs of the Zodiac associated with the four directions:

Facing East shout: **Aries, Leo, Sagittarius!** (Fire signs)

Turn to the South and shout: **Taurus, Virgo, Capricorn!** (Earth signs)

Turn to the West and shout: **Gemini, Libra, Aquarius!** (Air signs)

Turn North and shout: **Cancer, Scorpio, Pieces!** (Water signs)

**Prayers to use for the Invocation:**

**Invocation to the Creator God**

Dear Creator God, thank you for this day and for all the blessings you have given me. Thank you for your love, your grace, and your mercy. Thank you for your presence, your guidance, and your protection. I ask you to forgive me for mistakes I have committed, and to help me become a better person. I ask you to heal me from any pain, sickness, or sorrow, and to comfort me in times of trouble. I ask you to bless me with wisdom, strength, and peace, and to fill me with joy.

I pray for my family, my friends, and all the people in the world. I pray that you would watch over them, provide for them, and protect them from harm. I pray that you would draw them closer to you and reveal yourself to them in a personal way. I pray that you will use me as an instrument of your love, and that I will glorify you in all that I do. I thank you for hearing my prayer, and I trust in your goodness and faithfulness. I praise you and I worship you with all my heart. Namaste.

## Invocation to the Ancestors

Mighty and benevolent Ancestors, I invoke your presence and your power. You who have come before me and paved the way for my existence, I call upon you to guide me with your wisdom and experience. As I stand before you, I offer you my respect and gratitude, knowing that I am the fruit of your labor and sacrifice. From the depths of time and space, from all corners of the world, I honor and cherish your diversity and your richness.

May I learn from your example of courage, resilience, and perseverance, and cultivate the virtues that you embody. Bless me, O Ancestral Spirits, and may your light shine upon me always. May I honor your memory and your legacy, and strive to live up to your expectations. I ask for your protection and guidance, and I offer you my love and loyalty. I honor you and give thanks for your presence in my life. Namaste.

## Invocation to the Mother Earth

Bhumi, Great Mother Earth, I invoke your presence and your power. You who sustain me and nourish me, I call upon you to bless me with your abundance and your beauty. As I stand upon your sacred body, I offer you my gratitude and respect, knowing that you are the source of all life and all creation. From your mountains to your oceans, from your forests to your deserts, I honor and cherish your diversity and richness.

May I learn from your lessons of resilience, adaptability, and interconnectedness, and may I cultivate the virtues that you embody. Bless me, Mother Earth, and may your light shine upon me always. May I be good stewards of your gifts and your resources, and may I strive to restore and protect your balance and health. I honor you and give thanks for your presence in my life. Namaste.

## Invocation to the Sun

Surya, Great Sun, source of life and light, I invoke your presence and your power. You who bring warmth and vitality to all living beings, I call upon you to bless me with your radiance and your energy. As I stand before you, I offer you my gratitude and reverence, knowing that you are the giver of life and the sustainer of all things.

May I learn from your lessons of generosity and abundance, and may I cultivate the virtues that you embody. Bless me, O Great Sun, and may your light shine upon me always. I honor you and give thanks for your presence in my life. Namaste.

## Invocation to Venus

O Venus, Lord Sukra, whose beauty captivates the skies above, I call upon you in this sacred space, to grace us with your presence, charm, and grace. Planet of passion, pleasure, and delight, you shine with brilliance and heavenly light. Bestow upon me your creative force to nurture love and guide me on my path.

Venus, you who rule the hearts' desire, kindle within me your eternal fire. Inspire me to cherish and forge connections with others that will endure eternally. In harmony and balance may I live with an open heart. O Venus, Planet of love, bless my life and heart forever. Namaste.

## Invocation to Mars

Lord Mangala, Great Mars, Planet of war and courage, I invoke your presence and your power. You who govern the forces of action, strength, and perseverance, I call upon you to bless me with your bravery and your determination. As I stand before you, I offer you my respect and loyalty, knowing that you are the embodiment of discipline and leadership.

May I learn from your lessons of tenacity and focus, and may I cultivate the virtues that you embody. Bless me, O Mars, and may your light shine upon me always. I honor you and give thanks for your presence in my life. Namaste. Invocation to the

## North Node of the Moon

Rahu, North Node of the Moon, I invoke your presence and your power. You who govern the mysteries of destiny, karma, and spiritual growth, I call upon you to bless me with your guidance and your wisdom. As I stand before you, I offer you reverence and gratitude, knowing that you are the embodiment of purpose and evolution.

May I learn from your lessons of transformation and transcendence, and may I cultivate the virtues that you embody. Bless me, Rahu, North Node of the Moon, and may your light shine upon me always. I honor you and give thanks for your presence in my life. Namaste.

## Invocation to the South Node of the Moon

Ketu, South Node of the Moon, I invoke your presence and your power. You who govern the mysteries of the past, the subconscious, I call upon you to bless me with your insight and healing. As I stand before you, I offer you my humility and compassion, knowing that you are the embodiment of memory and release.

May I learn from your lessons of surrender, and may I cultivate the virtues that you embody. Bless me, O South Node of the Moon, and may your light shine upon me always. I honor you and we give thanks for your presence in my life. Namaste.

## Invocation to Saturn

Shani, Great Saturn, ruler of the cosmos, I invoke your presence and power. You who govern the cycles of time and lessons of life, I call upon you to guide me on my journey towards wisdom, maturity, and self-mastery. As I stand before you, I offer you my respect and devotion, knowing that you are the embodiment of discipline, responsibility, and the rewarder of hard work.

May I learn from your lessons of perseverance and determination, and may I cultivate the virtues that you embody. Bless me, O Saturn, and may your light shine upon me always. I honor you and give thanks for your presence in my life. Namaste.

## Invocation to the Moon

Lord Chandra, Great Moon, master of the night, I invoke your presence and power. You who govern the mysteries of intuition, emotions, and the cycles of life, I call upon you to bless me with your guidance and protection. As I stand before you, I offer you my reverence and gratitude, knowing that you are the embodiment of sensitivity and receptivity.

May I learn from your lessons of reflection and transformation, and may I cultivate the virtues that you embody. Bless me, O Moon, and may your light shine upon me always. I honor you and give thanks for your presence in my life. Namaste.

## Invocation to Mercury

Budha, Great Mercury, messenger of the gods, I invoke your presence and power. You who govern the realms of communication, travel, and commerce, I call upon you to bless me with your wisdom and agility. As I stand before you, I offer you my admiration and respect, knowing that you are the embodiment of intelligence and adaptability.

May I learn from your lessons of versatility and resourcefulness, and may I cultivate the virtues that you embody. Bless me, O Mercury, and may your light shine upon me always. I honor you and give thanks for your presence in my life. Namaste.

## Invocation to Jupiter

Guru, Great Jupiter, I invoke your presence and power. You who govern the forces of expansion, growth, and abundance, I call upon you to bless me with your wisdom and generosity. As I stand before you, I offer you my respect and devotion, knowing that you are the embodiment of leadership and authority.

May I learn from your lessons of justice and fairness, and may I cultivate the virtues that you embody. Bless me, O Jupiter, and may your light shine upon me always. I honor you and give thanks for your presence in my life. Namaste.

**Finish your invocation with a prayer for a Good Destiny and a Long and Healthy life,**

**Prayer for a Good Destiny**

Divine Creator, I come before you with a humble heart, seeking your guidance and your blessings. I ask that you bless me with a good destiny, one that is filled with purpose, joy, and abundance. May my path be guided by your wisdom, and may I be open to the opportunities and lessons that present themselves along the way. Help me to cultivate the virtues of kindness, compassion, and gratitude, and to use my gifts and talents to serve others and make a positive impact in the world. Protect me from harm and negativity and surround me with love and support. May my destiny be aligned with my highest good and the good of all beings. I trust in your divine plan for me, and I am grateful for all the blessings that you have bestowed upon me. Thank you for listening to my prayer. Namaste.

**Prayer for a long healthy life**

Gracious and loving Creator, I come before you with a prayer for a long and healthy life. As I journey through this world, guide me with your wisdom and keep me strong in body, mind, and spirit. Help me to make choices that will honor and preserve my life, so that I may continue to serve you and fulfill my purpose in this world. May I be blessed with good health, happiness, and vitality, and may I be surrounded by people who love and support me. Protect me from harm. Grant me the strength and resilience I need to care for myself and others. May my life reflect your grace and your goodness. May I be a source of inspiration and blessing to others. With gratitude and trust, I offer this prayer to you. Namaste.

## Conclusion

Facing East shout: **Aries, Leo, Sagittarius!** (Fire signs)

Turn to the South and shout: **Taurus, Virgo, Capricorn!** (Earth signs)

Turn to the West and shout: **Gemini, Libra, Aquarius!** (Air signs)

Turn North and shout: **Cancer, Scorpio, Pieces!** (Water signs)

**These invocations are NOT to be used in the formal calling of planetary forces. But I have included them if you plan to do invocations to the outer planets.**

### Invocation to Uranus

Great Uranus, ruler of innovation and change, I invoke your presence and power. You who govern the realms of creativity, intuition, and progress, I call upon you to bless me with your inspiration and your insight. As I stand before you, with curiosity and openness, knowing that you are the embodiment of originality and freedom.

May I learn from your lessons of unconventional thinking and radical transformation, and cultivate the virtues that you embody. Bless us, O Uranus, and may your light shine upon me always. I honor you and give thanks for your presence in my life. Namaste.

### Invocation to Neptune

Great Neptune, ruler of the ocean and the depths of the soul,

I invoke your presence and power. You who govern the realms of spirituality, creativity, and imagination, I call upon you to bless me with your intuition and empathy. As I stand before you, I offer you my sensitivity and vulnerability, knowing that you are the embodiment of transcendence and compassion.

May I learn from your lessons of surrender and transcendence, and may I cultivate the virtues that you embody. Bless me, O Neptune, and may your light shine upon me always. I honor you and give thanks for your presence in my life. Namaste.

Invocation to Pluto Great Pluto, lord of the cycles of life and death, I invoke your presence and power. You who govern the realms of transformation, power, and regeneration, I call upon you to bless me with your strength and resilience. As I stand before you, I offer you my courage and determination, knowing that you are the embodiment of rebirth and transformation.

May I learn from your lessons of release and renewal, and may I cultivate the virtues that you embody. Bless me, O Pluto, and may your light shine upon me always. I honor you and give thanks for your presence in my life. Namaste.

# PREPARATION FOR
# A SPIRITUAL BATH

Choose a time and place where you won't be disturbed for at least an hour. Your bath must be taken on the day and hour associated with the planet. There are apps like Delux Moon which will calculate sidereal planetary hours. Cleanse your bathroom and create a peaceful environment by lighting candles or incense, playing soothing music, or adding crystals to the space. Set an intention for your bath. This could be a specific goal or simply a desire for relaxation and cleansing.

Gather your supplies, such as epsom salt, herbs, essential oils, or crystals. Choose ingredients that align with your intention. Draw a warm bath and add your chosen ingredients. Stir the water clockwise to infuse it with your intention. Before getting into the bath, take a few deep breaths and visualize yourself being surrounded by a healing, protective light. As you soak in the bath, focus on your intention and allow yourself to fully relax and release any negative energy. Focus on your intention and just soak.

After your bath, take time to journal and reflect on any insights or feelings that came up during the experience.

**Methods**

You can take a spiritual bath one of three ways. First there is a pour over bath you can make in a large bowl, bucket, or basin if you only have a shower. The second is soaking in a bathtub. The third is using a magical / spiritual soap. With the pour over bath what you want to do is gather all the ingredients together with your bowl. As you recite your incantation or say your mantra, set your intention as you add each item to the bowl. Use your hands! Make sure to put your hands in the bath to mix the ingredients. Magic flows through your hands, your palms, that's how you infuse your ashe, chi, prana, or whatever you call personal energy. When you are ready to take the bath, get into the shower and clean yourself first. After you shower, turn off the water and take the bowl of mixture and pour it over your body. Air dry and try to sleep in white.

If you have a bathtub you can fill it with warm water and two cups of epsom salt. Through fresh herbs, not dried herbs, into the bath. Add 25-30 drops of your essential oil of choice. Get into the tub and set your intention. Bathe yourself with the fresh herbs as you recite your incantation or say your mantra. The last method for a spiritual bath is infusing liquid African Black Soap with essential oils.

African black soap, also known as "ose dudu" in Yoruba language or "alata samina" in Ghana, is a type of soap that originated in West Africa. It's typically handmade and used for both cleansing and healing purposes. The soap is traditionally made from the ash of locally harvested plants and barks such as plantain, cocoa pods, palm tree leaves, and shea tree bark. These ingredients are sun-dried and roasted, which gives the soap its characteristic dark color. Water, oils like palm oil, coconut oil, shea butter, or palm kernel oil, and sometimes honey, are then added to the mixture.

African black soap is known for its skin benefits. It's often used for the treatment of various skin conditions like acne, eczema, and psoriasis. It's also known to soothe skin irritations and help to fade skin discoloration. Moreover, it's gentle enough for all skin types. However, as with any skincare product, it's important to test it on a small area first as reactions can vary. I suggest buying a gallon of it in liquid form. You can infuse it with your choice of essential oils. Then place the bottle under the moonlight on a full moon. Keep it in the shower and use it when you feel like you need to clean yourself spiritually. This is not an everyday soap. It is a quick bath to do when you need to get spiritually clean immediately. Only wash yourself from the neck down.

**Here's how to prepare an astrological spiritual bath:**

Choose a time and place where you won't be disturbed for at least an hour. Your bath must be taken on the day and hour associated with the planet. There are apps like Delux Moon which will calculate sidereal planetary hours. Cleanse your bathroom and create a peaceful environment by lighting candles or incense, playing soothing music, or adding crystals to the space. Set an intention for your bath. This could be a specific goal or simply a desire for relaxation and cleansing. Gather your supplies, such as epsom salt, herbs, essential oils, or crystals. Choose ingredients that align with your intention.

Draw a warm bath and add your chosen ingredients. Stir the water clockwise to infuse it with your intention. Before getting into the bath, take a few deep breaths and visualize yourself being surrounded by a healing, protective light. As you soak in the bath, focus on your intention and allow yourself to fully relax and release any negative energy. After your bath, take time to reflect on any insights or feelings that came up during the experience.

**Essential oils and Herbs associated with Planets and Signs**

**Sun / Leo:** Bergamot, Lemon, Orange, Grapefruit, Lime, Rosemary, Cinnamon, Chamomile, Frankincense, Lavender.

**Moon / Cancer:** Jasmine, Sandalwood, Frankincense, Myrrh, Ylang-ylang, Neroli, Clary sage, Patchouli, Lavender, Chamomile

**Mars / Aries / Scorpio:** Black pepper, Ginger, Basil, Frankincense, Cedarwood, Rosemary, Patchouli, Clove, Pine, Juniper

**Mercury / Gemini / Virgo:** Peppermint, Lavender, Eucalyptus, Lemongrass, Tea tree, Bergamot, Lemon, Rosemary, Basil, Clary sage

**Venus / Taurus / Libra:** Rose, Geranium, Ylang-ylang, Jasmine, Sandalwood, Vanilla, Cardamom, Patchouli, Neroli, Palmarosa

**Jupiter / Sagittarius / Pisces:** Peppermint, Clove, Lemon, Rosewood, Bergamot, Cedarwood, Clary sage, Pine, Sandalwood, Nutmeg

**Saturn / Capricorn / Aquarius:** Cypress, Patchouli, Frankincense, Myrrh, Vetiver, Cedarwood, Sandalwood, Yarrow, Spikenard, Helichrysum

**Crystals associated with each planet:**

**Mercury:** Amazonite, Emerald, Agate

**Venus:** Rose Quartz, Emerald, Lapis Lazuli

**Earth:** Onyx, Agate, Jasper

**Mars:** Red Jasper, Garnet, Bloodstone

**Jupiter:** Citrine, Amethyst, Lepidolite

**Saturn:** Obsidian, Hematite, Jet

**Uranus:** Labradorite, Amazonite, Sodalite

**Neptune:** Aquamarine, Amethyst, Lapis Lazuli

**Pluto:** Garnet, Smoky Quartz, Obsidian

**Crystals associated with each sign of the Zodiac:**

**Aries:** Carnelian, Bloodstone, and Red Jasper.

**Taurus:** Emerald, Rose Quartz, and Kyanite.

**Gemini:** Agate, Citrine, and Chrysocolla.

**Cancer:** Moonstone, Rhodonite, and Calcite.

**Leo:** Tiger's Eye, Carnelian, and Sunstone.

**Virgo:** Amazonite, Jasper, and Peridot.

**Libra:** Lepidolite, Opal, and Aventurine.

**Scorpio:** Malachite, Obsidian, and Garnet.

**Sagittarius:** Turquoise, Sodalite, and Lapis Lazuli.

**Capricorn:** Garnet, Shungite, and Smoky Quartz.

**Aquarius:** Amethyst, Aquamarine, and Labradorite.

**Pisces:** Amethyst, Aquamarine, and Larimar.

**Incense associated with each planet:**

**Mercury:** Lavender, Lemongrass, Spearmint

**Venus:** Rose, Vanilla, Sandalwood

**Earth:** Patchouli, Vetiver, Pine

**Mars:** Dragon's Blood, Basil, Ginger

**Jupiter:** Sage, Clove, Cedar

**Saturn:** Myrrh, Patchouli, Vetiver

**Uranus:** Peppermint, Lemongrass, Frankincense

**Neptune:** Jasmine, Sandalwood, Ylang Ylang

**Pluto:** Dragon's Blood, Myrrh, Pine

**Incense associated with each sign of the Zodiac:**

**Aries:** Dragon's Blood, Frankincense, and Cinnamon.

**Taurus:** Storax, Musk, and Rose.

**Gemini:** Lavender, Peppermint, and Lemongrass.

**Cancer:** Jasmine, Camphor, and Lemon Balm.

**Leo:** Frankincense, Copal, and Orange.

**Virgo:** Patchouli, Sandalwood, and Cypress.

**Libra:** Cardamom, Thyme, and Vanilla.

**Scorpio:** Basil, Pine, and Patchouli.

**Sagittarius:** Sage, Cedarwood, and Clove.

**Capricorn:** Vetiver, Magnolia, and Cypress.

**Aquarius:** Star Anise, Pine, and Lavender.

**Pisces:** Sandalwood, Frankincense, and Ylang Ylang.

# VEDIC ASTROLOGY BIRTH CHARTS

In Hinduism, specifically in Advaita Vedanta (the non-dualistic teachings of the Vedas and Upanishads), your true self is called the Atma. Atma is pure consciousness or pure awareness. It is the real you unaffected by what happens to your physical body, your emotions, and your thoughts. It is the Atma that travels from lifetime to lifetime in the process of reincarnation. Sometimes it's also called the Jiva, or soul. A Jivamukta is a fully liberated soul after achieving moksha which means liberation. Today you're Johnny, tomorrow you're Jane. But your true self is immortal, unchanging, and connected to the source of existence. The problem is that we forget this fact when we are born. So, we start the cycle of life again and every time we do, we bring our past karma with us. Vedic Astrology is about understanding your purpose in life and what karma you bring from your past lives. In Hinduism the source of existence is called Brahman. The ultimate reality. Vedic astrology is also referred to as Jyotish, or the Science of Light. To Hindus a birth chart is extremely important as it gives parents a clue as to the universal forces at work when a child is born. Those forces, it is believed, will continue to play a role in the development of the soul as it journeys through life. Karma is a key concept in Hinduism, the law of cause and effect. And it is revealed in our birth chart what kind of karmic lessons we have been sent here to learn.

Some of the main components in a birth chart are the signs,

the houses, the planets, and the lunar mansions. The signs contain the consciousness of the planets that rule them and the planets are conscious beings. The lunar mansions are divine consciousness. Your birth chart reveals what planets are here to help you on your life path. It is these combinations that make you a special snowflake. At the moment you took your first breath, when your spirit entered your body, all the forces of the universe at play in that moment contributed to who you are today. Meditating and reflecting on your birth chart is very important. So please do not just read the chart for entertainment then disregard the jewels of wisdom contained in these pages. Take time to sit down and reflect on the chart as it will also help you understand how the signs, houses, and planets continue to fructify the karma you have accrued throughout your past lives. Sometimes Karma has immediate effects and sometimes it takes several lifetimes to fructify.

It is very important to understand that in Hinduism, Karma is not a "judgment" brought about by God in the same way Christians or Muslims conceive of punishment. God does not judge us, we judge ourselves. The Laws of Karma are completely unbiased. Positive actions have positive results and negative actions have negative results. What you put out comes back to you eventually, even if we do not understand why at the moment. Everything from winning the lottery to losing a loved one is based on the laws of karma not an angry or malevolent God. Karma and reincarnation are the Divine's way of allowing us to learn and reap the fruits of our action while having an unlimited amount of tries to get it right.

Vedanta is life affirming and a very positive philosophy that sees life as a journey, as an adventure. Thank you for allowing me to analyze your birth chart. I checked, double checked, and checked again to make sure that the information I am giving you is accurate according to the most revered Vedic astrologers who have been doing this from time immemorial until now.

At the end of this chart, I will give you the source material and references I used to compile the chart as well as the apps I used to calculate your chart. I will focus primarily on three areas that are overlooked in most astrological charts. Those are the North and South Nodes of the moon, the lunar mansions, and the outer planets. There is also a page on the Gayatri Mantra, a very important chant in Hinduism, that helps bring enlightenment to the seeker... you.

**Your life on a piece of paper**

There are twelve areas of life that are examined in the birth chart, and they are known as the twelve houses. Your rising sign, or ascendant, is always in the first house in a Vedic astrology chart. That rising sign is based on the sign of the Zodiac that was rising on the eastern horizon at the moment of your birth. This is the most important house and sign because it is you, the Native. The first house, whatever sign it is and whatever planets are placed in that house, sets the stage for your life. After we examine the first house, we will continue to explore the indications of the chart house by house. The planets are conscious beings, the signs of the Zodiac contain the consciousness of the planets that rule them, and the houses are not conscious. Thus, I have decided to explain your chart to you covering each house. We will break down that area of life examining the signs and planets ruling the house. A planet will behave differently whether it is happy or sad, active or sleepy, young or old, and that is calculated mathematically. The signs that each planet rules is going to reflect the state of mind it's Lord, or planet, is in. Each planet will also be judged by how well it fairs in the first, ninth, and sixtieth divisional charts. The divisional charts show us how well a planet will do over the long haul. The North and South Node of the Moon, Uranus, Neptune, and Pluto do not receive ranking in the divisional charts. It is not important for you to understand the divisional charts because they are very complicated and are what makes Vedic astrology so accurate. I will let you know how a planet ranks in the divisions in the analysis.

The houses reflect your needs and desires in every area of your life and are divided into four categories namely Dharma, Artha, Kama, and Moksha. Dharma is all about finding your path and purpose. Artha is about your resources such as what you will need to acquire to complete your destiny and accomplish your purpose in life. Kama is desire and the need for enjoyment in life. And Moksha means liberation. The Liberation houses can be rough since they pertain to spiritual matters and self-realization. The Dharma houses are one, five, and nine. The artha houses are two, six, and ten. The Kama houses are three, seven, and eleven. The Moksha houses are four, eight, and twelve. In Hinduism it is believed that all four areas of your life are equally important and that you should pursue the best of all of them. Remember that this analysis should be looked at holistically. You are a little bit of every sign and planet. Your birth chart just gives you clarity on the way YOUR planets behave in a positive and negative way. There is a light side and shadow side to each of your planet's personality which in turn are a part of your personality. Meditate and journal about what the indications in this chart are so you can work on improving your personality as you grow in spirituality.

## The Galactic Center in your birth chart

Our solar system spirals and pinwheels its way around the center of the galaxy. The Sun maintains the same relationship to the Galactic Center as the Earth does to the Sun. The Sun revolves around the Galactic Core taking roughly 240 million years to accomplish the task. The Galactic Center recently received verification that it contains a black hole at its center. The resulting energy squeeze emits a wide array of powerful radiation, most notably infrared in this instance. This infrared energy pressures the subconscious mind, providing the release of learned behavior and memories, both negative and positive, all in the interest of moving forward. - Philip Sedgwick

What is the Galactic Center and how does it relate to us on Earth? The Galactic Center, which sits at the center of our Milky Way Galaxy, is the source of energetic particles that bathe the Earth. With the recent years of the Sun being fairly quiet and Earth's magnetic field weakening a bit, these energetic particles (infrared and gamma particles) have been able to make their way into the Earth's energy field. These particles are thought to open up the subconscious mind, urging us to both release old emotional wounds and traumas and also to engage our new paradigm roles. In fact, the Galactic Center acts as a transmitter of Divine Consciousness. The Galactic Center sits at Sagittarius, which is a sign we know to be about freedom and truth. - Janet Hickox

There is much debate about how to calculate a birth chart, there always has been. Ancient astrologers based their consideration of the stars based on the visible sky. Dependending on how a birth chart is calculated will dramatically change the interpretation. I have decided to calculate your birth chart from the Galactic Center, Middle of Mula. Remember that the first Zodiacs were lunar based. Mula means root, as in the Muladhara chakra, your root chakra. The Nakshatra (lunar mansion) Mula is entirely in the sign of Sagittarius and is also called the "the original star" or "foundation star" where the Galactic Center resides. If we want to calculate the zodiac based on the center of the universe it would be the Galactic Center. The fact that ancient astrologers named this lunar mansion "the root" is pretty amazing since by visible observation there is no way to tell that the center of our galaxy resides there. I have calculated your birth chart with the Kala Vedic Astrology software created by Ernst Wilhelm. It is the most comprehensive Vedic Astrology tool on the market. I am fully confident in the calculation accuracy of your birth chart. As we gain a greater understanding of our universe we gain a greater understanding of ourselves.

## The Big Change Planets

Uranus, Neptune, and Pluto are normally not considered in a Vedic Astrology reading. They are not planets that are included in the classical text written thousands and thousands of years ago. But modern, innovative Vedic Astrologers do. Why? Because these forces control our universe. Astrology is an art and a science. As we learn more about our universe, we learn about ourselves. These planets are considered "transpersonal" planets. At least by considering them we have a lot to meditate on. We can say that the inner planets relate to a lot of external factors in our life while these three planets affect us on a deep internal level just like the Nakshatras.

## About Retrograde Planets

A lot of people get distressed when they hear a planet in their chart is in retrograde. Do not be alarmed if one or more planets are in retrograde. I am going to tell you my philosophy, based on the opinions of the Master astrologers I follow. When a planet is in retrograde in a natal chart it means that the energies of the planet, or its effects, are felt on an internal level not external. Let's use Pluto as an example because it's very common that one or three outer planets might be in retrograde in your chart. When Pluto shows up in any sign of the Zodiac it can mean that the native will experience life changing events in relation to the affairs of that house. That's the karma Pluto dishes out. It wrecks your ego. That could be in love, business, or whatever. When it is in retrograde those experiences are turned inwards and will be experienced mentally, emotionally, and spiritually. Not necessarily external events that impact the native. If Pluto is in your second house, which represents resources available for you as a child, it can mean you did not have access to those resources in the beginning of life. Poor parenting, poverty, illness, ect. If Pluto is in retrograde in the second house the native might struggle through life unable to pull the resources they need from inside themselves to accomplish their destiny. That could be addictions, mental and behavioral health problems, or just a shitty attitude towards life.

## Rahu and Ketu: The North and South Nodes of the Moon

To better understand what Rahu and Ketu may mean for us in our lives, the first step is to see what signs they occupy. The sign placement in our own individual charts will have specific meanings. They will indicate important issues and lessons we must learn in accordance with where our past lifetimes have led us through Ketu, and where Rahu will take us in this lifetime. Rahu and Ketu are always exactly opposite. Rahu is the ascending node, while Ketu is the descending node. You'll notice they are always in opposing signs, in the exact degree and minute opposite each other.

Rahu is our future and Ketu is our past. The polarity and opposite meanings of the signs are potent indicators, both of our current life and how our past life influenced the necessary lessons that had to be learned this time around. According to their sign placement in your own chart, Rahu and Ketu have particular lessons to teach us. The typical experiences are described below, both as they pertain to the past, and what we can do now to make a better future.

## The Ascendant

Just as the Sun rises in the East every morning due to the rotation of the Earth, so do all the signs of the Zodiac every 24 hours. Since there are 12 signs it takes about two hours for each one to rise. At the exact moment of your birth, depending on your location on Earth, one sign of the Zodiac is rising in the East. In Vedic astrology it is called the Lagna, your Ascendant, or rising sign. The Ascendant or Rising Sign is a key to self-discovery. In Vedic astrology this is your most important sign, not your Sun or your Moon sign. It tells how you express yourself as an individual. It is not so much your identity but more how you choose to express that identity - your primary motivation in life. The older you get, the more you strive to express yourself through the qualities of your Lagna/Ascendant.

## Your Atmakaraka Planet

Atma means the soul and karaka means significator. Atmakaraka is the significator of the soul's desire. According to the Vedic philosophy a soul is reborn because it has unfinished desires that were left unfulfilled in the previous lives and it is born again to get another opportunity to satisfy them. Your significator planet is based on which planet is holding the highest degree over the sky at the moment of your birth. So we can call this your "soul planet" because it represents your journey in this incarnation. Once the Atmakaraka is identified it's placement is of utmost concern. Whichever house your planet lands in will define your life's struggles and achievements.

Your karma is bound to the affairs of that house. Let's make something clear. Your Atmakaraka is not you, or a representation of you. The planet defines the nature of your mission, it's your duty to fulfill your life's purpose and achieve your destiny. So pay attention to the house your Atmakaraka is placed in and meditate on the implications. Your life will become easier once you realize your soul's mission and align yourself properly. The further you stray from your soul's purpose the more heartbreak you will bring on yourself. I know this from painful experience.

# THE BHAVAS / HOUSES

**The First House / Ascendant: Dharma - Body and Self-Projection**

Body and appearance, cognizance and caste, strength and weakness, comfort and pain, and one's own true state are looked at from the Lagna/Ascendant. The first house has an affinity toward Aries and Mars. The first house is angular and trinal which is considered to be auspicious. The angular houses are fixed. The trinal houses have a mixture of Divine masculine and feminine energies.

**The Second House: Artha - Wealth and Resources**

What you need to obtain your destiny. The second house has an affinity towards Taurus and Venus. The second house is generally considered neutral, but can bring misfortune under certain circumstances.

**The Third House: Kama - Mental Constitution**

Learning, communication, and abilities. This house also shows our baseline life energy. This house has an affinity towards Gemini and Mercury. The third house is considered neutral and planets that are difficult have the ability to improve with time and the right effort.

**The Fourth House: Moksha - Emotional Happiness**

Home life, the ability to attract comfort, and the kind of home you are attracted to. This house is about your wellbeing. It has an affinity towards Cancer and the Moon. The fourth house is an angular house and has a direct impact on the ascendant's life. Angular houses are important because they determine how you will behave under a variety of circumstances.

### The Fifth House: Dharma - Creativity and Innovation

This house is about your sense of identity. Your creative expression, feeling of security, and trust in yourself. The ability to take risks. It has an affinity with the Sun and Leo. The fifth house is trinal and considered to be auspicious. Planets located in this house have the capability of doing much good.

### The Sixth House: Artha - Health and Service to Others

Work, working relationships, and business partners. This house also tells us about our physical health. It has an affinity towards Virgo and Mercury. The sixth house is considered to be one of the houses of suffering. It is inauspicious and carries a lot of negative energy.

### The Seventh House: Kama - Partnerships

Marriage, long term relationships, and sexual partners. This house talks about all important relationships and our social lives. It has an affinity with Libra and Venus. The seventh house is an angular house which has a direct impact on the ascendant. It can bring misfortune under certain circumstances. Angular houses have a considerable influence on a person's life.

### The Eighth House: Moksha - The Hidden Side

Sex, death, the occult, and vice. This house is about the hidden part of life. Unspoken emotions we suppress during the day. It talks about our ability to show intimacy and the strength of sexual desire. Planets here reflect unresolved emotional issues. It has an affinity towards Scorpio and Mars. The eighth house is also considered inauspicious, a house of negativity and loss.

## The Ninth House: Dharma - Spirituality

This house talks about our ethics, morals, and opinions. It is about religion and philosophy. Reveals your spirituality. It is also a house of luck, good fortune, and grace. It has an affinity towards Sagittarius and Jupiter. The ninth house is trinal and is auspicious. The trinal houses have a mixture of Divine masculine and feminine energies.

## The Tenth House: Artha - Achievements

Public life, status, and achievements. Your life purpose or Dharma. These are the effects of our actions in the world. This house has an affinity towards Capricorn and Saturn. The tenth house is angular and considered to have the most impact in a person's life. Planets placed here are often the most influential in a person's life. This house also has the ability to improve over time with the proper effort.

## The Eleventh House: Kama - Life Gains

This house is about social integration, aspirations, and goals. All planets in the house do well. This house has an affinity towards Aquarius and Saturn. This house is considered neutral. The eleventh house is considered to be neutral. This house also has the ability to improve over time with proper effort.

## The Twelfth House: Moksha - The Inner World

The twelfth house is the most subtle. Planets placed here express energies in the most private matters. It is your subconscious, hidden emotions, and your true Nature. It has an affinity for Pieces and Jupiter. It is about self-realization, salvation, and liberation. This is the last inauspicious house and because of the internal nature of the house can produce much suffering. It is the house of breakthroughs.

# PLANET / SIGN ANALYSIS

**Aries**

**Sun in Aries**

**Analysis:** The Sun in Aries makes you a natural born leader. You are liberal, ambitious, and capable of achieving recognition for your efforts in life. You enjoy games, competitions, and sports. The Sun in Aries gives you a strong mental constitution and the ability to pioneer new frontiers. It makes you innovative. On the flip side if your fiery nature gets out of control you can be impatient, bossy, and authoritative. So you need to meditate on that. You can become easily excited and in your desire to achieve your goals burn yourself out. Your Aries Sun gives you the fire to stand up for yourself and others. Just do not overestimate your abilities which can lead to a brutal defeat.

**Moon in Aries**

**Analysis:** You enjoy being spontaneous. You require fun, travel, and vibrant people around you to thrive. You are able to make quick decisions and are a self starter. Moon in Aries brings you adaptability and the ability to resist disease. The shadow side is that you might have a short attention span. The indication is that you can be manipulative or say what you have to to get what you want, especially sex. And if boredom sets in you can generate risky situations to feel alive.

So there is a thrill seeker inside of you. You might even be good at starting projects, but never get around to completing them. Be careful of sexually transmitted diseases or unwanted pregnancy. These are important behavioral traits to meditate on. Act in your own best interest and do not allow your mind to create problems where there are none.

## Mars in Aries

**Analysis:** Mars in Aries gives you a pioneering attitude. You are bold, aggressive, and independent. Your Mars gives you the ability to organize events and be a strong leader. You must guard against ignoring others when they are giving you suggestions. You can be combative and belligerent when pushed. You also need to pay attention to your health and operating machinery. Mars in Aries can make you accident prone. Your fiery temper if left unchecked can lead to high blood pressure and heart problems. So take up mindfulness meditation and learn to count to ten when you feel anger coming on.

## Mercury in Aries

**Analysis:** Mercury in Aries makes you a fantastic problem solver, quick thinker, and very adaptable especially under pressure. The indication is that you also love dancing and music. There are some huge liabilities though that you should meditate on. Mar's influence on Mercury can make him erratic, frustrated, and angry easily. You might rush to accomplish goals too fast. When you get set back it frustrates you. It also makes you a gambler or risk taker. You might turn to substances to calm yourself down. So be careful with over using alcohol or cannabis to calm yourself. The combination of Mars and Mercurial energies makes you brilliant like a shooting star. But it also means that you are fast to heat up and fast to burn out.

## Venus in Aries

**Analysis:** Sex. Venus in Aries gives you a strong sex drive. Your Venus makes you affectionate, seductive, and charming. The liability is falling in love too fast or being hasty in choosing a romantic partner. Finding a partner that can keep up with you and satisfy all your needs is also a challenge. Venus in Aries makes you playful, adventurous, and spontaneous. It also makes you afraid of commitments which could lead to multiple failed relationships. In any case you are a sexual dynamo. The passions of Venus burn it up in Aries.

## Jupiter in Aries

**Analysis:** Your Jupiter in Aries gives you great earning potential. You hold strong ideologies and can be very strict in your rules and principles. Be careful because that can make you appear to be self righteous. Be on guard against being over optimistic. You dream big but if you do not have the means to go into a project do not take it on. Don't allow optimism to allow you to get into bad business partnerships or bad employment. You make a loyal partner.

## Saturn in Aries

**Analysis:** Saturn is debilitated and in the sign of his worst enemy. Saturn is not happy in Aries. That does not mean your entire chart goes to shit. There is light and shadow in every sign with every planet. Plus a difficult Saturn placement can get better with time. Like everything else in the Universe everything is constantly changing and transforming. The positive aspect you can receive is a hard working attitude, drive and determination to not quit or give up, and to accomplish your goals. You are also pretty organized. The shadow side of Saturn in Aries is getting frustrated too easily. You might plan things then experience setbacks and delays. That could lead you to depression, and depression is an indication in people who have Saturn in Aries. Keep your chin up, it's good for posture if nothing else.

## Rahu in Aries

**Analysis:** You have a strong desire to get things done and are action oriented. Be careful that you do not over extend yourself in your commitments personally and in business. Rahu in Aries can also get you into circumstances without thinking or without meditating on the consequences of your actions. So meditating on this is very important to increase the quality of your life. Do not allow other people to guilt trip you into taking on too much at the expense of your mental and emotional health.

## Ketu in Aries

**Analysis:** Ketu in Aries makes you a spiritual warrior. You have the ability to respond quickly to events. However you have to guard against making reckless decisions. Changes and unforeseen occurrences happen often to Ketu in Aries people. The indication is there is also a lot of travel or moving around from one place to another. These constant upheavals can diminish your spiritual growth. So create a schedule to do at least fifteen minutes a day of something spiritual to keep you grounded come hell or high water. Just fifteen minutes a day over a prolonged period of time is all you need to reach your destination. Be mindful in the face of adversity.

## Taurus

## The Sun in Taurus

**Analysis:** The Sun in Taurus makes you stay fixed on accomplishing your purpose. It gives you stamina and endurance on your journey through life. It makes you artistic with a love of music and literature. You also know how to deal and handle others well. The downside is that the Sun can make you hesitate or be overly cautious. It could mean missed opportunities based on your inability to act on decisions fast enough. Also not knowing when to quit because of the stubbornness famously attributed to the sign of Taurus.

## The Moon is Taurus

**Analysis:** You have an active imagination. You are attracted to sexual and sensual enjoyment. You also have a good influence over others. You have a generous, progressive, and grounded nature which is why you attract others to you. Just be careful with your imagination that you do not fall into a world deluded by fantasies. You also can get lazy real fast and have a tendency to be over indulgent in your pleasures. You like to accumulate things and live in comfortable surroundings. Pay attention that you do not become possessive and jealous in your relationships. Also do not become overly generous or you will end up giving everything you have away with nothing left for yourself. I mean that literally and also emotionally, mentally, and spiritually.

## Mars in Taurus

**Analysis:** You are charming, youthful, sensitive, and seductive. You care about others. You are a sweet talker and are very flirtatious. These are all beautiful qualities that Mars in Taurus blesses you with. On the flip side you can be too passionate and overly focused on obtaining short term pleasure. You need to be careful about rash, wasteful, and self-seeking. Relationships can get sour because of unfaithfulness to your partners. You act quick and this helps you catch opportunity when it comes knocking at the door. You have good earning abilities. Meditate on these indications.

## Mercury in Taurus

**Analysis:** Mercury in Taurus makes you practical and determined. You are creative with good reasoning skills. Reading, writing, and public speaking are all your forte. You enjoy being around intellectually stimulating and philosophically thinking people. You have a good sense of humor, are playful, and like being amused. Be careful that your natural youthful attitude does not make you a spoiled brat. You might lack motivation or tend to behave irresponsibly. You can also be stubborn about taking advice that may be in your best interest.

### Venus in Taurus

**Analysis:** Your Venus brings you all the good things in life. He is in his own sign and brings you wealth and prosperity. Venus makes you well educated, refined, good mannered, and artistic. You have expensive taste. If not in clothing than in food, wine, and other luxuries. Be careful that this blessing does not lead to extravagance and over indulgence. A liability of Venus in Taurus is expecting others to work for you not with you. You might expect your partner to do all the work in your relationship which leads to problems. You can also be a mooch on people. I know this because my Venus is in Taurus also. Meditate on that.

### Jupiter in Taurus

**Analysis:** Jupiter in Taurus makes you a natural educator. You are knowledgeable, gentle, and refined. You are drawn to humanitarian and spiritual causes. Your religious views do not change unless you have good reason based on convincing information presented to you. The shadow side to Jupiter in Taurus is that you can become stagnant. You can also miss opportunities to advance your life and career by not acting fast enough. You also must guard against spending too much money on pleasures and comforts.

## Saturn in Taurus

**Analysis:** Saturn in Taurus can bring self control, pleasure through hard work, and devotion to one's mate. On the flip side Saturn can also bring detachment, problems with love and intimacy, deceitfulness, and self isolating behavior. You feel comfortable around older people and might even choose a mate that is older or significantly older than you. Remember that Saturn's effects improve over the long haul and so will your ability to accumulate and maintain wealth.

## Rahu in Taurus

**Analysis:** Rahu in Taurus makes you very charitable. You have a love for those who are outcasted from society, neglected, and mistreated. You have the ability to advocate on their behalf. You are also fond of foreign peoples and can interact with people of other cultures easily. You like taking unconventional approaches to solving complex problems. You have to be careful with your finances because you can easily be deceived by people with bad motives surrounding your wealth. Protect yourself in business and in love when it comes to money. Make sure you are financially independent.

## Ketu in Taurus

**Analysis:** Ketu in Taurus makes you very spiritually inclined. A strong faith in God and also the desire to read scriptures. Money comes into your life unexpectedly and goes out just as fast. The shadow side is being conflicted inside about sex, sexuality, and spirituality. I recommend you buy the book Urban Tantra. That book will help you transmute spiritual energy into erotic energy and vice versa. Help balance you out. The indication is that you do not put enough attention on being financially stable. Make sure to keep your spiritual and mundane life balanced. Remember that the spiritual world and the physical world are one in the same, non dual. So every act you do is both material and spiritual in nature. Do not elevate one above the other. That kind of black and white thinking leads to a fractured view of God.

## Gemini

### Sun in Gemini

**Analysis:** The indication is that you have a good short term memory. That you are a fast learner. You also have the ability to hold a conversation about anything, even subjects that you might not be familiar with. That is because the intelligence and adaptability of Mercury is paired with the charming cheerful personality of the Sun. If you find something you like you are likely to buy two of the same item. Remember Gemini is the sign of the Divine twins so everything comes in two for you. Double your pleasure, double your fun. That can also mean holding double standards or being hypocritical. Sun in Gemini people can also be indecisive and hard to pin down. Meditate on that. Pick one cause and stick to it. Finish the projects you start.

### Moon in Gemini

**Analysis:** Moon in Gemini gives you a quick wit, a creative mind, and very humorous. You might come off as superficial due to your quickness of thought but you are very bright. You are sociable and would make a great community organizer. On the other hand you take on too many tasks. You think about too many possibilities and then do not take action to bring the idea to manifestation. Unfavorable qualities the Moon in Gemini brings is being too skeptical. You are prone to being emotionally overstimulated and restless. You should focus on reducing the amount of goals you have so that the most important ones are manageable. Your mental fog and confusion needs to be cleared out so you can focus. Finding ways to self-soothe and ground yourself are very important. A lot of these traits you exhibit are unconscious to you. They are intrinsic and unrecognizable to yourself because you lack the ability to be objective about yourself. The above mentioned are liabilities that you should journal about so that these traits become conscious to you and you have the ability to refine them.

**Mars in Gemini**

**Analysis:** The indication is that you have good problem solving abilities. That you have musical and literary interests, perhaps even theater. You are fond of change and have a strong desire to learn. You are clever but that can bring you trouble. If you are not careful you could become cynical. You have the tendency to burn out quickly or lose interest in projects. Mars in Gemini can make you restless and impatient. You should pursue mindfulness exercises to keep your mind active yet stable. Keep you on point. Download learning apps to your phone to give yourself something to do, like learn a second language.

**Mercury in Gemini**

**Analysis:** Mercury loves being in his own sign. Mercury in Gemini produces people with a quick wit, are good at communicating, resourceful, with a good sense of humor. The indication is that you are a master debater. You are also sexually curious and like to check things out. Because of Gemini's influence, it can lead to two of everything in your life, even partners. You have a tendency to talk more than you accomplish. The shadow side is acting superficial even if you are not. Being two faced or deceitful. You also get bored, almost stir crazy, when you are not being intellectually stimulated. So you go create problems for yourself. I know because my Mercury is in Gemini.

## Venus in Gemini

**Analysis:** Venus in Gemini gives you the ability to think abstractly. You have an interest in art. You are capable of accumulating wealth and respect in life. The shadow side of Venus in Gemini is being wishy washy in matters of love and relationships. Being indecisive. The indication is that you do not think ahead or plan for the future. Very important point to meditate on because this behavioral trait will affect your future.

## Jupiter in Gemini

**Analysis:** Jupiter in Gemini gives a person a good sense of humor. Also the ability to turn bad situations around to achieve a positive outcome. You are diplomatic in your affairs. The indication is that you are emotionally balanced. There is an idiot savant or nonchalant attitude you carry. The downside is that you could tend to be overly optimistic. You have to be careful that you do not become careless in your dealings with others.

## Saturn in Gemini

**Analysis:** Saturn in Gemini makes you conservative, scientific, very focused, and analytical. You might have a deep interest in literature, words, numbers, and organizing things. The shadow side of Saturn in Gemini is that you can act compulsively. The indication is that you might be gullible or take things too literally. You also need to guard against unnecessary worrying. Do not overthink or ruminate on matters.

## Rahu in Gemini

**Analysis:** Your mind is geared towards innovation. You might have an inclination for the macabre, things that are bizarre, maybe even conspiracy theories. Rahu in Gemini makes you oddly creative and mystically adventurous. The shadow side of Rahu in Gemini can lead you to work in shady industries and make your money through deceptive means. The indication is that you might suffer from behavioral and mental health issues. If so you must guard against self isolating behavior and try to surround yourself with positive, eccentric, and happy people.

## Ketu in Gemini

**Analysis:** Ketu's gift in Gemini is unbounded chaotic thinking. You have a mind that is creative and full of fresh ideas. However that mind can be fragmented, conflicted, and has problems with decision making skills. The spiritual side of Ketu in Gemini makes you transcendent and ethereal in your thinking abilities. That means your mind has the ability to perceive and construct very abstract thoughts. You have the ability to connect the dots mystically. You have a good mind for taking up the mystic arts.

## Cancer

## Sun in Cancer

**Analysis:** The indication is that you only take your own advice. You should listen to others because they have the ability to see things your ego might prefer to stay blind too. The Sun in Cancer makes you sensitive, feminine (even for guys by the way, does not mean they are gay), highly intuitive, and economical. The shadow side is someone who loses interest in things/people quickly. Sun in Cancer can also cause an erratic career with ebb and flow finances. I know because my Sun is in Cancer.

## Moon in Cancer

**Analysis:** Moon in Cancer makes you sensitive, perceptive, and affectionate. You have a gentle kindness to you that is very endearing. The indication is that you are forgiving, humane, and have a considerable amount of intuition. This points to psychic abilities and an affinity for the mystic arts. The liabilities are smothering others with your love or becoming too submissive to your partner. There is emotional neediness that should be kept in check. You are susceptible to other people's problems. You have weak boundaries. You need to empower yourself by meditating on the people around you and evaluating the boundaries, or lack thereof, that you have set with them. If the boundaries are poorly established they need to be reaffirmed. This can lead to relationship trouble because once you allow someone to overstep a boundary they become resentful towards you for trying to take back your personal power. Do not give away your personal power.

**Mars in Cancer**

**Analysis:** Mars shows his ass in Cancer. He can make you fickle, lack interest in your family, and unreliable. These are things you want to meditate on. It can also indicate inconsistent income. On the other hand Mars in Cancer gives you a sharp mind, a fascination with academic studies, and the ability to heal your body quickly after injury or illness.

**Mercury in Cancer**

**Analysis:** You have a strong imagination and would do well in creative pursuits. Artistic abilities like creative writing and playing music are good for you, even as a hobby. You have a lot of spiritual yearnings. You are sensual and open minded about trying new things sexually. Mercury in Cancer, if left unchecked, can lead to listlessness and rebellion. That leads to disregarding moral restraints and acting out in unhealthy ways. Acting out comes from being nervous and impatient. Meditate on this.

## Venus in Cancer

**Analysis:** You are artistic, elegant, royal, and enjoy the comforts of life. You are emotionally supportive and are kind hearted. The indication is that you have the ability to change negative situations into constructive and positive ones with your emotional intelligence. You are cultured with a great capacity to love. The shadow side is being overly emotional, fragile, and easily offended. Those are important things to meditate on.

## Jupiter in Cancer

**Analysis:** The keyword for Jupiter in Cancer is expansive. Everything you do is constantly expanding. Your personal life, your career, your family, your wealth, all have the ability to grow overtime and not in the general sense. You are a get the job done person. That attitude allows you to keep a steady incline despite obstacles and setbacks. The shadow side of Jupiter in Cancer is being left with a feeling of emptiness and discontent. Not knowing how to be happy. Never being satisfied with your end result. You might also be overly sensitive and offended easily. You should meditate on that.

## Saturn in Cancer

**Analysis:** Saturn in Cancer makes you consistent, steady, and reliable. Remember that nothing happens fast with Saturn and you will find success over time with sustained efforts. Worry about yourself and what you do. The shadow side to Saturn in Cancer can make you heartless and uncompassionate for others. There is a rigidity Saturn can bring that prevents you from openly expressing your feelings. Be more vocal to those around you about what you need emotionally, mentally, spiritually, and physically so you can thrive, not just survive.

## Rahu in Cancer

**Analysis:** Rahu in Cancer indicates you have a hard time making commitments and do not like domestic responsibilities. You care for the underdogs and for the suffering masses. It also suggests living in foreign lands or working with foreigners. Rahu in Cancer makes it difficult to make life decisions. It can make you unclear about educational goals. And if you chose higher education you would study and teach unconventional topics. You have to guard against depression and feelings of uncertainty. Please use extra care operating machinery and driving your car because you are accident prone.

## Ketu in Cancer

**Analysis:** You have intuitive abilities that make it easy to read people, places, and situations. Spiritual growth is important to you as well as a strong interest in religious knowledge. The shadow side to Ketu in Cancer is having anxiety, worrying too much, and being nervous all the time. Your feelings about matters change often. More than any other spiritual pursuit you need to be seeking balance and harmony. You need to relax and learn how to enjoy your life. Do not allow yourself to suffer unnecessarily.

## Leo

### Sun in Leo

**Analysis:** The Sun could not be happier sitting in his own sign. He is shining bright and gives leadership abilities. You are a capable opponent for your haters and have the ability to repel negativity around you. The Sun in Leo makes you very ambitious. You must guard against egotism and arrogance. Because that will screw you over. Listen to others when they speak and do not seek to dominate them. Nobody wants to be around a vain, self-centered, know it all. The Sun in Leo has the ability to make you fiercely independent in the most brilliant way as long as you keep your ego under control.

**Moon in Leo**

**Analysis:** You take pride in your work and have a need to be recognized for your accomplishments. You take a prominent position in the circles you run with. You are helpful, responsible, and know how to take charge in a leadership role. The shadow side could be that you overly seek out attention. You have to be on guard about arrogance, selfishness, and pride. Moon in Leo can give you a fickle personality. Take time to meditate on this and journal about it.

**Mars in Leo**

**Analysis:** Mars gets very aggressive in Leo because of the solar influence. You are self reliant, competitive, and resistant to disease. A real dynamo. Your Mars energy is unconstrained. The shadow side is acting like a dictator and not a wise benevolent king. The indication is that you can become impatient, adversarial, and egotistic if you do not keep yourself under control.

**Mercury in Leo**

**Analysis:** You have a bright mind literally. You might excel at public speaking or other situations where you can captivate an audience. You are ambitious and well known in your field. You have a progressive, think big, and be self -reliant. Your liabilities are thinking too fast, not paying attention to details, and getting disorganized. Think about how you can refine your actions to reflect the sublime qualities of your mind.

**Venus in Leo**

**Analysis:** Venus is a beautiful planet that affords its Native with luxury and wealth when well placed. Venus in Leo can bring those things through art, music, and dance. The fiery nature of Leo heats up Venus and impels it to create to deal with its frustration. Venus is not very happy in Leo. The Sun and Venus are enemies. This makes Venus more prone to act conceited, self absorbed, and indulgent. You need to be very careful about sexual activity and make sure you are always safe. Venus is a seductive planet and under this influence its seductive qualities are enhanced a hundred fold. Check out the book Urban Tantra. That book is very good in helping people transmute negative/destructive sexual drives into spiritually uplifting experiences.

## Jupiter in Leo

**Analysis:** Your Jupiter brings the gift of leadership abilities and independent thinking. You have the ability to think strategically. That can be used for good or for ill. If you are a CEO of a big business, that shrewdness can keep a company thriving. On the other hand when you feel slighted you can use that same strategy for exacting revenge on your enemies. Any way you play the game of life you definitely have staying power with this Jupiter. I have Jupiter in Leo also.

## Saturn in Leo

**Analysis:** Saturn does not like being in Leo, it is the house of his enemy the Sun. When Saturn is well placed he brings a hard working attitude to the Native. He cultivates inner discipline. When he is agitated he becomes conflicted between responsibilities. You take on too many responsibilities, all of them done poorly instead of just a few done to completion. Saturn can obstruct fortune in Leo. A poorly placed Saturn can make you sullen, depressed, and self isolating. At worst you can become calloused and heartless. So this is something you need to meditate on.

### Rahu in Leo

**Analysis:** You have incredible earning abilities. Rahu in Leo gives you a lot of potential. You find creative and innovative approaches to business and career. You like helping others get organized and become successful also. The shadow side to Rahu in Leo is feeling a lack of purpose or confusion about your path. You also have to be very cautious not to be taken advantage of. It would seriously benefit you to journal about what makes you feel confused, doubtful, and define clear objectives for your life. You also need to take an inventory of the people in your life and journal about whether or not they should have a place in your life. I have Rahu in Leo also.

### Ketu in Leo

**Analysis:** Ketu in Leo gives you the ability to make quick life changes. You are spiritually advanced and interested in higher levels of education. You love knowledge and seek it consistently. The shadow side of Ketu in Leo is that your life purpose might feel ambiguous. You may encounter a lot of uncertainty and unexpected upheavals on your journey.

### Virgo

### The Sun in Virgo

**Analysis:** The Sun in Virgo blesses you with a knowledge of numbers and letters, scientific thinking, and good analytical abilities. You are good at organizing things with a sense of service to others. Your best fields of business would be in science, legalities, designing, writing, and other jobs that require high functioning mental activity. The shadow side of that is not caring about your own needs. You could be taken advantage of by bosses and superiors. You might want to be happily married, but you don't know how to be happy. You must be very careful to guard against getting into a victim mentality. If you do, you can end up disappointed, angry, and critical.

## Moon in Virgo

**Analysis:** You are discriminating, honest, and pragmatic. You might come off frigid but warm up quickly. Moon in Virgo also makes you generous, empathetic, and gives you healing abilities. The Virgo in you makes you like the scientific method, makes you philosophical, and makes you resistant to aging. The dark side of the Moon in Virgo makes you depressed from unmet expectations. You might act like a victim or feel like a martyr. You may feel called to living a monastic life. You need to be on guard about compulsive behavior and cyclical thinking. My Moon is in Virgo also... so I know.

## Mars in Virgo

**Analysis:** You have the ability to get results quickly when you want something accomplished. You also prefer to do things yourself because you are afraid of others doing the job poorly. You have quick problem solving abilities, you are strategic, and like the scientific method. The shadow side to Mars in Virgo can give you an overactive mind, black and white thinking, and prone to exaggeration. You might actually be a liar or very good at lying. Mars in Virgo makes you very calm and calculating. When you serve up revenge you do it cold as ice. I know because my Mars is also in Virgo.

## Mercury in Virgo
**Analysis:** Mercury is very happy in his own sign. He is the master communicator and gives you intelligence, the resources you need to obtain your destiny, and the discrimination you need to use those resources wisely. The shadow side is you could expect too much, and think too

much. Your ability to enjoy life could be ruined by how analytical your mind works. You must always stay positive and guard against the urge to dwell on possible negative outcomes.

## Venus in Virgo

**Analysis:** Venus is debilitated in Virgo. Instead of romantic love you might have sublimated your sexual desires for something more religious in nature. You are unpretentious and unassuming. You make gains in life through establishing good partnerships. You might focus more on work and career rather than developing a personal life. You need to be on guard against negative self talk and work on your self esteem. It's possible to make poor choices in life because you have low self worth. Like getting into relationships that do not serve you or keep you subservient.

## Jupiter in Virgo

**Analysis:** You are methodical, enthusiastic, and sympathetic. You are always learning and have a good sense of humor. The shadow side to Jupiter in Virgo is not having a backup plan or being out of touch with practical reality. You might also give in to matters that you should stay firm in. Do not allow others to guilt trip you into behaving in any kind of way.

## Saturn in Virgo

**Analysis:** The indication is that you work better alone. You are service oriented, focused, and highly productive. You might lean conservative and maintain traditional values. Your life becomes more meaningful and rich in experience the older you get. The shadow side to Saturn in Virgo is not liking change, being resistant to change, and being pessimistic about the future. Obstinate is the word. You are also not a people person. I know because my Saturn is in Virgo.

## Rahu in Virgo

**Analysis:** Rahu in Virgo makes you resourceful and a survivor. He gives you the ability to think outside of the box. The indication is that you work well alone and need time alone to thrive. The downside to Rahu in this sign can prevent you from being of service to others. You must strive to overcome this and take all those talents you have to be of service to others, however that manifests.

## Ketu in Virgo

**Analysis:** Ketu in Virgo gives you advanced intuition, prediction abilities, sublime thoughts, and the ability to be innovative. You would be a good astrologer! You must hold onto your mental stability. Your primary focus spiritually should be maintaining balance and harmony if not you will become hypersensitive. Ketu also brings a lot of surprises in life.

## Libra

## Sun in Libra

**Analysis:** You are charming, alluring, soothing, and attractive as a mate although you may be poor at being in relationships. You give everyone the benefit of the doubt. You show compassion for those less fortunate than you. The shadow side of Sun in Libra is lacking motivation and not facing up to your responsibilities. The Sun is poorly placed and debilitated in Libra. This can affect your connection to the Self. You need to be careful about using drugs and alcohol because the indication is that you are prone to addiction. Sun in Libra can also make you deceitful and try to play both sides of the table. Those games never run well or end well. Meditate on these things.

## Moon in Libra

**Analysis:** You are diplomatic, smooth, and persuasive when you want to be. You are a chameleon and have the ability to use those charms to manipulate others. You try to avoid hurting other people's feelings. The indication is that you might be overly sensitive to criticism. Your personality is multifaceted and will react differently to the stimuli around you. To people who do not understand you your behavior can come across erratic and nonsensical. There can also be a tendency to mooch off others. Meditate on any fickle behavioral traits you have been accused of and investigate if those leanings are true.

## Mars in Libra

**Analysis:** You are passionate and love being around other passionate people. You have fiery love. You are affectionate, charming, and persuasive. The shadow side to Mars in Libra is being fickle, reckless, and deceptive. It's easy for you to be overcome by your passions. Compulsive behaviors surrounding love, sex, and relationships must be paid attention to. People perceive you to be friendly and warm. You enjoy a good challenge and are not afraid to take on more than you think you can handle.

## Mercury in Libra:

**Analysis:** You are fun loving, friendly, and curious by nature. You are a sweet talker and a persuasive speaker. You are also creative. You are inclined towards studying philosophy and religion. The shadow side to Mercury in Libra is being flaky and undependable. You also have a hard time taking responsibility for your actions. You will own up to your flaws but not after being put under pressure to do so. You are light hearted and like a bird. Not easy to pin down.

## Venus in Libra

**Analysis:** You are very fortunate to have Venus placed in his own sign. You are elegant, artistic, sensual, and balanced in thought and deed. You benefit from activities related to women since Venus rules all things feminine. You are a deep feeler, full of passion and enthusiasm. The shadow side you must be careful of is you are prone to extravagance and overindulgence. Venus supplies wealth and luxuries and those things can be exhausted because of a lack of gratitude. Having a gratitude journal is a healthy way of reminding yourself to appreciate all you have been gifted. You might also set your expectations too high for your lovers and partners. Entitlement is to be watched out for and the feeling that you should be served rather than to serve. That is just the nature of Libra ascendants with a strong Venus. Venus can bring you all the blessings in life, how you use those blessings is what will generate your karma.

## Jupiter in Libra

**Analysis:** Jupiter in Libra makes you impartial, mannerly, and humanitarian in nature. You are very competent to lead others and possess a refined intuition. The shadow side of Jupiter in Libra is that you can be too indulgent wanting to spend more time vacationing than working. You might feel misunderstood in relationships and prone to get entangled in sloppy romances.

## Saturn in Libra

**Analysis:** Saturn is exalted in Libra and he makes you very well organized. You are clever, focused, and self-sufficient. Your reputation and achievements get stronger over time. Things will get better for you as you get older because Saturn slows down development in the house he lands in.

So that also means the affairs of this house will also take a long time to fructify. You might feel restrictions in romance and partnerships. Delayed commitments as well as marriage. Saturn in Libra also can make you afraid of change. These are things to meditate on.

### Rahu in Libra

**Analysis:** You have a love and acceptance for the unusual. You might even have a kinky streak. You might find success dealing with foreign lands and foreign people. The shadow side of Rahu in Libra is being misunderstood or judged for your unusual taste. The indication is that you can act self centered and put your needs before the people around you. So meditate on those points.

### Ketu in Libra

**Analysis:** The indication is that you are very adaptable in business. You have the ability to deal with a variety of personality types. Ketu in Libra also gives you a love for all things spiritual. Ketu in Libra can also give you conflicts between love and spirituality.

### Scorpio

### Sun in Scorpio

**Analysis:** Scorpio is ruled by Mars and when the Sun is in Scorpio he will take on some of Mar's attributes. You are a strong leader, in the dictator sense of the word. You are militaristic in your pursuits. You are a ride or die partner. You would drive off the edge of a cliff in a relationship just like the end of Thelma and Louise. So you have a very strong inner drive to succeed and you will try to achieve your goals by any means necessary. So you have a laundry list of destructive unconscious behavioral patterns to journal about. Be on guard for acting possessive, jealous, vengeful, or harboring grudges. Those traits are all bad for your health. Meditate deeply on those indications.

## Moon in Scorpio

**Analysis:** You need to be cautious about getting too intimate too early in a relationship. You are a take charge kind of person, you do not beat around the bush. Moon in Scorpio can make you a reformer, give you the ability to fight adversity alone, and make revolutionary changes. The shadow side to Moon in Scorpio is not being able to break bad emotional attachments. You might also have trouble expressing your needs properly. You might also hold grudges. You might be afraid of being embarrassed by others. Meditate on those things.

## Mars in Scorpio

**Analysis:** You will try anything once, if not twice. You are adventurous and passionate with a sharp mind. You enjoy resolving opposition. You would make a great detective, secret agent, or investigator. You have an affinity for research and researching. The shadow side is you might get impatient with people who are slower than you in thought and action. You can be challenging, arrogant, and selfish. So you need to meditate on this and journal about it. Mars in Scorpio gives you a warrior's spirit. That spirit can make you very heroic and also a big pain in the ass.

## Mercury in Scorpio

**Analysis:** Mercury in Scorpio gives you a sharp mind, sharp as a knife. You have the ability to make rapid decisions, even under pressure. You are interested in investigating, researching, and getting to the bottom of matters. You are a clever strategist. You are the real Sherlock Holms... or perhaps Professor Moriarty. In this case you can swing either way.

You are incredibly adaptable in this area of life. You question authority and demand proof for religious and philosophical dogmas. The shadow side to Mercury in Scorpio is that you can be deceitful and 100% rationalize your behavior. So lying or not telling the whole truth should be examined. You might seek instant gratification in relationships than lose interest quickly. Creating sustainable relationships is a challenge. These are some things to meditate on.

## Venus in Scorpio

**Analysis:** Venus in Scorpio indicates that you desire love but can live independently. There is a strong need to protect what is sacred to you, protect your own interests. You are also slow to age. You have a strong desire for action and adventure. You are also not afraid of getting into a debate. You have to be careful that heated arguments do not go south which could result in a lot of damage in partnerships. You also need to remember that life is not just about you, your feelings, your desires. You have a tendency to be selfish and only focus on your satisfaction in relationships.

## Jupiter in Scorpio

**Analysis:** Jupiter in Scorpio makes you articulate, competent, and persuasive. You always find opportunities for growth. You have a strong sense of self and purpose. The shadow side is getting into debt too easily. You can also hold on to past mistakes. You have to be careful not to lose wealth on poor investments. Wealth does not just mean money, it also means your time, energy, and emotional health. Jupiter in Scorpio also tends to make one stuck up, or perceived to be self-absorbed.

## Saturn in Scorpio

**Analysis:** You have the capacity to work hard and fast. You have a strong ability to focus. Your analytical skills are sublime. The shadow side to Saturn in Scorpio is you could be mistreated. The indication is that you should not be around weapons or people who use them because they can harm and kill you. As far as health is concerned you can get depleted by overwork and not caring for yourself. Be on guard against feeling depressed, angry, and frustrated too easily.

## Rahu in Scorpio

**Analysis:** Rahu in Scorpio can make you very aggressive. He also gives you a higher level of intuition. You feel driven to learn the mysteries of life. On the flip side you might not know the appropriate way to respond when met with confrontation. The indication is that you may hold grudges, be vindictive, and live to extremes. On the spiritual path you should be seeking balance and harmony. You need to meditate and practice mindfulness of your feelings. That way you can react appropriately when upset or put on the spot.

## Ketu in Scorpio

**Analysis:** Ketu in Scorpio can leave you feeling vulnerable, hypersensitive, angry, and make you behave deceptively. On the other hand it also makes you quick to react, quick minded, and intuitive. You need to seek balance and harmony in this area of life. Not be pulled to extremes. Recognize that all feelings, situations, and "things" are impermanent and not get stuck in all or nothing thinking.

## Sagittarius

## Sun in Sagittarius

**Analysis:** You are concerned about impartiality and fairness. Sun in Sagittarius gives you a strong sense of justice. That means that you are idealistic and resolute in your religious,

165

spiritual, and ethical standards. You don't like feeling restrained in relationships or career. You want to be free. You are strong willed, honest, and sincere. The shadow side to Sun in Sagittarius is the inability to cooperate and be subordinate when you need to be. Your personal freedom is important, but not at the expense of a great opportunity. So you need to be more yielding. Compromise in matters does not equate to abandoning your ideals. It means you recognize not everyone shares your same ethics or beliefs. You also have to resist saying whatever comes to your mind and blurting it out. Not everything you think needs to be expressed.

**Moon is Sagittarius**

**Analysis:** You are idealistic, expansive, and deeply intuitive. That can manifest in both positive and negative qualities. The Moon in this sign makes you gracious, brave, energetic, and determined. You have a strong focus on fulfilling your desires. That positive attitude about life can lead to the benefit of all around you. On the other hand Moon in Sagittarius can make you argumentative, blunt without consideration for others feelings, and overly sensitive. You enjoy learning new things and have a desire to understand religion and philosophy. Traveling is very good for you. The downside is that you might have a tendency to change jobs often and behave in an unreliable manner. So these are qualities that you need to meditate on.

**Mars in Sagittarius**

**Analysis:** You have the ability to recognize opportunities and jump on the bandwagon. You are a quick thinker and can make difficult decisions without hesitation. That makes a good leader. You are straight forward and like to get things done. You want your work to be done so you have the time to play. The shadow side to Mars in Sagittarius is trying too hard to succeed. You might be so honest that you hurt others feelings.

The indication is that you can become overstimulated easily and impatient on top of it. Meditate on those things.

## Mercury in Sagittarius

**Analysis:** You enjoy learning and the indication is that you are well organized, an original thinker, competent, and respectable. Someone who leads by example. The shadow of Mercury's fiery nature could lead you to exaggerate things, be consumed in your point of view, and have a superiority complex. So you need to meditate on how you interface with others from day to day and make sure that you are not talking down to others or acting condescending. You have a brilliant mind. Having a mind as sharp as yours can make you intolerant of others who can not problem solve as quickly as you.

## Venus in Sagittarius

**Analysis:** You are a visionary. You like good food, good clothes, good friends, and good sex. You like soothing and pleasant surroundings. You are sensual and romantic and stay on the bright side of life. You must guard against becoming overly indulgent and extravagant. You might even get lazy and miss good opportunities because of lack of motivation.

## Jupiter in Sagittarius

**Analysis:** When Jupiter is in his own sign, exalted, or at an angle he can manifest his highest qualities. Your Jupiter is influential, cultured, trustworthy, and wise. You have the ability to give good advice to others. You speak well and can communicate your thoughts and feelings clearly. You also feel drawn to religion and spirituality. Having a daily spiritual practice is very good for you like a mantra or prayer. The shadow side to an overactive Jupiter is being overly optimistic, indulgent, and making poor investment choices.

## Saturn in Sagittarius

**Analysis:** Saturn in Sagittarius makes you serious, respectful, and have humanitarian interests. The indication is structured and progressive spiritual growth over time. You have to be on guard about getting frustrated on your path and realize that your journey is a marathon not a sprint. Do not be in a hurry to get anywhere fast. Take your time. You are also slow to trust others which is a good thing. But holding out for too long makes you miss opportunities to create friendships and partnerships. Allow yourself to take more risks.

**Rahu in Sagittarius**

**Analysis:** Rahu has the ability to bring good material rewards in life. However, that growth can be perplexing and confusing for you. You are very clever which gives you a good mind for higher education, legal, and ethical matters. You have a taste for out of the ordinary spiritual experiences. The detrimental effects of Rahu in Sagittarius is misguidance on the spiritual path. That means ending up on the wrong spiritual path by not listening to your guides. Not being able to manage your financial affairs. These are things to meditate on.

**Ketu in Sagittarius**

**Analysis:** You are a natural born mystic. Ketu in Sagittarius gives you a burning desire to study the magical arts. You are drawn to intellectual undertakings such as studying philosophy and religion. Taking pilgrimages to mysterious and spiritual places is good for you. The shadow side of Ketu in Sagittarius is that you take up too many philosophies without mastering any. That you become an "armchair magician" and fill your mind with knowledge you never apply. Ketu can also cause you to become unethical. Be careful when traveling. Always be alert or you could get into an accident by day dreaming or not paying attention.

## Capricorn

### The Sun in Capricorn

**Analysis:** You feel uber responsible for others around you. You have a strong sense of duty. A Capricorn Sun blesses you with practicality and makes you a hard worker. You have to guard against burn out. You must remind yourself that it's not just up to you to get things done. Allow other people to help you accomplish tasks. If they are lazy you must tell them they have to help you because it's not fair to put all the pressure on you to perform. So you can be too accommodating to others to the point that you are treated like a doormat. That can lead to resentment towards others around you. You also must guard against being overly skeptical and self isolating. Pay attention to your mental health especially when it comes to getting bummed out. You may be prone to depressive bouts.

### The Moon in Capricorn

**Analysis:** You make a devoted companion and friend. You are dependable for the most part. You tend to be orthodox, pragmatic, and methodical. You also have an affinity for things that are historic, ancient, and old. You have respect for antiquity. Spending time outdoors, especially in the mountains, is good for your soul. The dark side to the Moon in Capricorn is being coldhearted or lacking mercy. Doing whatever you need to do to succeed even if that means stepping over others to get there. Living your life by rules and not principles. Being unyielding. These are very important things to meditate on.

### Mars in Capricorn

**Analysis:** Mars is exalted in Capricorn this indicates the highest manifestation of Mar's qualities. Mars is the warrior planet and you come with undefeatable energy. You would make a fantastic political activist. Mar's admirable qualities are generosity, a hardworking attitude, and being very protective of others. Mars is feared as being the most violent of all the malefics but he is at an angle and radiates the positive side of his nature to you.

## Mercury in Capricorn

**Analysis:** Mercury in Capricorn makes you logical, rational, and analytical. You take a systematic approach to all your projects. You ponder deeply into matters. You also like to stick to the rules. The shadow side to Mercury in Capricorn is losing sight of the big picture. You must guard against negative self talk and low self esteem. You also have a tendency to create a lonely path for yourself. You need to put effort into surrounding yourself with positive, healthy, happy people. You also need to do things for yourself.

## Venus in Capricorn

**Analysis:** Venus in Capricorn makes you loyal, responsible, and mature. The indication is that you prefer mature lovers. You have democratic ideals but also love tradition and traditional values. You are also not afraid of being alone and enjoy being by yourself at times. The shadow side of Venus in Capricorn is that you might be hesitant pursuing romantic relationships. You might struggle with a lack of pleasure, feeling frigid, or averse to love. You should buy the book Urban Tantra. That book will help you create neural pathways to bring together the sexual and spiritual aspects of your true nature.

## Jupiter in Capricorn

**Analysis:** Jupiter in Capricorn makes you very structured and organized. You get pissed when your schedule gets thrown off or interrupted. You are someone who does well when working within set parameters. You have to guard against dogmatism and black and white thinking. You're brilliant but might lack positivity. You need to let go of unrealistic ideals. You need to learn to relax and allow things to just be. The indication is that you might be OCD or a control freak. Meditate on these points and determine if any of it rings true.

## Saturn in Capricorn

**Analysis:** Saturn makes you hardworking, deliberate, practical, and have the ability to work by yourself or for yourself. You also are ok with aloneness or being by yourself. The downside is that you might not be much fun. You have a hard time letting go to relax and enjoy life. Perfectionism can drive you to disappointment and depression. So you must balance your practicality with pleasures and enjoyment. Remember it is the little things that make life worth living and you are entitled to enjoy those things.

## Rahu in Capricorn

**Analysis:** Rahu in Capricorn makes you unconventional, goal oriented, persistent, and hardworking. Once you set your mind to a project you do not stop until you accomplish your goals. You are drawn to unusual occupations but have a knack for making money. You also work best alone, unsupervised, and on your own set schedule. The shadow side to Rahu in Capricorn is being unclear about your life purpose. At worst you might tend to take advantage of people and situations and then get taken advantage of in return. You must guard against becoming self-isolating.

## Ketu in Capricorn

**Analysis:** Ketu in Capricorn makes you innovative. You also have the ability to achieve heightened spiritual states. The indication is that you can be successful following traditional approaches to work and career. The shadow side to Ketu in Capricorn is not having steady work or a lot of ups and downs with finances. So focusing on being stable in work is very important.

## Aquarius

### Sun in Aquarius

**Analysis:** Sun in Aquarius makes you brilliant and intelligent. Aquarius people tend to be philanthropic and humanitarians. They act on behalf of the masses. There is a universal outlook you have that gives you perspective. At your best you are hardworking, dedicated, and have staying power. The shadow side to Sun in Aquarius is being too secretive, having low self esteem, and lacking the ability to promote yourself. Be careful that you stay grounded and don't become disconnected from reality. The indication is that you could get up in a victim mentality. These are very important things to meditate on.

### Moon in Aquarius

**Analysis:** The Moon in Aquarius gives you the desire to fulfill your dreams. It makes you an innovator, creator, and a scientific disposition. It also makes you a seer, philosopher, and humanitarian. The Moon represents the mind and Aquarius gives the native the "big picture" mentality. Aquarius minded people tend to do their work on behalf of humanity helping large groups of people at a time. It is written in the stars for you to be a seer, a philosopher, and even become an astrologer. You age gracefully and have a mystical presence. The shadow side of Moon in Aquarius is being reluctant, full of self doubt, being a loner, and at the extreme paranoid. Studying magic, the mystic arts, and Yoga is very good for you. Those emotional/mental disciplines will give you the knowledge you need to thrive, not just survive.

## Mars in Aquarius

**Analysis:** You have a strong capacity for action. You are energetic and have to keep busy to feel productive in life. Everything you do is extra. You win big and lose big. You get angry fast and forget about conflict fast. The shadow side of Mars in Aquarius is setting your expectations too high. You must guard against burn out. The indication is that at worst your behavior can be erratic and manic. So pay attention to those points.

## Mercury in Aquarius

**Analysis:** Mercury in Aquarius gives you a strong interest in metaphysics. You are intellectual, philosophical, and like the scientific method. Being an administrator, researcher, or scholar are good careers for you. Your thinking capability gets better over time and with age. The shadow side to Mercury in Aquarius is being too critical or a micromanager. The indication is that you over analyze everything and have trouble dealing with uncertainty.

## Venus in Aquarius

**Analysis:** Venus in Aquarius makes you a loyal and valued friend. In relationships you seek maturity and stability in a partner. You are attracted to the mysteries of the universe, unusual philosophies, and magic. The shadow side to Venus in Aquarius is being attracted to lost causes as partners. You might be drawn to unusual erotic experiences which might or might not be healthy for you. The indication is that you need to be very careful about your partners. You might be inclined to get involved with people who are emotionally and behaviorally dysfunctional. Be on guard about getting into relationships that are not reciprocal. If you bring 100% to a relationship then your partner should equally bring their 100%. Take time to meditate this week about the people you are surrounded by and ask yourself whether or not these people give back as much as you give. If the answer is no then you have a lot of choices to make about keeping them in your life.

## Jupiter in Aquarius

**Analysis:** You are orderly and organized. You are oriented toward the light and are a reformer. You have the desire to work towards the benefit of all. You are diplomatic in your dealings, are self-sufficient, and have political skills. The shadow side to Jupiter in Aquarius is being too legalistic, perfunctory, and reluctant to expand and grow into new territory. You must be careful not to become self isolating. You need to put effort into maintaining your friendships.

## Saturn in Aquarius

**Analysis:** Saturn is happy in his own sign and manifests his highest qualities by being dependable, deliberate, and respectable. Saturn in Aquarius is here for the long haul, looking to the endgame. He gives you the ability to be patient because your spiritual growth happens slowly and over time. So do not be in a hurry or rush any of your processes. The shadow side to Saturn in Aquarius is being robotic, dispassionate, and alienated. The indication is that the "ends justify the means'. Be on guard about lacking compassion for others.

## Rahu in Aquarius

**Analysis:** Rahu in Aquarius gives you the creative ability to fulfill your desires. You think of unusual ways to make things work. You work well with foreigners and people at long distances. The big indication from Rahu in Aquarius is that you are easily taken advantage of. You have to be very careful about choosing your associates. You might have the tendency to fall into the wrong circles. You need to be social and actively involved with the world to be successful. You just need to put up healthier and harder boundaries with others.

## Ketu in Aquarius

**Analysis:** Ketu in Aquarius is sublime development. In business you think creatively to increase profits. You are oriented towards spiritual life. You might even use a mixture of politics and religion to get yourself ahead. You have the ability to make money appear. The shadow side to Ketu in Aquarius is being all over the place, not being able to finish projects you start, and getting caught up in schemes that lead to nowhere. You might feel cut off and isolated often. You also might not have many friends. Ketu in Aquarius will make you a mystic and the older you get the more passionate you will feel towards the transcendental. My Ketu is also in Aquarius.

## Pisces

## Sun in Pisces

**Analysis:** You give good aid and support to others. You are flexible and adaptable. The indications are that you have an impressive inner life, are contemplative, and philosophical. You are also endearing to your lovers. The shadow side to the Sun in Pisces is being too submissive. Squandering opportunities because you lack focus. Volunteers too much then become a victim. The indication is that you need to focus on planning and setting goals for yourself.

## Moon in Pisces

**Analysis:** You have an ability to feel and comprehend emotions deeply. You are intuitive, but you must be sure that your abilities as an empath do not turn to codependency. Moon in Pisces gives you humanitarian desires. When your

Moon is shining bright you radiate idealistic, visionary, and empowering light to those around you. When that light is obstructed you can feel betrayed, full of doubt, and emotionally despondent. Because you have a Pisces Moon, the Mind/Heart of an empath, you must guard against being taken advantage of or becoming subservient to others.

## Mars in Pisces

**Analysis:** Mars in Pisces gives you fast gains in wealth but you need to be careful not to be over generous with your money. Mars in this sign could make you a political activist or interested in fighting challenging legal battles. Mars makes you excited for life and enthusiastic to see what is going to happen next. Like I said before you need to be careful about overspending and not try to live large. You also need to pay attention to alcohol and drug use because you have an inclination for addiction.

## Mercury in Pisces

**Analysis:** You have a spiritual nature, are imaginative, and versatile. You are sensitive, intuitive, and open-minded. You can also be a little spaced out and indecisive. Your mind has great potential for humanitarian and philanthropic work. The shadow side to Mercury in Pisces is being indecisive and not being able to manifest by thought only. You must engage in mental effort and find others that can give you advice. You might not have the ability to make proper decisions for yourself when it comes to your wealth or wellbeing. Find supportive people to be around who will encourage you to achieve your goals.

## Venus in Pisces

**Analysis:** Venus in Pisces makes you gentle, cultivated, and unpretentious. You love luxury, beauty, and refinement.

Because of your charming and knowledgeable nature you always get pushed to the front of the line. You are deeply compassionate for others. The shadow side to Venus in Pisces is you might be easily taken advantage of. You give more than you get back. You sacrifice your own needs mentally, emotionally, spiritually, and physically for people who can not recognize the value of it and are not capable of reciprocating the same. Be on guard about becoming overindulgent.

## Jupiter in Pisces

**Analysis:** Jupiter in Pisces represents wisdom, wealth, and expansion. At your best you are spiritual, supportive, and highly regarded. You are intuitive. The shadow side of Jupiter in Pisces is being overly optimistic. Getting fooled by people with grandiose ideas and going down dead end roads. You might also overspend on spiritual development.

## Saturn in Pisces

**Analysis:** You are down to earth and concerned with the affairs of the common person. You are good for your word and have a charitable disposition. Your wealth builds up over time so you need to be patient. You are a gracious person who makes a great friend. The shadow side to Saturn in Pisces is not defending your acquisitions, your assets. You can be too trusting. You need to keep track of details and not try to hide your problems. You might be drawn to or attract the wrong kind of people.

## Rahu in Pisces

**Analysis:** You have a big heart and are inclined to do humanitarian services as well as finance or support philanthropic adventures. Working internationally or having dealings internationally are also indicated. You must be careful with your Rahu in Pisces concerning the ability to manage your wealth and finances. You might have big dreams but you might not have the ability to manage your money very well. This could result in big loss and having to become dependent on friends and family. It is my high recommendation that you find someone to help you manage your affairs. That is a tax person or a counselor in finances. You need someone with objectivity to give you good counsel on how you budget your money and invest it.

## Ketu in Pisces

**Analysis:** Ketu in Pisces indicates enlightened and chaotic behavior. You are naturally drawn to the spiritual side of life and carry inherent wisdom carried over from past lives. You enjoy living a simple life and are inspirational to those around you. You do not like surprises. The downside is that you might experience a lot of upheavals during life which throws off your delicate Nature. You need to have a plan in life, which is not your strong suit. Your income might be erratic which leads to debts and bills piling up. You also need to pay attention to your wealth because you are prone to be taken advantage of, even having your money stolen from underneath you. You have great intuition which is your strength. You must use that to preserve your life gains. You have the ability to convert challenges into opportunities with Ketu in Pisces.

# YOUR PAST LIVES - RAHU AND KETU

To better understand what Rahu and Ketu mean in your life, we can start by looking at the signs they occupy in your chart. The sign placement will have specific meanings for each person, indicating important issues and lessons we must learn in accordance with our past lifetimes that have led us through Ketu, and where Rahu will take us in this lifetime. Rahu and Ketu are always exactly opposite each other, with Rahu being the ascending node and Ketu being the descending node. They are always in opposing signs, in the exact degree and minute opposite each other. Here are the oppositions of Rahu and Ketu:

**Rahu and Ketu in Aries/Libra**

**Rahu and Ketu in Taurus/Scorpio**

**Rahu and Ketu in Gemini/Sagittarius**

**Rahu and Ketu in Cancer/Capricorn**

**Rahu and Ketu in Leo/Aquarius**

**Rahu and Ketu in Virgo/Pisces**

Rahu is our future and Ketu is our past. According to their sign placement in your birth chart, Rahu and Ketu have particular karmic lessons to teach us. The typical experiences are described below, both as they pertain to the past, and what we can do now to make a better future.

### Rahu in Aries, Ketu in Libra

In this lifetime, you are meant to develop your own skills and be independent. You need to stand on your own two feet without relying on others. You are a self-starter and a pioneer, always going into new ventures and exploring the unknown to realize your full potential. In your last lifetime, you were all about taking care of others and making them feel supported and secure. You became so involved in their lives that you lost your own individuality and identity. This lifetime, you are meant to reclaim your Self and become whole and complete, without the need for a dependent relationship. You can master relationships this time around without being codependent.

### Rahu in Libra, Ketu in Aries

You are here to grow and learn through your relationships. It is important to understand yourself through the way you interact with others. How others make you feel is a reflection of your own inner world. You will not feel whole or complete without love and commitment in a lasting relationship. In previous lifetimes, you may have given too much of yourself to others, neglecting your own needs. This time around, you are empowered to focus on your own personal growth and development. You are supported by others who believe in you and want to see you succeed. You have the power to create the life you desire. Embrace this new chapter in your life and step into your own personal power. You are ready to shine bright!

### Rahu in Taurus, Ketu in Scorpio

This is a good placement for manifesting desires in the physical plane. Material things are important to you and you are able to easily acquire them. You have a sweet and gentle temperament and love beauty and nature. You love life and the gifts of the material world, which gives you a sense of happiness and contentment. Financial security gives you a sense of achievement and the ability to provide for your family without hardship, stress, or worry. You are gifted with the comforts of this world due to strong desires to achieve and seek power in previous lifetimes. Your struggles from previous lifetimes have brought you comforts in this lifetime. You were forced to share your wealth before, but now your earnings are yours to keep.

## Rahu in Scorpio, Ketu in Taurus

Rahu in Scorpio can make you intensely desire material wealth and power. If you don't achieve these things, you may feel unhappy and unfulfilled. However, your intense desire can also help you to achieve your goals. Rahu in Scorpio can also make you jealous of others who have what you want. You may be passionate and intense, but you may have trouble expressing your feelings. You may also feel insecure and inadequate, which can make it difficult to find true love. You may try to buy love with material things, but this will only lead to superficial relationships. It's important to learn to love yourself for who you are, not for what you have.

## Rahu in Gemini, Ketu in Sagittarius

In this life, you are here to develop your mental skills, especially in learning and communicating. You have the gift of gab and can easily connect with people from all walks of life. You are also a natural teacher and can explain complex concepts in a way that is easy to understand. In your past lives, you were a philosopher and teacher. You are to teach people how to live their lives in a meaningful way. In this life, you are here to share your experiences with others and teach them about the world. You thought you knew everything and were always trying to prove it to others. In this life, you are here to learn to be more humble. You are to develop non-judgment and accept others for who they are.

### Rahu in Sagittarius, Ketu in Gemini

You are now on a journey of self-discovery and enlightenment. You are meant to share your wisdom with others, but you must be humble and avoid arrogance. You must be compassionate and understanding, and not judge others. You must travel the world to teach your message, but you must do so with love and compassion, not judgment or rigidity. Through life's experiences, you will become more understanding, aware, and compassionate.

### Rahu in Cancer, Ketu in Capricorn

Cancer is the sign of family and security. People with this sign are often very nurturing and protective of their loved ones. They have a strong need for stability and security, and they often put their family first. In this life, Cancers are learning to balance their need for family with their need for independence. They are also learning to let go of the past and forgive themselves and others. As they do this, they will find more peace and happiness in their lives. Focus on your family and friends. They are your biggest source of support and happiness. Find a balance between your work and personal life. Don't neglect your family for your career. Forgive yourself and others. Holding on to anger and resentment will only hurt you in the long run. Let go of the past. Focus on the present and the future. Live in the moment. Don't worry about the future or dwell on the past. Enjoy the present.

### Rahu in Capricorn, Ketu in Cancer

You are driven to provide for and care for your family. In past lives, you were the emotional provider, but now you are driven to provide for them financially. You are determined to never feel the deep sense of lack that you felt in previous lifetimes. However, it is important to balance your work ethic with the time you need to spend with your family. You will be very successful financially because of your determination. You have the power to achieve financial security for your family. In this life, you will never lack the emotional commitment and security that you craved in past lives.

**Rahu in Leo, Ketu in Aquarius**

You are a natural leader with a thirst for achievement. You are driven and ambitious, and you always strive to be the best that you can be. However, in your pursuit of success, you can sometimes forget to take the time to listen to others. You may feel like the world revolves around you, but it is important to remember that everyone has their own needs and desires. When you learn to value others and their opinions, you will become a more effective leader and friend. In your past lives, you were often taken advantage of by others who did not appreciate your kindness and generosity. As a result, you have become more self-protective and less trusting of others. However, it is important to remember that not everyone is out to hurt you. There are many people who care about you and want to see you succeed. If you can learn to open your heart to others, you will find true happiness and fulfillment.

**Rahu in Aquarius, Ketu in Leo**

In past lives, you were all about being in control and being in command. Now, you are intellectualizing about many things, especially about human behavior. It feels better to share your thoughts rather than to keep to yourself as you did in previous lives. You gave of your heart in the last life and were hurt and your loyalties betrayed. So now, you feel better staying wrapped up in your head to better protect your heart. You are very intellectual and incredibly smart, but you can be arrogant when you are with others who are not as brilliant as yourself. Be open to others' thoughts, because you're not the ultimate authority of all knowledge. Compassion for humanity is real when it truly comes from the heart.

### Rahu in Virgo, Ketu in Pisces

You are a person who pays close attention to details. This can be a great strength, but it can also sometimes make it difficult for you to see the big picture. In previous lifetimes, you may have blamed others for your problems and seen the world as a negative place. However, you now have the power to change this. You can choose to focus on the positive and solve your own problems. In the past, you may have allowed others to take advantage of you. This has made you cautious and guarded in relationships. However, you don't need to let your fears control you. You can learn to give without fear and form lasting, sincere relationships. Just remember to set healthy boundaries. In this lifetime, you can use your organizational skills to create a happy and fulfilling love life. Just remember to be open to new experiences and be willing to put in the effort.

### Rahu in Pisces, Ketu in Virgo

In your past lives, you were constantly worried and created problems. This made you a more compassionate and loving soul in this life. You are now able to express your feelings openly, but your lack of boundaries can make you vulnerable to aggressors. It is important to take responsibility for your own feelings and not blame others for the way you feel. You should also look within yourself to understand how your actions affect others. In the past, your criticism destroyed your relationships. In this life, you should be open-hearted and accepting of others' shortcomings. This will help you overcome your past and prevent you from being a victim again.

# NAKSHATRAS ASCENDANT QUALITIES

In Vedic astrology, the Ascendant Nakshatra indicates the pattern of life. The Ascendant Lord indicates the direction of life.

**Ashwini** is the first Nakshatra in Vedic astrology and is associated with the celestial twins, the Ashvins. Here are some qualities, both positive and negative, of individuals born under this star:

**Positive Qualities:**

**Energetic**: Ashwini-born individuals are often full of energy, making them active and enthusiastic.

**Quick**: They are known for their speed and agility, both mentally and physically.

**Healing**: They often have an affinity for healing professions and can be found in fields such as medicine or therapy.

**Adventurous**: They are risk-takers, love to explore new things, and are unafraid of trying out novel ideas.

**Creative**: They have a knack for creativity and can be good at arts and crafts.

**Negative Qualities:**

**Impulsive**: Their quick nature can sometimes turn into

impulsiveness, leading to hasty decisions.

**Restless**: They may struggle with restlessness and can find it hard to stick to one task for a long time.

**Overzealous**: Their enthusiasm can sometimes be too much, causing them to become overly zealous or intense.

**Lack of Consistency**: Their love for novelty and change can sometimes lead to inconsistency in their work or relationships.

**Difficulty with Details**: While they're great at starting projects, they might struggle with the details or the follow-through.

**Bharani** is the second Nakshatra in Vedic astrology, ruled by the planet Venus and the deity Yama. Those born under this star possess several distinct qualities:

**Positive Qualities:**

**Determined**: Individuals born under Bharani are known for their determination and strong willpower.

**Honest**: They are generally straightforward and value honesty in their communication.

**Creative**: Bharani natives often have a flair for creativity, whether it's in arts, music, or any form of self-expression.

**Responsible**: They are known to take their responsibilities seriously and are often reliable.

**Patient**: They are capable of waiting for the right time to act, showcasing a sense of patience.

**Negative Qualities:**

**Stubborn**: Their determination can sometimes morph into stubbornness, making them inflexible.

**Impatient for Results**: While they're patient in waiting for the right time to act, they can be impatient when it comes to seeing the results of their efforts.

**Possessive**: They can sometimes get possessive about the

people or things they care about.

**Intense**: Their strong emotions can occasionally be intense and overwhelming for others around them.

**Struggle with Change**: They often prefer stability and can struggle when faced with changes in their lives.

**Krittika** is the third Nakshatra in Vedic astrology, ruled by the Sun and associated with the deity Agni, the fire god. Here are some qualities, both positive and negative, of individuals born under this star:

## Positive Qualities:

**Courageous:** Krittika-born individuals are often brave and ready to take on challenges.

**High Achievers:** They are ambitious and driven, and often aim for high achievements.

**Honest:** They are straightforward and appreciate honesty, often speaking up for what they believe is right.

**Protective:** They are often protective of their loved ones and stand up for those in need.

**Sharp Intellect:** They often possess a sharp mind and excellent analytical abilities.

## Negative Qualities:

**Overly Critical**: Their analytical nature can sometimes make them overly critical of themselves and others.

**Impatient**: Their drive to achieve can lead to impatience, leading them to act hastily at times.

**Stubborn:** They can be set in their ways and resistant to change, which can be perceived as stubbornness.

**Temperamental:** They can be quick-tempered or easily provoked, which sometimes leads to conflicts.

**Intense:** Their strong personality can sometimes come off as too intense or overpowering to others.

**Rohini** is the fourth Nakshatra in Vedic astrology, ruled by the Moon and associated with the deity Prajapati, the creator. Here are some qualities, both positive and negative, of individuals born under this star:

**Positive Qualities:**

**Loving**: Rohini-born individuals are often caring and affectionate, making them great partners and friends.
**Creative**: They have a flair for creativity and can excel in fields like art, design, and music.
**Practical**: They are pragmatic and often have a good understanding of the material world.
**Persuasive**: They are good communicators and can persuade others with their charm and eloquence.
**Patient**: They are known for their patience and ability to wait for the right moment to act.

**Negative Qualities:**

**Materialistic**: Their practical and material-oriented nature can sometimes make them overly focused on wealth and possessions.
**Stubborn**: They can be set in their ways and resistant to change.
**Jealous**: They can sometimes exhibit jealousy, especially in personal relationships.
**Overindulgence**: Their love for material comforts can lead to tendencies of overindulgence.
**Possessive**: They can become possessive of their loved ones or their possessions.

**Mrigashira** is the fifth Nakshatra in Vedic astrology, ruled by Mars and associated with the deity Soma, the Moon god. Here are some qualities, both positive and negative, of individuals born under this star:

**Positive Qualities:**

**Curious**: Mrigashira-born individuals are often curious and inquisitive, always seeking knowledge.
**Adaptable**: They are adaptable and flexible, able to adjust to change quite well.
**Pleasant**: They are generally pleasant and amiable, making them likable to people around them.
**Creative**: They often have a strong creative streak and can excel in artistic fields.
**Spiritual**: They may have a deep interest in spirituality and philosophical matters.

**Negative Qualities:**

**Restless**: Their curiosity can often lead to a sense of restlessness, always seeking something new.
**Indecisive**: They can sometimes struggle with decision-making due to their constant exploration of options.
**Overly Sensitive**: They can be extremely sensitive, which may lead to emotional instability at times.
**Inconsistent**: Their love for change can sometimes lead to inconsistency in their actions.
**Fickle**: Due to their adaptive nature, they can sometimes be fickle, changing their minds frequently.

**Ardra** is the sixth Nakshatra in Vedic astrology, ruled by the planet Rahu and associated with the deity Rudra, the storm god. Individuals born under this star possess a variety of qualities:

**Positive Qualities:**

**Intelligent**: Ardra natives are known for their sharp intellect and keen understanding of complex concepts.
**Innovative**: They often possess a unique, innovative approach

to problem-solving and are not afraid to think outside the box.

**Empathetic**: They are capable of understanding and sharing the feelings of others, which makes them good listeners and friends.

**Determined**: They are known for their determination and ability to persevere in challenging situations.

**Courageous**: Ardra individuals are brave and ready to face any challenge head-on.

**Negative Qualities:**

**Unpredictable**: Their innovative and out-of-the-box thinking can often make them unpredictable.

**Impulsive**: They can sometimes act on impulse without thoroughly considering the consequences.

**Volatile**: Like the storm god Rudra, they can be volatile and have quick shifts in mood or behavior.

**Stubborn**: Their determination can often turn into stubbornness, making them resistant to change.

**Tendency towards Negativity**: They can sometimes have a pessimistic outlook and may struggle with negative emotions.

**Punarvasu** is the seventh Nakshatra in Vedic astrology, ruled by the planet Jupiter and associated with the deity Aditi, the mother of the gods. Here are some of the qualities, both positive and negative, of individuals born under this star:

**Positive Qualities:**

**Generous**: Punarvasu individuals are often known for their generosity and willingness to help others.

**Optimistic**: They tend to have a positive outlook on life and are able to see the good in every situation.

**Intellectual**: They often possess a sharp intellect and a love for learning.

**Spiritual**: Many Punarvasu-born individuals have a deep interest in spirituality or philosophy.

**Adaptable**: They are flexible and can easily adjust to changes and new circumstances.

**Negative Qualities:**

**Naive**: Their optimism can sometimes make them naive and they may trust others too easily.
**Indecisive**: They may struggle to make decisions, often wavering between different options.
**Unpredictable**: They can be unpredictable, with sudden changes in mood or behavior.
**Lack of Focus**: Their interest in many things can sometimes lead to a lack of focus or direction.
**Procrastination**: They may tend to delay tasks and decisions, leading to procrastination.

**Pushya** is the eighth Nakshatra in Vedic astrology, ruled by the planet Saturn and associated with the deity Brihaspati, the god of wisdom. Here are some qualities, both positive and negative, associated with individuals born under this star:

**Positive Qualities:**

**Nurturing**: Pushya individuals are often caring and nurturing, always ready to lend a helping hand.
**Wise**: They are known for their wisdom and are often sought after for advice.
**Reliable**: They are dependable and can be relied upon to fulfill their responsibilities.
**Spiritual**: Many Pushya-born individuals have a deep interest in spirituality and may pursue paths of self-realization.
**Peaceful**: They usually prefer peace and harmony, avoiding conflict whenever possible.

**Negative Qualities:**

**Stubborn**: They can be quite set in their ways and resistant to change.

**Overprotective**: Their nurturing nature can sometimes make them overly protective, which can come off as controlling.

**Pessimistic**: Under the influence of Saturn, they may sometimes adopt a negative or pessimistic view of life.

**Slow**: They tend to take their time in doing things, which can sometimes be frustrating to others.

**Overly Serious**: They can sometimes be overly serious, forgetting to enjoy life and have fun.

**Aslesha** is the ninth Nakshatra in Vedic astrology, ruled by the planet Mercury and associated with the deity Sarpa, the serpent god. Individuals born under this star are known to possess certain qualities:

**Positive Qualities:**

**Intelligent**: Aslesha natives are often highly intelligent with a sharp intellect.

**Persuasive**: They possess strong communication skills and can be very persuasive.

**Determined**: They are known for their determination and willpower to achieve their goals.

**Passionate**: They often have a deep passion and intensity for whatever they pursue.

**Resourceful**: They are good at finding creative solutions to problems and are known for their resourcefulness.

**Negative Qualities:**

**Manipulative**: Their persuasive nature can sometimes lead them to be manipulative.

**Secretive**: They tend to be secretive and may not always share their thoughts and feelings openly.

**Possessive**: They can become overly possessive in personal relationships.

**Vengeful**: If wronged, they can hold grudges and seek revenge.

**Intense**: Their intensity can sometimes be overwhelming for others and can lead to conflicts.

**Magha** is the tenth Nakshatra in Vedic astrology, ruled by the planet Ketu and associated with the Pitris, the forefathers or ancestors. Here are the qualities of individuals born under this star:

**Positive Qualities:**

**Ambitious**: Magha natives are often ambitious and are willing to work hard to achieve their goals.
**Respectful**: They have a deep respect for traditions and ancestors.
**Loyal**: They are loyal to their friends and loved ones.
**Generous**: They are known for their generosity and willingness to help others.
**Leadership**: They often have strong leadership skills and are good at taking charge.

**Negative Qualities:**

**Arrogant**: Their ambition and leadership skills can sometimes make them come across as arrogant.
**Stubborn**: They can be quite stubborn and resistant to change.
**Domineering**: Their strong personality can sometimes be overbearing for others.
**Impulsive**: They can often act on impulse without considering the consequences.
**Overly Traditional**: Their respect for traditions can sometimes make them resistant to new ideas or changes.

**Purva Phalguni** is the eleventh Nakshatra in Vedic astrology, ruled by the planet Venus and associated with the deity Bhaga, the god of delight. Here are the qualities, both positive and negative, associated with individuals born under this star:

**Positive Qualities:**

**Charismatic**: Purva Phalguni natives often have a natural charm and charisma that draws people to them.
**Artistic**: They possess a strong aesthetic sense and often have talents in arts, music, or other creative fields.
**Generous**: They are known for their generosity and willingness to help others.
**Sociable**: They enjoy socializing and are often popular within their social circles.
**Romantic**: They are deeply romantic and value love and relationships.

**Negative Qualities:**

**Indulgent**: Their love for the finer things in life can sometimes lead to excess indulgence.
**Lazy**: They may have a tendency to procrastinate and avoid hard work.
**Materialistic**: They can be overly focused on material comforts and pleasures.
**Impulsive**: They may act on their emotions without considering the consequences.
**Overly Sensitive**: They may take criticism or negative feedback very personally.

**Uttara Phalguni** is the twelfth Nakshatra in Vedic astrology, ruled by the Sun and associated with the deity Aryaman, the god of contracts and relationships. Here are some qualities, both positive and negative, of individuals born under this star:

**Positive Qualities:**

**Warm-Hearted**: Uttara Phalguni natives are often warm-hearted and friendly, making them well-liked by others.
**Reliable**: They are known for their reliability and can be

trusted to fulfill their responsibilities.

**Generous**: They are often very generous and willing to help those in need.

**Balanced**: They tend to seek balance and harmony in their lives, avoiding extremes.

**Responsible**: They often have a strong sense of duty and responsibility.

**Negative Qualities:**

**Stubborn**: They can be quite stubborn and set in their ways, making them resistant to change.

**Overly Cautious**: Their desire for balance and stability can make them overly cautious and resistant to taking risks.

**Possessive**: They can be possessive in their personal relationships.

**Over-Reliant on Others**: They may depend too much on others for support or validation.

**Lack of Initiative**: They may lack the initiative to take action, preferring to wait for others to lead.

**Hasta** is the thirteenth Nakshatra in Vedic astrology, ruled by the Moon and associated with the deity Savitar, the Sun god who imparts creative and transformative energy. Here are some qualities, both positive and negative, associated with individuals born under this star:

**Positive Qualities:**

**Skilled**: Hasta natives are often very skilled, especially in crafts and artistic pursuits.

**Humorous**: They often have a good sense of humor and enjoy making others laugh.

**Practical**: They are practical and grounded, often with a good sense of what's achievable.

**Friendly**: They are sociable and enjoy the company of others.

**Versatile**: They have the ability to adapt and excel in different situations.

**Negative Qualities:**

**Manipulative**: Their skill and versatility can sometimes be used to manipulate others.
**Impatient**: They may lack patience, wanting results immediately.
**Materialistic**: They may be overly focused on material possessions and comforts.
**Overly Critical**: They can be overly critical of others, focusing on flaws and mistakes.
**Inconsistent**: Their versatility can sometimes make them inconsistent, changing their minds or plans frequently.

**Chitra** is the fourteenth Nakshatra in Vedic astrology, ruled by Mars and associated with the deity Vishwakarma, the celestial architect. Here are some traits, both positive and negative, associated with individuals born under this star:

**Positive Qualities:**

**Creative**: Chitra natives are often very creative, with a knack for design, architecture, art, and other creative fields.
**Skilled**: They excel in their chosen fields and are often seen as experts.
**Independent**: They are known for their independence and prefer to work on their own terms.
**Honest**: They are usually straightforward and honest in their dealings.
**Charismatic**: They often have a natural charm and charisma that attracts others.

**Negative Qualities:**

**Impulsive**: They can be impulsive, making decisions without considering the consequences.

**Overly Critical**: They can be overly critical of themselves and others.

**Perfectionist**: Their desire for perfection can lead to dissatisfaction and stress.

**Stubborn**: They can be quite stubborn and resistant to others' opinions.

**Competitive**: Their competitive nature can sometimes make them unsociable or uncooperative.

**Swati** is the fifteenth Nakshatra in Vedic astrology, ruled by Rahu and associated with the deity Vayu, the wind god. Here are some qualities, both positive and negative, of individuals born under this star:

**Positive Qualities:**

**Independent**: Swati natives are known for their strong sense of independence. They like to do things their own way and don't like being controlled.

**Flexible**: Just like the wind, they are adaptable and can adjust to different situations easily.

**Intelligent**: They are often intelligent and knowledgeable, with a keen interest in learning.

**Peace-loving**: They prefer harmony and avoid conflict whenever possible.

**Business-minded**: They often have a knack for business and are good at making profitable deals.

**Negative Qualities:**

**Restless**: Their independent nature can also make them restless and they may have trouble sticking to one thing for long.

**Indecisive**: They can sometimes be indecisive and have trouble making decisions.

**Detached**: They may come off as detached or aloof, making it hard for others to connect with them emotionally.

**Overly Analytical**: They may overthink things and get caught up in details, missing the bigger picture.
**Impatient**: They may lack patience and want quick results.

**Visakha** is the sixteenth Nakshatra in Vedic astrology, ruled by Jupiter and associated with the deities Indra and Agni, the gods of lightning and fire, respectively. Here are some qualities, both positive and negative, of individuals born under this star:

**Positive Qualities:**

**Determined**: Visakha natives are known for their perseverance, determination, and willpower.
**Charismatic**: They often possess a certain charm and charisma that draws others towards them.
**Successful**: They are ambitious and often successful in their endeavors, thanks to their hard work and dedication.
**Spiritual**: Many of them have a strong spiritual inclination and may be drawn to philosophy, religion, and the pursuit of truth.
**Generous**: They are generous and often willing to share their resources with others.

**Negative Qualities:**

**Stubborn**: Their determination can sometimes turn into stubbornness, making it difficult for them to accept other people's opinions.
**Impulsive**: They can be impulsive, often acting on their desires without thinking of the consequences.
**Aggressive**: They can be prone to aggression, especially when they feel their goals are being threatened.
**Overly Ambitious**: Their strong desire to succeed can sometimes make them overly competitive or ambitious.
**Restless**: They can be restless and always in need of change, which can lead to instability.

**Anuradha** is the seventeenth Nakshatra in Vedic astrology, ruled by Saturn and associated with the deity Mitra, the god of friendship and partnership. Here are some qualities, both positive and negative, of individuals born under this star:

**Positive Qualities:**

**Friendly**: Anuradha natives are often known for their friendly and sociable nature. They usually get along well with others and are good at building and maintaining relationships.

**Loyal**: They are loyal and reliable, which makes them trustworthy partners and friends.

**Adaptive**: They are adaptable and flexible, capable of adjusting to different situations and environments.

**Spiritual**: Many of them have a strong interest in spirituality and may be drawn to philosophical and metaphysical pursuits.

**Persevering**: They often exhibit great perseverance and determination, especially when working towards their goals.

**Negative Qualities:**

**Possessive**: Their loyalty can sometimes turn into possessiveness, which can cause problems in their relationships.

**Stubborn**: They can be quite stubborn and resistant to change, even when it's necessary.

**Secretive**: They often keep their thoughts and feelings to themselves, which can make them seem distant or aloof.

**Insecure**: They may struggle with feelings of insecurity and self-doubt.

**Overly Sensitive**: They can be overly sensitive to criticism or negative feedback.

**Jyeshta** is the eighteenth Nakshatra in Vedic astrology, ruled by Mercury and associated with the deity Indra, the king of the gods. Here are some qualities, both positive and negative, of individuals born under this star:

**Positive Qualities:**

**Leadership**: Jyeshta natives often possess natural leadership qualities. They are usually confident, decisive, and command respect from those around them.

**Intelligent**: They are known for their intelligence and quick thinking. They have a knack for problem-solving and are often successful in their chosen fields.

**Protective**: They have a strong protective instinct towards their loved ones and will go to great lengths to ensure their safety.

**Courageous**: They are brave and are not afraid to take risks or face challenges.

**Resourceful**: They are often resourceful and able to make the best out of any situation.

**Negative Qualities:**

**Dominating**: Their strong leadership traits can sometimes turn into a tendency to dominate others.

**Jealous**: They can be prone to feelings of jealousy and may struggle with envy.

**Impatient**: They can be impatient and may want things done their way without delay.

**Stubborn**: They can be quite stubborn and resistant to other's opinions.

**Overly Critical**: They may be overly critical of themselves and others, which can lead to strained relationships.

**Mula** is the nineteenth Nakshatra in Vedic astrology, ruled by Ketu and associated with the deity Nirriti, the goddess of destruction and dissolution. Here are some qualities, both positive and negative, of individuals born under this star:

**Positive Qualities:**

**Research Oriented**: Mula natives are often interested in research and investigation. They have a natural curiosity and a desire to get to the bottom of things.

**Honest**: They are known for their honesty and straightforwardness. They value truth and transparency.

**Spiritual**: They often have a deep interest in spirituality, mysticism, and the metaphysical aspects of life.

**Hardworking**: They are usually hardworking and dedicated, often achieving success through their perseverance.

**Intuitive**: They are often intuitive and can pick up on things that others might miss.

**Negative Qualities:**

**Uncompromising**: They can be uncompromising and rigid in their views, which can create conflict with others.

**Detached**: They may come across as detached or aloof, as they are often more focused on their inner world than their surroundings.

**Impulsive**: They can be impulsive and may make decisions without thinking through the consequences.

**Destructive**: Just like their ruling deity, they can sometimes bring about destruction, especially when they are not in control of their emotions or desires.

**Stubborn**: They can be stubborn and resistant to change, even when it's necessary.

**Purvashada** is the twentieth Nakshatra in Vedic astrology, ruled by Venus and associated with the deity Apas, the goddess of water. Here are some qualities, both positive and negative, of individuals born under this star:

**Positive Qualities:**

**Artistic**: Purvashada natives often have a deep appreciation for beauty and art. They may be talented in various forms of artistic expression.

**Charismatic**: They are known for their charisma, charm, and likability. They are often popular and attract others towards them.

**Optimistic**: They are generally optimistic and have a positive view of life, which helps them overcome challenges.

**Generous**: They are generous and kind-hearted, often going out of their way to help others.

**Diplomatic**: They are good at resolving conflicts and can handle difficult situations with grace and diplomacy.

## Negative Qualities:

**Indecisive**: Due to their desire for balance, they can sometimes be indecisive and find it hard to make decisions.

**Overindulgent**: They have a love for luxury and comfort and may be prone to overindulgence.

**Impatient**: They can be impatient and may want things to happen instantly.

**Egotistical**: Their charisma and popularity can sometimes lead to an inflated ego.

**Sensitive**: They can be overly sensitive to criticism and may take things personally.

**Uttarashada** is the twenty-first Nakshatra in Vedic astrology, ruled by the Sun and associated with the deities called the Vishvadevas, the universal gods. Here are some qualities, both positive and negative, of individuals born under this star:

## Positive Qualities:

**Ambitious**: Uttarashada natives are often ambitious and driven. They have a strong desire to achieve their goals and succeed in their endeavors.

**Generous**: They are known for their generosity and willingness to help others. They often use their success to benefit others.

**Optimistic**: They have a positive outlook on life and tend to be optimistic, even in challenging situations.

**Courageous**: They are brave and courageous, often willing to face any challenge head-on.

**Honest**: They value honesty and integrity, and always strive to do what is right.

**Negative Qualities:**

**Stubborn**: They can be stubborn and inflexible, often insisting on doing things their own way.

**Arrogant**: Their success and ambition can sometimes lead to arrogance.

**Overly Competitive**: They have a strong competitive streak, which can sometimes lead to conflict with others.

**Impatient**: They can be impatient and want to achieve their goals as quickly as possible.

**Insensitive**: They can sometimes be insensitive to the feelings and needs of others, especially when focused on their own goals.

**Shravana** is the twenty-second Nakshatra in Vedic astrology, ruled by the Moon and associated with the deity Vishnu, the preserver. Here are some qualities, both positive and negative, of individuals born under this star:

**Positive Qualities:**

**Knowledge Seekers**: Shravana natives are often avid seekers of knowledge. They have a love for learning and are often very well-read.

**Good Listeners**: They are known for their listening skills. They are patient and give their undivided attention to others when they speak.

Compassionate: They are compassionate and understanding, often showing great empathy towards the feelings of others.

Calm: They usually have a calm and tranquil demeanor, not

easily swayed by emotional turmoil.

Diligent: They are often meticulous and diligent in their work, with a strong attention to detail.

**Negative Qualities:**

Overly Sensitive: They can be overly sensitive and may take things personally. This can lead to emotional instability.

Pessimistic: They can sometimes be pessimistic, tending to focus on the negative aspects of situations.

Insecure: They may suffer from feelings of insecurity and self-doubt.

Indecisive: They can sometimes be indecisive, finding it hard to make decisions.

Gossipy: Due to their love for communication, they may sometimes indulge in gossip or unnecessary chatter.

**Dhanishta** is the twenty-third Nakshatra in Vedic astrology, ruled by Mars and associated with the deity Vasu, the god of wealth. Here are some qualities, both positive and negative, of individuals born under this star:

**Positive Qualities:**

**Ambitious**: Dhanishta natives are often ambitious and driven. They have a strong desire to succeed and achieve their goals.

**Wealthy**: They have a knack for accumulating wealth and often do well financially.

**Charitable**: Despite their wealth, they are often very generous and charitable, and like to use their resources to help others.

**Musical**: Dhanishta is often associated with music and dance. Those born under this star may have a natural talent in these areas.

**Courageous**: They are brave and don't shy away from taking risks to achieve their goals.

**Negative Qualities:**

**Stubborn**: They can be stubborn and inflexible, insisting on doing things their way.

**Materialistic**: Their desire for wealth and success can sometimes make them overly materialistic.

**Impulsive**: They can be impulsive and may make decisions without thinking them through.

**Competitive**: They have a strong competitive streak, which can lead to conflicts with others.

**Arrogant**: Their success can sometimes lead to arrogance, making them seem self-centered or egotistical.

**Satabisha** is the twenty-fourth Nakshatra in Vedic astrology, ruled by Rahu and associated with the deity Varuna, the god of cosmic waters. Here are some qualities, both positive and negative, of individuals born under this star:

**Positive Qualities:**

**Intelligent**: Satabisha natives are often intelligent and possess a deep thirst for knowledge.

**Compassionate**: They tend to be compassionate and caring, often going out of their way to help those in need.

**Creative**: They are creative and inventive, often coming up with unique ideas and solutions.

**Spiritual**: They are often deeply spiritual or philosophical and may have an interest in the mysteries of the universe.

**Healers**: They have a natural knack for healing, whether it be physical, emotional, or spiritual healing.

**Negative Qualities:**

**Secretive**: They can be secretive and may find it hard to open up to others.

**Stubborn**: They can be very stubborn and may resist change.

**Detached**: They may come across as detached or aloof, which can make it difficult for them to form close relationships.

**Pessimistic**: They can at times be pessimistic, focusing more on the negatives rather than the positives.

**Impulsive**: They can be impulsive, sometimes acting without thinking of the consequences.

**Purva Bhadrapada** is the twenty-fifth Nakshatra in Vedic astrology, ruled by Jupiter and associated with the deity Aja Ekapada, a form of Shiva's vehicle, Nandi. Here are some qualities, both positive and negative, of individuals born under this star:

**Positive Qualities:**

**Intellectual**: Purva Bhadrapada natives are often intellectual and possess a deep thirst for knowledge. They are curious and love to learn.

**Generous**: They are generous and giving, often willing to share their resources with others.

**Spiritual**: They are often deeply spiritual and may have an interest in the mysteries of the universe.

**Creative**: They are creative and have a unique way of thinking. They often excel in fields that allow them to use their creativity.

**Loyal**: They are loyal and trustworthy. They value their relationships and are often reliable friends and partners.

**Negative Qualities:**

**Restless**: They can be restless and may find it hard to stay still or focus on one thing for a long period.

**Impulsive**: They can be impulsive, sometimes acting without thinking of the consequences.

**Overly Sensitive**: They can be overly sensitive and may take things personally. This can lead to emotional instability.

**Pessimistic**: They can sometimes be pessimistic, tending to focus on the negative aspects of situations.

**Rebellious**: They can be rebellious and may resist authority or traditional norms.

**Uttara Bhadrapada** is the twenty-sixth Nakshatra in Vedic astrology, ruled by Saturn and associated with the deity Ahir Budhnya, the serpent of the deep sea. Here are some qualities, both positive and negative, of individuals born under this star:

**Positive Qualities:**

**Patient**: Uttara Bhadrapada natives are often patient and persevering. They can handle difficult situations calmly and with determination.
**Compassionate**: They are compassionate and kind-hearted, often showing empathy and understanding towards others.
**Reliable**: They are reliable and dependable. People often count on them to fulfill their responsibilities.
**Intuitive**: They are often intuitive and have a deep understanding of human nature. This helps them in their interpersonal relationships.
**Generous**: They are generous in nature and willing to help others without expecting anything in return.

**Negative Qualities:**

**Stubborn**: They can be stubborn and resistant to change. This can make them inflexible in their viewpoints.
**Overly Serious**: They can be overly serious, which can make them seem unapproachable or unsociable.
**Pessimistic**: They can be pessimistic and may focus on the negatives rather than the positives in situations.
**Detached**: Their serious nature can sometimes cause them to be detached from others, making it difficult for them to form close relationships.
**Overly Critical**: They can be overly critical, nitpicking minor details which can be frustrating for others.

**Revati** is the twenty-seventh and final Nakshatra in Vedic astrology, ruled by Mercury and associated with the deity Pushan, the nurturer and protector of flocks and herds. Here are some qualities, both positive and negative, of individuals born under this star:

**Positive Qualities:**

**Kind-Hearted**: Revati natives are often kind-hearted and caring. They are well-liked for their gentle and compassionate nature.
**Intellectual**: They are intelligent and have a love for knowledge. They are often drawn to academic and intellectual pursuits.
**Creative**: They are highly creative and imaginative and may excel in artistic fields.
**Generous**: They are generous and giving, often willing to help others without expecting anything in return.
**Reliable**: They are reliable and trustworthy, often making them good friends and partners.

**Negative Qualities:**

**Overly Sensitive**: Revati natives can be overly sensitive and may take criticism or negative feedback to heart.
**Indecisive**: They can often be indecisive, finding it difficult to make decisions.
**Overly Protective**: Their caring nature can sometimes make them overly protective, which can be smothering for others.
**Pessimistic**: They have a tendency to worry and can sometimes focus on the negative aspects of situations.
**Naive**: Due to their kind and trusting nature, they can sometimes be naive and easily deceived.

# HERBAL PREPARATIONS

Traditional healing is not only concerned with curing physical illness, but also takes into account the mental, emotional, and spiritual well-being of a client. When preparing medicinal plants, it is believed that illness begins in the spiritual realm and manifestation ultimately results in the mental/physical body. Traditional healers take into account psychological, emotional, and social contexts when preparing their treatments. The Sancista has an entire arsenal of tools for healing, protection, defensive, and offensive magic. When "it" hits the fan, we do not have to stand around and wait to see what happens. We don't just pray and hope bad things go away. No! We bust out the herbs and start practicing our magic — creating potions, lotions, and baths charged and powered by our spirits. There is so much more magic in this tradition, but for the purpose of this book for non- initiates, we are sticking to herbal magic and preparation.

## Recognizing Quality Herbs

If you are going to buy herbs online or at the health food store, I want to give you advice on determining the quality of the plants. To determine the quality of your herbs, check for color, taste, effect, and scent. Ed Smith of Herb Pharm, explains it this way; "when you go into a grocery store you look for the freshest quality lettuce; the head with the youngest, most tender green leaves. If the lettuce looks brown or rotting, you don't buy it." Shopping for herbs requires the same level of discernment. Dried herbs should look, taste, and smell almost exactly as they do when they are fresh, and they should be effective. Here are the rules we follow according to Rosemary Gladstar, the most respected traditional herbalist in America.

## Color

The herb should retain the same color as when it was fresh with very little color variation. If you are buying green leaves such as peppermint or basil, they should be vivid, bright, and alive looking. If buying blossoms, they should retain almost the same color as when fresh. Roots are generally not as colorful as leaves or flowers, but they should be true to their original color.

## Smell

All herbs have distinctive odors that are effective means to determine their quality. Becoming an herbalist means being able to recognize a plant and its distinctive scent. Smell your herb before purchasing. They should smell strong but not necessarily "good." Not all herbs smell good. Good quality dried peppermint will smell as fragrant and astringent as the fresh herb.

## Taste

Herbs should have a distinct, fresh flavor. Not all herbs taste good, some are very bitter. Do your herbs taste fresh? Do they taste strong? That is a very good way of determining its potency. This is an art and as you begin to study herbal medicine you will learn by working with the herbs. Trial and error are your teachers.

## Effects

Herbal remedies made with quality herbs are incredibly effective. If the herb you are using is not working, scrutinize the herbs for quality first. If the herbs seem good, then re-examine your extraction process. You might not have allowed the herbs to soak long enough to pull all its medicinal qualities.

There are other concerns when shopping for herbs. Herbs that are commercial and harvested in bulk may retain pesticides and other toxic substances. Words like "natural," "high quality," "pure," and even "organic" have become meaningless sales pitches in the food industry. High quality herbs are expensive in themselves and usually are not found in expensive commercial type packaging. Finding locally grown herbs from small farmers and growers is your best bet. Actually, growing them yourself is the ideal.

**Working with Herbs**

Making herbal preparations is very simple. Anyone can do it, including me! Becoming an herbalist and aromatherapist is something I always wanted to do, but was overwhelmed by the amount of work I thought it took. It's not that hard and you can do it too. All you need is fresh or dried herbs, water, oil, vinegar, or high proof liquor for herbal extraction. You will need empty glass amber bottles to store your concoctions or Mason jars. Heat and light destroy the quality of herbs and herbal preparations. Store your herbs and concoctions in a cool dark place such as a closet or pantry. Always store your herbal formulations in glass containers, nothing else. Make sure you label and date the Mason jars, so you do not forget what is in there! We're keeping it very simple. The herbs listed in this manual are easy to use and are the ones most commonly found at a grocery store or health food store. The herbs that are listed in this manual are generally recognized as safe and for the most part do not have adverse reactions in the human body. There is always an exception though, so be careful.

Remember that whenever you're treating an individual patient, you need to find out what their pre-existing health conditions are, if they're taking medications, and encourage them to check in with their healthcare provider to let them know whether using herbal remedies is safe for them. Always err on the side of caution. You are a spiritual healer, but these plants also have very real medicinal properties. If you are interested in getting a more in-depth education of herbalism, I recommend that you sign up for an online certification such as Rosemary Gladstar's The Science and Art of Herbalism. Why wait though? Start trying to make your own herbal remedies and magical oils immediately!

## Cannabis sativa

Cannabis is listed in this book, but working with cannabis is not as easy as working with other herbs. First, there are the legalities of possessing cannabis. In Massachusetts, where I live, every adult is allowed to grow marijuana plants for home cultivation and use. It also can be given as gifts to friends and family, but cannot be sold without having an approved cannabis business. So, understand that you must craft cannabis products in harmony with your state and local laws.

Cannabis has to be decarboxylated to release its THC and CBD properties. That is beyond the scope of this book, but I will recommend buying the book "The Marijuana Medical Handbook" by Ed Rosenthal as well as "The Cannabis Spa at Home" by Sandra Hinchliffe. The best book for learning how to grow is "The Cannabis Grow Bible: The Definitive Guide to Growing Marijuana for Recreational and Medicinal Use" by Greg Green. Hopefully soon the prohibition against this plant will end and every American will be able to have safe access to the medicine or even cultivate it themselves without fear of arrest or stigma. It is disgusting that in this country there are marijuana dispensaries that look like Apple stores with employees serving up weed like baristas while there are still people sitting in jail for holding a joint in a prohibited state.

## Where to Find Herbs and Storage

If you are going to be making tinctures, tonics, and herbal oils, you will need to buy herbs in bulk. Mountain Rose Herbs and other online bulk herb suppliers like Jean's Greens or Starwest Botanicals are trusted sources. Store your herbs in a cool dry place. The kind of herbs you can use are in dried, crushed, and powder form. We would prefer freshly cut herbs for spiritual baths, although that's not always possible in today's world. Use what's available and affordable to get started. Some of the herbs listed are for topical use only and can make you very sick if consumed! All of those plants are clearly titled for topical use only.

## Cooking with Herbs

Be creative, find recipes online that use the specific herbs you want to use. For spiritual purposes, of course, you want to charge the herbs before you cook with them. Then after you make your food, pray over it and bless it — asking for help from your spirits. Yes, cooking is magic! Buy a few books on Creole seasoning because it was the Tainos who invented it! The book "Puerto Rican Cookery" by Carmen Aboy Valldejuli is a must-have in your kitchen. My grandmother had that book and I remember flipping through it when I was a little boy. It's available on Kindle now.

## Herbal Tea/Infusion/Decoction

These extractions use water as a solvent. Put a heaping teaspoon full of herbs in a cup or buy individual empty tea bags. Add boiling water, stir, cover, and let steep for 10 minutes. Strain, drink, and use the infusion within 24 hours. The standard dosage is one to two cups. An herbal tea is considered an infusion. A decoction is a stronger tea made with tougher plant materials. Decoctions are used for extracting the medicinal properties of roots such as dried herbs, seeds, roots, rhizomes, and bark. Put plant matter into a saucepan and add one and a half cups of cold water. After bringing to a boil, cover and simmer for 15 minutes. Strain and drink. This will last about 72 hours if you refrigerate it.

## Tincture

A tincture is when you extract the medicinal properties of plants using 80 to 100 proof alcohol such as vodka, gin, or brandy. Place the herbs into a mason jar and fill with the alcohol of your choice. Stir well, cap the jar, and put it in a cool dark place. Shake the jar vigorously once or twice a day for 14 days. The longer the herbs steep, the stronger the tincture becomes. When you are ready to strain out the herbs, use a cheesecloth. Try to get all the liquid you can out of the herbs. Discard the compost and store the tincture in an amber glass dropper bottle. The tincture will keep for several years. You can add several drops of tincture into any beverage of choice or take directly under the tongue.

## Apple Cider Vinegar Tonic

You can make an apple cider vinegar tonic by filling a Mason jar half full of herbs, saturating it, and filling the rest of the jar with apple cider vinegar. Use a plastic lid to cover. Just like you would a tincture, shake the mason jar once or twice a day for 14 to 30 days. The longer the herbs soak in apple cider vinegar, the stronger it becomes. Like the tincture, strain all of the plant matter through a cheesecloth; also, squeeze the herbs to get all of the vinegar out. You can refrigerate the tonic, but it does not have a long shelf life. It should be used within 30 days.

## Oil Infusion/Solar and Slow Cooker

Put herbs into a Mason jar and cover with high-quality, cold-pressed olive oil. Stir and make the consistency of a mud pie, leaving about an inch of oil on top. Keep it in a warm place of approximately 100°F, such as on a windowsill, to receive direct sunlight for a solar infusion. Shake frequently throughout the day for 10 to 14 days. Strain. Press the remaining oil out as much as you can and store it in a cool place. If you feel pressed for time, you can also take the herbs and oil and put it in a slow cooker. Make sure there is one to two inches of oil on top of the herbs. Turn the slow cooker on and let it cook for 24 hours on low or until the oils take the color and scent of the herbs. Strain the oil and you have made an herbal oil. You can use the oil on salads, while cooking, and even topically as an herbal massage oil or you can make a salve. You can use the herbal oil to anoint anything you want for magical purposes.

**Liniment for Topical Use Only!**

To make a liniment, the method is the same as a tincture except you're making it with much higher proof alcohol. This is an ethanol extraction and the liquor used is called Everclear. You can't get Everclear in some states because it's high proof. It's not drinkable. It's for extracting plant material only. After making the liniment, you can put some on a rag with hot water and place it over the area of the body that needs treatment.

**Foraging For Beginners**

Learning to forage your herbs is a great way to connect with nature, but it's also important to do so responsibly and safely. Here's a general outline to get started:

**Educate Yourself:** Start by reading books or online resources about foraging. Some recommended books include "The Forager's Harvest" by Samuel Thayer or "Edible Wild Plants" by John Kallas.

**Attend Workshops or Classes:** Look for local foraging workshops, classes, or guided walks. Learning from an expert in-person can be very beneficial.

**Learn to Identify Plants:** Invest time in learning how to accurately identify plants. Some plants have toxic look-alikes, so correct identification is vital.

**Know Your Area:** Understand the seasons, climate, and ecosystems in your local area. This will help you anticipate what plants you can forage.

**Follow Laws and Regulations:** Familiarize yourself with local laws about foraging. Some parks and public lands may have restrictions.

**Practice Sustainable Foraging:** Only take what you need, never over-harvest, and be mindful not to damage the habitat.

**Safety First:** Never consume a plant unless you're 100% sure of its identification and safety. Some wild plants can be poisonous.

Remember, it's a gradual learning process and it's perfectly okay to go slow and be cautious. Happy foraging!

# MATERIA MEDICA - THE MEDICINE

The herbs listed below are the most commonly used herbs in Puerto Rico and the United States for medicinal and spiritual use. The criteria for an herb to make it into this book is it had to be used in Puerto Rican traditional healing, American herbalism, and have a religious, magical, and spiritual use. I have also listed appropriate crystals and gemstones you can use with your herbal magic. It also had to be easily obtainable by the novice practitioner and be somewhat familiar. Buying a bunch of herbs from a botanica and not knowing what to do with them is a waste of money and is bad for the environment. I recommend you pick up a copy of "Earth and Spirit: Medicinal Plants and Healing Lore from Puerto Rico" by Maria Benedetti. That book primarily interviews traditional Puerto Rican herbalists and gives a wealth of information on treating conditions with herbal remedies. It is not a magic book. Ms. Benedetti also leads retreats in Puerto Rico and has an apprenticeship program for those wishing to study with her. The herbs will be listed as "Topical Use" if they are poisonous to ingest or could be dangerous.

**Disclaimer:** *None of these herbs should be smoked. Some are for topical use only and are noted accordingly. Use responsibly! Also, do not use these if you have serious health conditions without consulting a doctor or other qualified medical professional.*

**Aloe** (Topical Use)

*Aloe vera*

**Medicinal:** Speeds the healing of burns and wounds. Can be used to treat insect bites, eczema, dry skin, and poison ivy.

**Contraindications:** Do not take internally without checking with the doctor. Do not take during pregnancy or breast-feeding. This plant could cause diarrhea or worse when ingested.

**Spiritual:** Aloe as a house plant is used to prevent accidents and misfortunes around the home. It is also used for love and beauty and spells.

**Crystals/Stones:** Jade, Citrine, Rose Quartz

## Angelica Root

*Angelica archangelica*

**Medicinal:** Angelica is used for heartburn, flatulence, loss of appetite, arthritis, circulation problems, and trouble sleeping.

**Generally recognized as safe.**

**Spiritual:** Ward off evil, break jinxes, brings good luck, to ensure good health and wellbeing.

**Crystals/Stones:** Black Tourmaline, Amethyst

## Anise

*Pimpinella anisum*

**Medicinal:** Abdominal pain, chronic diarrhea, flatulence, and intestinal ailments.

**Generally recognized as safe.**

**Spiritual:** Protection and purification. Fresh anise wards off evil spirits and averts the evil eye. The seed can be combined with bay leaves in a spiritual bath to call for spirits aid in magical operations.

**Crystals/Stones:** Citrine, Onyx

## Anise seed

*Pimpinella anisum*

**Medicinal:** Anise is used for upset stomach, intestinal gas, runny nose, and as an expectorant to increase productive cough. It is also used as an appetite stimulant.

**Generally recognized as safe.**

**Spiritual:** Increases psychic abilities, wards off the evil eye.

**Crystals/Stones:** Citrine, Onyx

## Annatto

*Bixa orellana L.*

**Medicinal:** Used for diabetes, diarrhea, fevers, fluid retention, heartburn, malaria, and hepatitis. It is an antioxidant and bowel cleanser. Annatto is sometimes put directly on an affected area to treat burns and vaginal infections.

**Contraindications:** Do not use during pregnancy or breast-feeding.

**Spiritual:** Brings courage, helps with lack of decisiveness. Use if you need stealth.

**Crystals/Stones:** Bloodstone, Obsidian, Carnelian

## Arrowroot

*Maranta arundinacea*

**Medicinal:** Arrowroot is used as a nutritional food for infants and for people recovering from illness. It is also used for stomach and intestinal disorders including diarrhea.

**Generally recognized as safe.**

**Spiritual:** Money drawing and good luck.

**Crystals/Stones:** Aventurine, Citrine

## Arnica (Topical Use)

*Arnica montana*

**Medicinal:** Relieves aches and pains.

**Contraindications:** Poisonous if ingested. Must be diluted in a carrier oil. Do not put on broken skin.

**Spiritual:** To create boundaries, cope with trauma, or ease disappointments.

**Crystals/Stones:** Garnet, Carnelian, Rose Quartz, Tigers Eye, Lapis Lazuli

## Ashwagandha

*Withania somnifera*

**Medicinal:** Used as a tonic and aphrodisiac. Sexual function and hormonal balance. It is also called Indian ginseng and is used in Ayurveda to treat cerebral function in the elderly.

**Contraindications:** Should be avoided for people with thyroid conditions or on thyroid medications.

**Spiritual:** Strengthens spiritual endurance. Protects the aura and energy body.

**Crystals/Stones:** Green Jade, Peridot

## Balsam Apple

*Momordica balsamina*

**Medicinal:** A liniment is made by adding the pulped fruit without the seeds to almond oil. This is useful for burns and chapped elbows, knees, and hands.

**Contraindications:** Abdominal pain, diarrhea, headache, or fever with excessive amounts.

**Spiritual:** Removes spirit attachments in spiritual baths.

**Crystals/Stones:** Black Tourmaline, Rose Quartz

**Basil**

*Ocimum basilicum*

**Medicinal:** Prevents cellular damage. Relieves vomiting, diarrhea, and constipation. Good for the digestive system. Also fights acne and itchy skin.

**Contraindications:** Generally recognized as safe.

**Spiritual:** Powerful herb in magic that brings balance and harmony. Brings wealth if carried in your pocket.

**Crystals/Stones:** Black Tourmaline, Clear Quartz, Polished Selenite

**Bay Laurel** (Topical Use)

*Laurus nobilis*

**Medicinal:** Used to treat arthritic aches, back pain, and sore muscles.

**Contraindications:** Ingesting Bay Laurel is dangerous; it is a strong stimulant and has narcotic properties. If consumed it will cause increased blood pressure and vomiting.

**Spiritual:** Bay Leaves are used in divination, clairvoyance, and helps induce visions. Burning a bay leaf can cleanse ritual space, banish negativity, and ward off evil.

**Crystals/Stones:** Amethyst, Super Seven

**Black Nightshade** (Topical Use)

*Solanum nigrum*

**Medicinal:** Is applied directly to the skin for psoriasis, hemorrhoids, and deep skin infections (abscesses). Bruised fresh leaves are put on the skin to treat swelling, burns, and ulcers.

**Contraindications:** Poisonous. Causes irregular heartbeat, trouble breathing, dizziness, twitching in the arms and legs, and possibly paralysis and death.

**Spiritual:** Chthonic powers and travel to the underworld. Black nightshade is also used in offertory rites for the spirits of the dead.

**Crystals/Stones:** Lapis Lazuli, Rose Quartz, Yellow Tigers Eye

**Burdock Root**

*Arctium*

**Medicinal:** Primarily used as a blood purifier. Herbalists use it to treat liver disorders. It is a diuretic and laxative.

**Contraindications:** Slows blood clotting should be avoided by persons with bleeding disorders

**Spiritual:** Helps let go of victim mentality. Powerful herb for protection and healing. Wards off negativity if casted around the home.

**Crystals/Stones:** Labradorite, Amethyst

**Calendula**

*Calendula officinalis*

**Medicinal:** Calendula flower is used to prevent muscle spasms, start menstrual periods, and reduce fever. It is also used for treating sore throats and duodenal ulcers.

**Generally recognized as safe.**

Spiritual: Inspiration, optimism, and good vibes. Repels negativity. It is used to comfort those who have experienced shock or trauma. Brings balance and harmony.

Crystals/Stones: Amber, Citrine

**Camphor** (Topical Use)

*Cinnamomum camphora*

**Medicinal:** Mostly used for sprains, muscular aches, and pains. It is the most active ingredient in my favorite salve, Tiger Balm. Also has anti-bacterial and anti-fungal properties.

**Contraindications:** Absolutely do not ingest. Can cause seizures and death. Do not apply to broken skin.

**Spiritual:** Psychic protection. Put in a floor wash to ward off negativity.

**Crystals/Stones:** Lodestone, Black Tourmaline, Obsidian

## Cannabis

*Cannabis sativa*

**Medicinal:** Cannabis fights cancer cells. Aids in long term memory function although it impairs short term memory when used. Can treat severe stomach and digestive disorders such as crohn's disease. Help with glaucoma. Eases nausea due to chemotherapy and helps with appetite. Also reduces chronic pain and neuropathy. Best used as an edible for medicinal purposes in small doses to reduce the chance of a panic attack. People panic from using too much cannabis because it affects the amygdala, your flight or fight response in the brain. Do not go to the hospital if you overdose you will not die. Drink orange juice and get fresh air in case of anxiety. There is a link between cannabis use and the onset of schizophrenia in pre-disposed people that scientists have not been able to figure out yet.

**Warning:** The drug is federally illegal and only legal in certain states. There might be an allergic reaction such as a rash. This plant is intoxicating. Can cause anxiety if taken in large doses. Should not be used in conjunction with Valerian or within 24 hours of use because it can intensify the intoxicating effects and be unpleasant.

**Spiritual:** One of the five teaching plants given to mankind from the gods. It is a visionary plant used by Yogis in meditation to become one with the divine. When used during sexual activity can increase sensations and bring powerful orgasms.

**Crystals/Stones:** Citrine, Sodalite, Rose Quartz, Amethyst

# Cardamom

*Elettaria cardamomum*

**Medicinal:** Antioxidant. Anti-inflammatory. Good for heart and digestive function. Good for metabolism. Also boosts men's sexual health.

**Contraindications:** Generally recognized as safe. It might cause intestinal spasms if you have irritable bowel syndrome.

**Spiritual:** Can inflame lust in a man.

**Crystals/Stones:** Pink Tourmaline, Pyrite, Garnet

# Catnip

*Nepeta cataria*

**Medicinal:** Catnip is a nervine and tonic. It makes cats crazy but has the opposite effect on humans. It can be used in tea for relaxation and helps with sleep disorders.

**Generally recognized as safe.**

**Spiritual:** Calls good spirits and can be used to bring good luck.

**Crystals/Stones:** Jade, Citrine, Rose Quartz

# Cayenne Pepper

*Capsicum annuum*

**Medicinal:** This is a very powerful stimulant it has the ability to irritate the skin. It can treat severe colds and is best used if you feel like you are starting to get sick. Put a sprinkle of Cayenne Pepper in hot water with a splash of lemon juice and honey to stimulate body heat. It increases circulation and makes you sweat.

**Warning:** Keep away from the eyes. Rinse with cold water immediately if contact is made.

**Spiritual:** Acceptance. Helps resistant people embrace change.

**Crystals/Stones:** Apatite, Apache Tears

## Chamomile

*Matricaria chamomilla*

**Medicinal:** This is one of the most pleasant sedatives available and one of the safest. It is completely harmless and will relax you for a good night's sleep.

**Generally recognized as safe.**

**Spiritual:** Chamomile is very powerful! It is used in spiritual warfare fighting against curses and black magic. Use it in a spiritual bath with other herbs to banish negativity or remove a jinx.

**Crystals/Stones:** Black Tourmaline, Clear and Smoky Quartz, Bloodstone

## Cinnamon

*Cinnamomum verum*

**Medicinal:** Cinnamon treats a variety of illnesses. Good for stomach and digestive issues. It relieves gas and works to stop vomiting. Boots men's sexual health.

**Contraindications:** May cause low blood sugar and interact with certain diabetic medications.

**Spiritual:** Helps overcome anxiety and fear. Cinnamon raises spiritual vibrations.

**Crystals/Stones:** Red Spinel, Carnelian, Tigers Eye

**Clove**

*Syzygium aromaticum*

**Medicinal:** Used as an antimicrobial to help kill bacteria. Can treat digestive upset and relieve respiratory conditions such as cough and asthma.

**Generally recognized as safe.**

**Spiritual:** Used for psychic enhancement. Drives away hostile and negative forces. It also brings comfort to those who have experienced loss.

**Crystals/Stones:** Celestite, Amethyst

**Comfrey** (Topical Use)

*Symphytum*

**Medicinal:** Used in a variety of treatments including bruises, burns, sprains, and broken bones.

**Warning:** Poisonous if ingested.

**Spiritual:** Apply to the body or carry to ensure safety during travel. You can also put some in your luggage to make sure they are not stolen.

**Crystals/Stones:** Rutilated Quartz, Azurite

**Cumin**

*Cuminum cyminum*

**Medicinal:** Improves metabolism, lowers cholesterol, and promotes weight loss.

**Generally recognized as safe.**

**Spiritual:** Use for protection, fidelity, or to attract a lover.

**Crystals/Stones:** Pink Tourmaline, Pyrite, Garnet

## Echinacea

*Echinacea purpurea*

**Medicinal:** Good for the immune, lymphatic, and respiratory systems. Used to treat acute bacterial and viral infections as well as poison ivy and venomous bites.

**Contraindications:** Should not be taken by people with tuberculosis, HIV, leukemia, multiple sclerosis, lupus, or autoimmune disease.

**Spiritual:** Releases old patterns and welcomes change. Echinacea was used by American Indians as an offering to the spirits.

**Crystals/Stones:** Selenite, Green Aventurine, Apache Tears

## Elderflower

*Sambucus*

**Medicinal:** Elder flowers have an anti-inflammatory effect on the upper respiratory system when under stress from colds, flu, or sinusitis.

**Contraindications:** Do not use high dosages. Can cause digestive upset or rash.

**Spiritual:** Elder is one of those plants surrounded by mystery, magic, and superstition. Elderflower wards off spiritual attacks of every kind. It fights against sorcery and is highly useful in spiritual warfare.

**Crystals/Stones:** Black Tourmaline, Smoky Quartz, Onyx

## Fennel

*Foeniculum vulgare*

**Medicinal:** Used as a digestive aid and to treat gastrointestinal problems.

**Contraindications:** Should be avoided in high doses during pregnancy.

**Spiritual:** Aids in Communication.

**Crystals/Stones:** Lapis Lazuli, Rose Quartz, Tigers Eye

**Garlic**

*Allium sativum*

**Medicinal:** The healing properties of garlic are too many to name. Helps treat colds, flu symptoms, and relieves chest congestion. It is diuretic and also treats digestive problems.

**Generally recognized as safe.**

**Spiritual:** Protection and banishment. Wards off evil.

**Crystals/Stones:** Black Tourmaline, Bloodstone, Carnelian

**Ginger**

*Zingiber officinale*

**Medicinal:** Improves digestive and cardiovascular health. Fights colds and flu. Boosts men's sexual health.

**Generally recognized as safe.**

**Spiritual:** Personal power. Sex magic. Brings prosperity and good luck. Promotes healthy relationships.

**Crystals/Stones:** Pink Tourmaline, Pyrite, Garnet

**Goldenseal**

*Hydrastis canadensis*

**Medicinal:** Digestive problems such as gastritis, peptic ulcers, and inflamed colon.

**Contraindications:** Goldenseal should not be taken for a prolonged period of time. This herb should not be used in cases of kidney disease including kidney failure.

**Spiritual:** Brings mental clarity of past, present, and future. Increases potency of spells.

**Crystals/Stones:** Celestite, Amethyst

**Holy Basil/Tulsi**

*Ocimum tenuiflorum*

**Medicinal:** Calms the stomach and nervous system. It is a very important herb in Ayurvedic medicine. It is adaptogenic and a good all-purpose herb.

**Contraindications:** Not recommended for people taking medications that slow blood clotting.

**Spiritual:** Balances the energy body. Brings joy, positivity, and hope. Wards off negative energy.

**Crystals/Stones:** Amber, Citrine

**Lavender**

*Lavandula*

**Medicinal:** Lavender has antiseptic and anti-inflammatory properties. Useful in treating anxiety, insomnia, depression, and restlessness. Some studies suggest that consuming lavender as a tea can help digestive issues such as vomiting, nausea, intestinal gas, upset stomach, and abdominal swelling. Lavender is one of Nature's most powerful medicinal plants.

**Generally recognized as safe.**

**Spiritual:** Increases spiritual awareness and sensitivity.

**Crystals/Stones:** Clear and Rose Quartz, Amethyst

**Lemongrass**

*Cymbopogon*

**Medicinal:** Helps reduce spasms in the digestive tract. Can help with vomiting, cough, fever, and cold. Is an astringent.

**Generally recognized as safe.**

**Spiritual:** Repels evil. Increases psychic abilities. Good for cleansing and healing spells.

**Crystals/Stones:** Black Tourmaline, Blue Lace Agate, Blue Kyanite

**Licorice**

*Glycyrrhiza glabra*

**Medicinal:** Licorice contains constituents that are similar to natural steroids in the human body and affects the endocrine system. It's used for upper respiratory conditions such as congestion, coughs, and bronchitis.

**Contraindications:** Is a blood thinner and must be taken with caution. It can elevate blood pressure and can be dangerous for persons with high blood pressure.

**Spiritual:** Used in binding spells to restrict your enemies or gain control over a situation.

**Crystals/Stones:** Citrine, Onyx

**Mugwort**

*Artemisia vulgaris*

**Medicinal:** Has a reputation for helping people to achieve more vivid dreams. You can put mugwort in herbal tea and drink it about two hours before you go to sleep.

**Generally recognized as safe.**

**Spiritual:** Increased lucid dreaming and psychic awareness.

**Crystals/Stones:** Selenite, Super Seven, Clear Quartz

**Nettle**

*Urtica dioica*

**Medicinal:** Very useful aphrodisiac. It's been known to stop bleeding and is used for purifying the kidneys and removing toxic substances from the kidneys. Nettle can be used in the treatment of jaundice.

**Contraindications:** Persons with high blood pressure, diabetes, kidney disease, or bleeding disorders should avoid this plant.

**Spiritual:** Uncrossing and jinx breaker. Protective. Used for love and luck spells.

**Crystals/Stones:** Black Tourmaline, Obsidian, Smoky Quartz

## Peppermint

*Mentha × piperita*

**Medicinal:** Peppermint is excellent for treating nausea, vomiting, and headaches. It's wonderful in herbal teas and gives everything a crisp clean flavor.

**Generally recognized as safe.**

**Spiritual:** Treats mental, emotional, and spiritual lethargy. Uncrossing and jinx breaker.

**Crystals/Stones:** Calcite, Rainbow Fluorite Grid

## Rosemary

*Salvia rosmarinus*

**Medicinal:** The health benefits for rosemary are too many to name. It can help someone who is having trouble sleeping. Has been used to help alleviate muscle pain, improve memory, boost the immune and circulatory system, and promote hair growth.

**Contraindications:** Encourages menstrual bleeding and may cause miscarriage. Do not use in large doses.

**Spiritual:** Reconnects the soul and spirit after traumatic events. All healing and protection spells.

**Crystals/Stones:** Hematite, Blue Chalcedony, Sodalite

## Sage

*Salvia officinalis*

**Medicinal:** Helpful for relieving constipation.

**Generally recognized as safe.**

**Spiritual:** Protection and purification. Fresh starts. Mental clarity. Used in banishing work.

**Crystals/Stones:** Clear Quartz, Obsidian

## Saw Palmetto

*Serenoa repens*

**Medicinal:** Good for the urinary, nervous, and digestive systems. It enhances male sex hormones and is used to treat the prostate. Excellent for men's sexual health.

**Generally recognized as safe.**

**Spiritual:** Controls passions and worn by women to keep their husbands faithful.

**Crystals/Stones:** Red Jasper, Rhodochrosite

## Skullcap

*Scutellaria*

**Medicinal:** Skullcap is a sedative and antispasmodic. It is a reliable and safe nervous system tonic.

**Contraindications:** Do not use this herb in high dosages.

**Spiritual:** Used in recovery from a spiritual attack. Combats nightmares and other nighttime disturbances.

**Crystals/Stones:** Garnet, Carnelian, Rose Quartz, Tigers Eye,

Lapis Lazuli

## Thyme

*Thymus*

**Medicinal:** Thyme is excellent for treating upset stomach. It can also help with arthritis and rheumatism.

**Contraindications:** Can slow blood clotting. Not recommended for persons using blood thinners.

**Spiritual:** Grants the ability to see spirits and other entities. Gives strength in spiritual warfare.

**Crystals/Stones:** Clear and Smoky Quartz, Obsidian, Black Tourmaline

## Turmeric

*Curcuma longa*

**Medicinal:** Turmeric is one of the most powerful herbs on the planet. It is most reputable for reducing inflammation.

**Generally recognized as safe.**

**Spiritual:** Healing, protection, and banishing magic.

**Crystals/Stones:** Aquamarine, Rose Quartz

## Valerian

*Valeriana officinalis*

**Medicinal:** Regulates nerve cells and calms anxiety. Put the herb in tea to promote sleep.

**Contraindications:** Should not be used if using other sleep aids. Do not drive or operate machinery after taking this herb.

**Spiritual:** Protection and love magic. Can bring lucid dreams due to its aid in restful sleep.

**Crystals/Stones:** Rainbow Fluorite, Celestite

## Yarrow

*Achillea millefolium*

**Medicinal:** Yarrow has been known to stop bleeding and assist in the healing process. It's good for treating colds and fevers.

**Generally recognized as safe.**

**Spiritual:** Brings compassionate feelings towards others.

**Crystals/Stones:** Lapis Lazuli, Rose Quartz, Tigers Eye

# CARIBBEAN SOUL FOOD

**Avocados**

*Persea americana*

**Medicinal:** One of the healthiest fats you can eat. Contains more potassium than bananas, can lower cholesterol, lower risk of depression, and improve digestion. Avocados are also an aphrodisiac!

**Generally recognized as safe.**

**Spiritual:** Luck, abundance, and attraction. Grow a plant from the pit of an avocado to bring love to your home.

**Cassava**

*Manihot esculenta*

**Medicinal:** Cassava is a good source of vitamin C, thiamine, riboflavin, and niacin.

**Generally recognized as safe.**

**Spiritual:** Love, confidence, and courage.

**Coconut**

*Cocos nucifera*

**Medicinal:** Healthy fat, supports heart health, reduces blood pressure, and is a great source of hydration.

**Contraindication:** Some people are allergic to coconuts.

**Spiritual:** Use coconut water or cream in a spiritual bath for purification and removing negativity.

## Coffee

*Coffea*

**Medicinal:** Helps burn fat, improves physical performance, contains essential nutrients, may lower risk of type two diabetes, Alzheimer's and dementia, and Parkinson's disease. May prevent strokes and is a powerful antioxidant.

**Contraindications:** Generally recognized as safe. Can cause elevated heartbeat or jitters if consumed in large amounts.

**Spiritual:** Add to a spiritual bath to remove spiritual blockages and bring clarity.

## Chocolate

*Theobroma cacao*

**Medicinal:** Powerful source of antioxidants improves circulation, lowers blood pressure, improves brain function, relieves anxiety. Especially dark chocolate.

**Generally recognized as safe.**

**Spiritual:** Resolves conflicts in love or with enemies.

## Honey

*Honey*

**Medicinal:** Can be put on a wound to slow bacterial growth. Is a cough suppressant. Eat locally grown honey to improve your immune system and combat seasonal allergies.

**Contraindications:** Some people have an allergic reaction. Is not Vegan.

**Spiritual:** Great for sex magic. Used to attract a lover.

## Horseradish

*Armoracia rusticana*

**Medicinal:** Strengthens the immune system, treats urinary tract infections, may regulate blood pressure.

**Generally recognized as safe.**

**Spiritual:** Used in spiritual warfare, cleansing, drives out evil.

**Lemon**

**Medicinal:** Great source of vitamin C, improves digestive health, detoxifier.

**Generally recognized as safe.**

**Spiritual:** Used to remove negative vibrations and cleanse objects. You can take a lemon and put it in your ritual space, or any room, leave it out. If it starts to decay quickly there's bad juju. You need to clean and freshen the room. If there's good energy the lemon will keep even for a couple of weeks.

**Vinegar**

*dilute acetic acid*

**Medicinal:** Kills harmful bacteria, lowers blood sugar, fights diabetes, improves weight loss, lowers cholesterol.

**Contraindications:** Can affect blood sugar. Do not take if using diabetic medication. Dilute in water to drink, it is highly acidic and can irritate the throat.

**Spiritual:** Prevents magical attacks, protects against evil, can be used in spiritual warfare.

**Sweet Potato**

*Ipomoea batatas*

**Medicinal:** Great source of fiber. It is packed with vitamins and minerals, promotes good gut health, and has antioxidants.

**Generally recognized as safe.**

**Spiritual:** Spiritual nourishment, can be enchanting to bring love and friendship. Eat when you need to feel grounded and connected to the earth.

### Rice

*Oryza sativa*

**Medicinal:** Stabilizes blood sugar levels, provides essential sources of vitamin B 12.

**Generally recognized as safe.**

**Spiritual:** Protection, money, and fertility.

### Plantains

Musa × paradisiaca

**Medicinal:** Useful remedy for coughs, inflamed skin, and dermatitis. Can be used topically to treat insect bites, stings, eczema, and small cuts or sores.

**Generally recognized as safe.**

**Spiritual:** Excites sexual passion.

# ESSENTIAL OILS

You want to buy real steam distilled essential oils and not perfumed or fragrance oil. Essential oils are made by collecting bulk plant matter and putting it into a copper still. The copper still is heated and as water boils underneath the plants the steam passes through the plant matter and distills out the aromatic waters and oil. The oil floats to the top of the water and they are separated. Hydrosols (aromatic waters) are fascinating and wonderful in themselves and you can buy them online. We are going to confine our lesson to essential oils only and ones that are easily obtained.

I cannot recommend the book "Aromatherapy Anointing Oils: Spiritual Blessings, Ceremonies, and Affirmations" by Joni Keim and Ruah Bull enough. For any Sancista who wants an in-depth study of anointing oils for mental, emotional, and spiritual well-being, pick up a copy. "The Healing Intelligence of Essential Oils: The Science of Advanced Aromatherapy" by Kurt Schnaubelt is the absolute best book on aromatherapy and has a clinical approach if you are a serious student. To become a clinically certified aromatherapist, I recommend the New York Institute of Aromatic Studies online school.

### Synergy / Anointing Oil / Body Oil

A synergy is when you select two or more essential oils and blend them in a carrier oil. As an example, you would take tea tree essential oil and put 10-20 drops into a one-ounce bottle of almond oil. Thus, you would have a small bottle of oil to use on candles, objects you wish to bless, or put into a spiritual bath. If you made body oil you would take a large bottle, four to eight ounces, and increase the amount of essential oil. You would use it as a massage oil or after shower oil.

## Lotion

Today, you can buy pre-made plain organic lotions and body butters in a tub to add essential oils to and bottle yourself. You do not want cheap unscented lotions with synthetic ingredients containing alcohol in them. Websites like Essential Wholesale and Labs, or a company like them, have "ready" lotions for you to buy with vegan all-natural ingredients to purchase. Making lotion is a lot of work and it is just as simple to buy a quality mixture and add your own herbal oils and essential oils.

## Bath Salt / Salt Scrub

You can go to the pharmacy and buy a bag full of Epsom salt or go online and buy a large bag of coarse sea salt for bath and body. Then, after putting the salt into a container of choice, add a few drops of essential oil or your synergy for a ready to go cleansing spiritual bath. You can also add dry herbs to your bath salt. You make a salt scrub just like making a bath salt, but you add oil to it until the salt and oil make a paste.

## Salves / Ointments

A salve is a balm that is made with a combination of liquid and solid oils, butters, wax, and essential oil.

## Directly into Baths

You can put drops of essential oils directly into a bath. To be honest when I am making a spiritual bath, I will turn on the water to start to fill my tub and as the water rises, I will cast in the ingredients while making my incantations. That's the easiest way to make a bath for me but then again, I am kind of lazy! However, not all essential oils are safe to be applied directly to the body. And some have health contraindications for women who are pregnant or nursing. After the description of the medicinal use and magical use of the oil is listed there will also be any warnings.

## The Essential Oils

These oils are meant for topical use only. Essential oils are highly concentrated when undiluted. It is best not to apply directly to the skin when starting out. If there is an allergic reaction, they may cause rash, redness, and discomfort. I always recommend a small test on a non-sensitive part of the skin, such as the hand, to ensure there are no reactions. These oils can be used to anoint your candles or put into a spiritual bath for therapeutic or spiritual purposes.

## Anise

*Pimpinella anisum*

**Medicinal:** Can be used to treat a runny nose and is an expectorant.

**Generally recognized as safe.**

**Spiritual:** Dispels limiting thoughts. Also helps you let go of old beliefs. Allows messages from higher level spirits to be received clearly.

**Crystals/Stones:** Citrine, Onyx

## Allspice

*Pimenta dioica*

**Medicinal:** Can relieve gas, bloating, and upset stomach. Has antioxidants and anti-inflammatory properties. Can ease menstrual cramps.

**May irritate the skin. Must be dilute in a carrier oil.**

**Spiritual:** Strengthens aura.

**Crystals/Stones:** Citrine, Onyx

## Balsam of Peru

*Myroxylon Pereirae*

**Medicinal:** This wonderful aroma helps soothe out-of-control emotions, calms nervous tension, and can promote a tranquil environment. It can be used during times of respiratory congestion to help you breathe easier.

**Generally recognized as safe.**

**Spiritual:** Protects from emotional, mental, and physical disturbance.

**Crystals/Stones:** Rose Quartz, Ruby

## Bay Rum

*Pimenta racemosa*

**Medicinal Properties:** Clarifying for the skin.

**May irritate the skin. Must be dilute in a carrier oil.**

**Spiritual:** Clarity. Purification. Used in spiritual baths for cleansing. Draws helping spirits.

**Crystals/Stones:** Clear Quartz, Obsidian, Black Tourmaline

## Bergamot

**Medicinal:** Antispasmodic, antiseptic, analgesic, pain relieving.

**May irritate the skin. Must be dilute in a carrier oil. Do not use it before going in the sun.**

**Generally recognized as safe.**

**Spiritual:** Prosperity, happiness, confidence, and courage. Helps those dealing with grief, loss, and sadness. Releases energetic blocks.

**Crystals/Stones:** Carnelian, Moss Agate, Amber, Black

Tourmaline

## Black Pepper

*Piper nigrum*

**Medicinal:** Relieves aches and pains, has antiviral properties, eases feelings of anxiety, and reduces cigarette cravings.

**May irritate the skin. Must be dilute in a carrier oil.**

**Spiritual:** Makes someone receptive to spiritual guidance. Fearlessness, motivation, spiritual strength, cleansing, protection, and purification.

**Crystals/Stones:** Prehnite, Clear/Smoky/Rose Quartz

## Cannabis

*Cannabis sativa*

**Medicinal:** Antimicrobial, analgesic, and anti-inflammatory. Good for the nervous system and aids in relaxation.

**Generally recognized as safe.**

**Spiritual:** Enhances sex magic, protection, and healing.

**Crystals/Stones:** Citrine, Sodalite, Rose Quartz

## Cedarwood

*Cedrus atlantica*

**Medicinal:** Improves mental clarity, increases cerebral activity, and relaxes the body. Enhances concentration and decreases hyperactivity.

**May irritate the skin. Must be dilute in a carrier oil.**

**Spiritual:** Use when feeling spiritually weak or when you need help making decisions. To heal emotional wounds.

**Crystals/Stones:** Green Jade, Amber

## Chamomile

*Matricaria chamomilla*

**Medicinal:** Wound healing including ulcers and sores. Skin conditions like eczema or rashes. Anti-inflammation and pain relieving. Promotes restful sleep. Anxiety relief.

**Generally recognized as safe.**

**Spiritual:** Powerful in magic! Used in spiritual warfare and to break curses. Soothes feelings of loneliness.

**Crystals/Stones:** Smoky Quartz, Apache Tears, Aquamarine, Selenite

**Cinnamon**

*Cinnamomum verum*

**Medicinal:** Increases circulation and nourishes the skin.

**May irritate the skin. Must be dilute in a carrier oil.**

**Spiritual:** Helps you accomplish your goals. Aids in accessing old memories. Helps to be more assertive and supports will power.

**Crystals/Stones:** Jade, Citrine, Onyx

**Clary Sage**

*Salvia sclarea*

**Medicinal:** Antibacterial properties, natural antidepressant, helps relieve symptoms in menopause, and reduces menstrual cramps. Stress reduction.

**Generally recognized as safe.**

**Spiritual:** Helps with clairvoyants, channeling, divination, and getting through emotional difficulty or painful situations.

**Crystals/Stones:** Ametrine, Iolite

**Clove**

*Syzygium aromaticum*

**Medicinal:** Antimicrobial that kills bacteria. Pain reliever. Aids respiratory conditions like coughs and asthma.

**May irritate the skin. Must be dilute in a carrier oil.**

**Spiritual:** Psychic enhancer, releases old thoughts and patterns. Great for energy work and distance healing.

**Crystals/Stones:** Celestite, Amethyst

**Copaiba**

*Copaifera*

**Medicinal:** Anti-inflammatory, wound healing, pain relief. Treats infections from parasites. Can be an aphrodisiac.

**May irritate the skin. Must be dilute in a carrier oil.**

**Spiritual:** Balancing, grounding, protective, and heals emotional wounds.

Crystals/Stones: Selenite, Super Seven, Clear Quartz

**Eucalyptus**

*Eucalyptus globulus*

**Medicinal:** Antiseptic, cleansing and purifying agent, treatment for respiratory ailments, fevers, cold, flu, and asthma. Mental clarity.

**Generally recognized as safe.**

**Spiritual:** All healing spells. Purification. Helps when feeling overwhelmed or disillusioned.

**Crystals/Stones:** Labradorite, Blue Lace Agate, Amethyst, Obsidian, Black Tourmaline

**Frankincense**

*Boswellia*

**Medicinal:** Expectorant, clears nasal passages, and alleviates congestion. Enhances mood. Diminishes feelings of stress, anxiety. Improves concentration and memory.

**May irritate the skin. Must be dilute in a carrier oil.**

**Spiritual:** Blessing oil for the dead, funerals, and rites of passage. Use when feeling spiritually depleted.

**Crystals/Stones:** Iolite, Black Tourmaline, Moldavite, Amber

### Ginger

*Zingiber officinale*

**Medicinal:** Detoxifier, clears respiratory tract, and reduces inflammation.

**May irritate the skin. Must be dilute in a carrier oil. Do not use it before going in the sun.**

**Spiritual:** Mental clarity, abundance spells, use when feeling trapped or when needing confidence.

**Crystals/Stones:** Pink Tourmaline, Pyrite, Garnet

### Grapefruit

*Citrus × paradisi*

**Medicinal:** Appetite suppressant, promotes weight loss, improves mood, has antibacterial and antimicrobial effects.

**May irritate the skin. Must be dilute in a carrier oil.**

**Spiritual:** Stops mental chatter/confusion, helps you hear your inner voice and develops intuitive powers. Psychic awakening. Cleanses aura. Use when processing through difficult emotions.

**Crystals/Stones:** Rainbow Fluorite, Rhodochrosite

### Jasmine

*Jasminum*

**Medicinal:** Aphrodisiac, antispasmodic, anti-depressant, and reduces cramps due to menstruation.

**Generally recognized as safe.**

**Spiritual:** Love spells, sexual attraction, angelic connection, use when feeling agitated, also helpful when feeling creative.

**Crystals/Stones:** Rose Quartz, Ruby, Ametrine, Iolite

### Juniper

**Medicinal:** Air purifier, detoxifying agent. Supports urinary and kidney function.

**Generally recognized as safe.**

**Spiritual:** Wish granting, curse breaker, and jinx removal. Aids in healing from spiritually caused sickness. Stops damaging thoughts and beliefs. Use when feeling stuck or trapped.

**Crystals/Stones:** Obsidian, Black Tourmaline, Smoky Quartz, Hematite, Selenite

### Lavender

*Lavandula*

**Medicinal:** Promotes relaxation, treats anxiety, fungal infections, allergies, depression, insomnia, eczema, nausea, and menstrual cramps.

**Generally recognized as safe.**

**Spiritual:** Peace in the home, stops gossip. Use when feeling unbalanced or unable to forgive others.

**Crystals/Stones:** Amethyst, Rose Quartz

### Lemon

*Citrus × limon*

**Medicinal:** Antiseptic, astringent, calming, disinfectant and antifungal. Refreshing and energizing.

**May irritate the skin. Must be dilute in a carrier oil. Do not use it before going in the sun.**

**Spiritual:** Used for calling spirits in healing work. Purifying, cleansing, and protecting. Use to feel more optimistic and positive.

**Crystals/Stones:** Citrine, Amber

## Lime

*Citrus × aurantiifolia*

**Medicinal:** Antiseptic, good disinfectant, antibacterial, antiviral, astringent, anti-depressant.

May irritate the skin. Must be dilute in a carrier oil. Do not use it before going in the sun.

**Spiritual:** To keep a partner faithful, when needing clarity, when a memory needs to be released and let go of. To move on.

**Crystals/Stones:** Green Tourmaline

## Myrrh

Commiphora myrrha

**Medicinal:** Boost immunity, antioxidant, anti-inflammatory, boost mood, controls cough, treats insomnia, and sore throats.

**May irritate the skin. Must be dilute in a carrier oil.**

**Generally recognized as safe.**

**Spiritual:** Guards against evil forces. Use when dealing with feelings of resentment or to make a relationship more cooperative.

**Crystals/Stones:** Amber, Tigers Eye

## Palo Santo

*Bursera graveolens*

**Medicinal:** Can treat headaches, depression, anxiety, emotional pain, and inflammation, relieves common colds, flu symptoms, and reduces stress.

**Generally recognized as safe.**

**Spiritual:** Mental, emotional, physical and psychic healing. Energetic protection, removes negativity, spiritually purifying.

**Crystals/Stones:** Clear and Smoky Quartz

## Patchouli

*Pogostemon cablin*

**Medicinal:** Stimulates growth of new skin.

**Generally recognized as safe.**

**Spiritual:** Aphrodisiac, psychic enhancement, body acceptance, uniting the sensual and the spiritual.

**Crystals/Stones:** Carnelian, Angelite

## Peppermint

*Mentha × piperita*

**Medicinal:** antibacterial, antispasmodic, disinfects, soothes inflamed skin, expectorant, breaks up congestion due to colds and flu, immune support.

**Generally recognized as safe.**

**Spiritual:** Helps create positive change in one's life. Strengthens your magic for fighting curses. Use when needing more self-esteem.

**Crystals/Stones:** Amethyst, Ametrine

## Rose

*Rosa*

**Medicinal:** Clears up acne, reduces the signs of aging, minimizes appearance of scars, helps treat eczema and rosacea.

**Generally recognized as safe.**

**Spiritual:** Attracts love and affection, fertility spells, health, and protection magic. Helps heal heartbreak, feelings of being disconnected or lonely, and creates healthy boundaries.

**Crystals/Stones:** Clear and Rose Quartz

## Rosemary

*Salvia rosmarinus*

**Medicinal:** Improves brain function, stimulates hair growth, relieves pain, increases circulation, reduces joint inflammation, helps concentration and focus.

**May irritate the skin. Must be dilute in a carrier oil.**

**Spiritual:** Banishing oil especially combined with sage. Helps create appropriate boundaries. Strengthens faith. Use when redefining your values.

**Crystals/Stones:** Obsidian, Black Tourmaline

## Sage

*Salvia officinalis*

**Medicinal:** Muscular and joint pain, bacterial infections, antispasmodic, detoxifier, promotes digestive relief, alleviates skin conditions like dermatitis and athlete's foot.

**May irritate the skin. Must be dilute in a carrier oil.**

**Spiritual:** Divination and protection.

**Crystals/Stones:** Obsidian, Black Tourmaline

**Sandalwood**

*Santalum*

**Medicinal:** Helps promote restful sleep.

**May irritate the skin. Must be dilute in a carrier oil.**

**Spiritual:** Psychic enhancement, healing sexual wounds, improves self-esteem, heals relationships. Use when you don't trust yourself.

**Crystals/Stones:** Smoky Quartz, Garnet Citrine, Hematite

**Spruce**

*Picea*

**Medicinal:** Supports upper respiratory function, expectorant, helps fight against cough, congestion, and the flu.

**May irritate the skin. Must be dilute in a carrier oil.**

**Spiritual:** Brings feelings of security, balances mood, and helps overcome emotional barriers. Grounds you when feeling chaotic and all over the place.

**Crystals/Stones:** Garnet, Aquamarine, Tigers Eye, Bloodstone

**Tea Tree**

*Melaleuca alternifolia*

**Medicinal:** Antibacterial, anti-inflammatory, antiviral, antifungal, treat athlete's foot, contact dermatitis, and head lice. Detoxifier. Also promotes healthy respiratory function, fights colds and flus, helps with asthma.

**Generally recognized as safe.**

**Spiritual:** Clears away energy blockages. Protection, use when feeling stuck, use to understand someone else's perspective.

Helps overcome resistance to change.

**Crystals/Stones:** Clear/Smoky/Rose Quartz, Citrine, Lapis Lazuli

## Ylang Ylang

*Cananga odorata*          ·

**Medicinal:** Natural insect repellent, promotes wound healing, diminishes the appearance of scars on the skin.

**Generally recognized as safe.**

**Spiritual:** Improved self-esteem, to find employment, also an aphrodisiac, helps you to embrace your sensuality. Aids in becoming more creative and experiencing new perspectives.

Crystals/Stones: Rose Quartz, Jade

## Bulk Oils, Wax, Salt, and Soap

Below is a list of the carrier oils, wax, salt, and liquid soap I buy to make my products. Bulk Apothecary and J Edwards International sell these oils in bulk. It is cheaper to buy a bottle of liquid coconut oil by the gallon than going to the grocery store. You can buy a gallon of unscented pure castile liquid soap also. You can also find any of these things being sold on Amazon. Let me tell you, it's worth being a Prime member for two day guaranteed delivery and free shipping!

## Avocado oil

*Persea gratissima*

Almost 70% of avocado oil consists of heart-healthy oleic acid, a monounsaturated omega-9 fatty acid. This fatty acid is also the main component of olive oil and believed to be partly responsible for its health benefits. Additionally, around 12% of avocado oil is saturated fat and about 13% is polyunsaturated fat. The application of Vitamin B12 cream containing avocado oil has considerable potential as a well-tolerated, long-term topical therapy of psoriasis.

## Castor Oil

*Ricinus communis*

The use of castor oil goes as far back as the ancient Egyptians, who used it to treat eye irritations and as a powerful natural skin care remedy. In India, castor oil has been prized for its skin-healing, digestive-soothing, antibacterial properties and is commonly used in traditional Ayurvedic medicine practices. As an unsaturated fatty acid, ricinoleic acid found in castor oil, has many healing abilities including increased circulation, helping to kill ringworm, abrasions and fungal infections, reducing itching and swelling on the skin. One of the major reasons castor oil has strong immune-enhancing effects is because it supports the body's lymphatic system.

## Coconut Oil/MCT Oil (Medium Chain Triglyceride)

*Caprylic-Capric TG*

Coconut oil is famous throughout the world, not only as an edible oil and hair tonic, but also as an excellent massage oil and to smoothen the skin. Coconut oil can also be used as a makeup remover. This is not common, but women have begun using it for removing the makeup of the face and eyes, without worrying about the harsh chemicals of other removers getting into delicate or sensitive areas. Predominantly, these saturated fats are medium chain fatty acids or triglycerides. When applied on the skin, they keep it smooth to the touch. Due to the presence of these fats, coconut oil also retains the moisture content of the skin, as the fats eliminate moisture loss through the pores on skin.

Some people have a severe coconut allergy. Ask before putting it into a client's product.

## Hemp Seed Oil

Cannabis sativa

As a superfood, hemp seeds are a complete protein and rich in polyunsaturated fatty acids, omegas 3, 6, and 9. They are packed with potassium, magnesium, iron, zinc, calcium, and phosphorus. Hemp seed oil's similar composition to skin lipids makes it an excellent natural emollient and moisturizer. It is especially useful for dry, tired, or dehydrated skin and nails. It increases skin elasticity as well as the water retention capacity of the tissues and can be used to treat dry hair.

## Jojoba Oil

*Simmondsia chinensis*

This oil is extracted from seeds of the jojoba plant, scientifically known as Simmondsia chinensis, which are indigenous to the southern United States and northern Mexico. Jojoba oil is non-toxic, non-comedogenic and non-allergenic. This means that it will not clog pores and will not cause any allergic reactions. It is also not an irritant, so it can safely be used around the eyes and on the skin. Most bacteria including Staphylococcus aureus and the fungus Candida albicans cannot reproduce and die when they come into contact with jojoba oil.

## Shea Nut Oil

*Vitellaria paradoxa*

This oil is extracted from the shea nut, a plant native to West Africa. Shea nut oil has many of the same benefits of shea butter as it may be useful in mitigating skin conditions such as dermatitis, eczema, and burns. Since the oil contains an abundance of oleic and stearic essential fatty acids, it provides many benefits for those who use it. During the expeller process for the butter, a small amount of fractionated liquid oil is extracted directly from the nut. This oil is thick and can be slightly cloudy because of the fat content. Shea nut oil has been used for thousands of years as a valuable ingredient to nourish skin and hair.

May be dangerous for people with severe nut allergies.

## Sweet Almond Oil

*Prunus dulcis*

This is a mild hypoallergenic oil; it's safe for sensitive skin. Absorption is best when the oil is warmed to body temperature before application. Probably due in large part to its antioxidative properties, sweet almond oil is known for protecting skin against UV radiation damage and keeping skin soft and supple. It can be used to gently dislodge debris from deep within skin pores and follicles, and also may help prevent future acne because of its vitamin A content. When you apply a few warm drops beneath your bottom eyelid before bed, you can expect to see brighter, less puffy eyes. Applied all over the face, almond oil can also delay general signs of aging as it renews the cells of your facial skin.

May be dangerous for people with severe nut allergies.

## Vitamin E

*gamma-Tocopherol*

Vitamin E benefits skin by strengthening the capillary walls and improving moisture and elasticity, acting as a natural anti-aging nutrient within your body. Vitamin E also helps the healing process in the skin. It's absorbed by the epidermis layer of the skin and can be used to treat sunburn, which is one of the leading causes of skin cancer, among other factors. Because it speeds up cell regeneration, it can be used to treat scars, acne and wrinkles; this makes your skin look healthier and younger. Aloe vera produces two substances used for medicine: The gel is obtained from the cells in the center of the leaf, and the latex is obtained from the cells just beneath the leaf skin. Most people use aloe gel as a remedy for skin conditions, including burns, sunburn, frostbite, psoriasis, and cold sores, but there are a host of other benefits. Aloe vera is used for treating osteoarthritis, bowel diseases, fever, itching, and inflammation.

## Candelilla Wax

*Euphorbia antisyphilitica*

Candelilla wax (plant-based vegan wax) is a hard and brittle wax extracted from the wax-coated stems of Candelilla shrubs. The plant grows wild in northeastern Mexico and the plains and foothills of the Chihuahuan Desert. The plant has traditionally been harvested from the wild to extract the thick wax coating, originally used to make candles, giving candelilla its name "little candle." Mass production for commercial use began in Mexico in the early 20th century.

## Shea Butter

*Vitellaria paradoxa*

Shea butter aids numerous skin conditions such as blemishes and wrinkles, stretch mark minimization, muscle fatigue, dermatitis, and radiation treatments for certain medical problems. Because raw shea butter is extremely moisturizing and very hydrating, when applied to the skin, it provides immediate softness and smoothness.

May be dangerous for people with severe nut allergies.

## Dead Sea Salt

Since ancient times, the waters of the Dead Sea have been renowned for their therapeutic properties and healing qualities. People of long ago used it to naturally treat a variety of illnesses and skin conditions. What makes the Dead Sea special is its high salt content which is super rich in minerals. Dead Sea Salt contains a boatload of minerals, including magnesium, calcium, sulfur, bromide, iodine, sodium, potassium, and zinc, which are easily absorbed by the skin. Because of its dense mineral content, dead sea salt is extremely bitter and isn't edible — but it does have amazing benefits for the skin, hair, and more. It promotes cell metabolism, speeds up the healing of skin tissue, soothes damaged skin, protects skin from microbes that cause allergies, cleanses skin, relieves stiff and sore muscles, fights off skin cell degenerating free radicals, exfoliates dead cells, and detoxifies the skin.

## Castile Soap

*Sapo hispaniensis*

Castile soap has been around for a very long time and was created just following the popular Aleppo, which is quite possibly one of the most important soap and household cleaning products ever made. An all-natural chemical-free soap, Aleppo was made from mixing oil from laurel (bay) trees with olive oil and soda. This is where castile got its inspiration, however. Castile soap managed to establish such popularity because the Spanish city of Castile had an abundance of olive oil, which was a crucial ingredient used in the production of this high-quality soap. While the original recipe for Aleppo soap required laurel oil, this type of oil was in short supply; however, the city of Castile had easy access to olive oil and that enabled the creation of a pure white soap that was very mild and effective. The whiteness was seen as purity, which made it very popular with Spanish royalty. As centuries went by, Castile soap made its way all over Europe, entering the British market during the mid-1500s by sea. Castile soap is very popular among vegans and vegetarians since it is plant-based. Also, it does not lose potency with time and is often seen in the form of liquid Castile soap or pure Castile soap as a bar.

# MORE PLANETARY CORRESPONDENCES

**Sun / Leo:** Calendula, St. John's Wort, Chamomile, Bergamot, Lemon, Orange, Grapefruit, Lime, Rosemary, Cinnamon, Frankincense, Lavender, Sunflower, Orange Peel

**Moon / Cancer:** Jasmine, White Willow, Mugwort, Jasmine, Sandalwood, Frankincense, Myrrh, Ylang-ylang, Neroli, Clary sage, Green sage, Patchouli, Lavender, Chamomile

**Mercury / Gemini / Virgo:** Lavender, Eucalyptus, Peppermint, Lemon Balm, Chamomile, Lemongrass, Tea tree, Bergamot, Lemon, Rosemary, Basil, Clary sage

**Venus / Taurus / Libra:** Rose, Yarrow, Damiana, Thyme, Patchouli, Violet, Rose, Geranium, Ylang-ylang, Jasmine, Sandalwood, Vanilla, Cardamom, Patchouli, Neroli, Palmarosa

**Mars / Aries / Scorpio:** Basil, Nettle, Thistle, Black pepper, Ginger, Frankincense, Cedarwood, Rosemary, Patchouli, Clove, Pine, Juniper. Cayenne, Ginger, Mugwort

**Jupiter / Sagittarius / Pisces:** Sage, Clove, Cinnamon, Cedar, Frankincense, Chamomile, Seaweed, Sandalwood, Peppermint, Clove, Lemon, Rosewood, Bergamot, Cedarwood, Clary sage, Pine, Sandalwood, Nutmeg

**Saturn / Capricorn / Aquarius:** Mullein, Comfrey, Juniper, Echinacea, Lemon Verbena, Cypress, Patchouli, Frankincense,

Myrrh, Vetiver, Cedarwood, Sandalwood, Yarrow, Spikenard, Helichrysum

**Uranus / Aquarius:** Lavender, Frankincense, Hyssop

**Neptune / Pisces:** Seaweed, Blue Lotus, Passionflower

**Pluto / Scorpio:** Wormwood, Belladonna, Black Cohosh

Please note that these associations can vary depending on different astrological or crystal healing traditions. There isn't a universally accepted list, and this is a topic where a lot of personal beliefs and interpretations come into play.

# ANCESTOR VENERATION

Ancestor veneration, also known as ancestor worship, is a practice found in many cultures around the world where individuals show respect and honor to their ancestors. This can involve rituals, ceremonies, and offerings made to the spirits of the deceased. Practices can vary widely among cultures, but often include maintaining ancestral altars, making food and other offerings, holding ceremonies on death anniversaries, and observing certain holidays or festivals dedicated to ancestors. The belief behind this practice is that the ancestors continue to have an interest in the world of the living and can influence their descendants' fortunes, either positively or negatively. Therefore, maintaining good relationships with ancestors is considered important for well-being and prosperity.

**Genealogy Research:** Use online resources, libraries, or hire a professional genealogist to trace your lineage.

**Ancestral Rituals:** Some cultures have rituals to connect with ancestors, often involving offerings or ceremonies.

Storytelling: Ask older family members for stories about your ancestors.

**Create a Family Tree:** Visualize your lineage, it can help create a sense of connection.

**Visit Ancestral Locations:** Travel to places where your ancestors lived.

**Ancestry DNA Test:** Gain insights into your heritage.

**Preserve Family Artifacts:** Old photos, letters, and objects can help you feel connected.

**Write a Family History:** Documenting your family's past can help you understand your ancestors better.

**Cook Traditional Foods:** Preparing meals your ancestors ate can be a form of connection.

**Practice Ancestor Meditation:** Some people find meditation or prayer focused on their ancestors to be comforting.

Remember, different cultures have different beliefs and practices when it comes to ancestors, so it's important to be respectful and considerate. I highly recommend you buy Bad Ass Ancestors by Patti Wigington and Ancestral Medicine by Daniel Foor to start your ancestral journey.

**Mesa Blanca - The White Table**

An Ancestral/spirit guide altar is usually a white tablecloth draped over a small end table. It is fine to place offerings for your spirits such as a black cup of coffee, candy, tobacco, money, or other things your spirits enjoyed when they were alive. I am going to list the traditional items put on the Cuban and Puerto Rican table first then tell you how that can be modified to fit your own cultural heritage. In the Cuban Boveda there are one, seven, or nine glasses of water. One large glass with a crucifix inside for God and smaller glasses for spirit guides. However, the Puerto Rican fuente espiritual just has one glass with the crucifix inside surrounded by our spirit guide's items to work with them. If you are going to work more magically with your guides, having the one glass is better to conserve space and pack more of your spirits on the table. You can run your candle novenas on this altar. To protect your candle from harmful outside influences, wrap your Rosary around the bottom of the base.

**On the altar, you can have:**

Fresh flowers

A large glass filled with cold water (tap is fine)

A seven-day white candle, white tea light,  or plain white candle

A standing metal cross or crucifix to submerge in the goblet of water

A Rosary

Florida Water, Kolonia 1800, or both. You can also buy them cologne, perfumes, and room sprays. Incense and essential oils are also good since spirits love sweet smelling things.

Holy water, rain, lake, or ocean water

Crushed eggshell powder known as Cascarilla (pronounced Kas-Ka-Ree-Ugh)

A Bible, Holy Books, or Prayer Books like the Selected Prayers of Allan Kardec

Image candles or figurines reflecting the guides with whom you are working with after they are revealed to you

Anything else your spirits want placed on the shrine

You do not need to run out and buy everything at once. The best way to start your Ancestral altar is taking a white cloth and placing a single white candle and a single glass of water on it. You might have to get the help of a spiritualist to get started. This happens by booking a reading with a medium. When your spirit guides and ancestral spirits communicate with your spiritualist, they will tell her/him how they want you to represent them on the Ancestral altar unless you already are working with your spirits and know what they want. If you have a warrior spirit, then you might have a figurine of a toy soldier etc. Therefore, every practitioner's Ancestral altar will be different and vary from person to person. I cannot tell you what images to use because that information must be divined by a medium or revealed to you directly from the spirits. Keep the Ancestral altar plain until you are instructed otherwise.

## A metal cross submerged in the glass of water

The central focal point of the Ancestral altar usually is a metal cross or crucifix with Jesus on it within the large goblet of water. Craft stores like AC Moore and Michael's sell oversized glass wine goblets that are perfect for this. I just use a large clear glass. The metal cross acts as a conductor of spiritual energy for your spirits. The metal crucifix within the goblet represents Nzambi the first Ancestor according to my tradition. You can buy one on Amazon for fifteen dollars. Some also will say it represents the "first man who ever died".

## The Rosary

The Rosary is a meditation on the life of Jesus from the standpoint of his mother Mary using Catholic prayer beads known as the Rosary. It is a set of recitations that summarize the entire gospel. It can be recited in about 15 minutes once you memorize all the prayers. Praying the Rosary is purifying for the soul and comforting to the spirits. I devoted myself to the Virgin Mary and when I need her healing and protection, I invoke her with it. I also bind my spells and novenas with my Rosary for protection.

## Seven-day white candle, novena candles, vigil candles

A seven-day white candle or plain white candle is needed. The most important gift we can give to our spirits, according to my mentor, is light. Light, prayers, and water. As we elevate, so do they. When we sit down and light the candle, we are communicating with our guides. We are signaling to them that we are ready to do the work. It is this Sacred Flame, which has been used as the symbol of the Secret Fire, that connects us to the Divine since time immemorial. We can also run a Novena on the altar to get our spirits to help us. We can even say a prayer and light a small church candle for friends, family, and others in need. It's a way of offering our support if our spirits can help them.

## Holy water(s), Florida water, and cascarilla

You can sprinkle Holy Water around your home, Ancestral altar, and on yourself to spiritually cleanse and protect you. You can do the same with Florida Water or Kolonia 1800. Cascarilla usually is bought in a pack and contains little cups filled with the powder. Spiritualists will use Cascarilla like chalk for drawing protective circles and sigils. To protect yourself before leaving your home you can take the Cascarilla and draw a cross on your chest, on the soles of your feet, and on your wrists. Whenever you need to feel spiritually refreshed, splash Florida water in your hands and give yourself a dry bath. Put some Cascarilla and Florida Water on the back of the neck for protection.

## A bell, cologne, and incense

These tools are used to call on your spirits. Ringing the bell will scare off lower-level entities, while spritzing cologne or burning incense draws in your spirits. Spirits love fragrant smells, aromatic colognes, fine incense, and essential oils.

Some also like the smell of burning tobacco. It is common for a cigar to be placed on the Ancestral altar, lit, and the smoke blown around for clearing the space.

## The Bible and other holy/inspirational books

The Bible is considered a source of power to a lot of people who are into spiritualism, folk magic, and conjure traditions. Many practitioners use passages from the Psalms as well as the Gospels to perform incantations and healings. We also practice Bibliomancy, using the Scriptures as a tool of divination. The New Devotionary of Spiritist "Collection of Selected Prayers" by Allan Kardec is standard among practitioners of Spiritism, and the prayers are used privately as well as during larger ceremonies with other Spiritualists which is called a Misa. You might also have other Holy Books that are relevant to working with your spirits.

## Fresh flowers

It's nice to have a vase with fresh flowers in it such as white roses or carnations. If you cannot afford roses, you can buy baby's breath or put out some fresh basil leaves. But the point is that you have something living to honor your spirits with. Thus, you will have all four of the elements represented on the altar. Earth (flowers, herbs, tobacco); Air (bell, cologne, incense); Fire (white candle); and Water (goblet of water, holy water). This is a basic Ancestral altar set up. In the beginning of your journey, that is all you need.

## Candles, statues, and dolls for spirit guides and ancestors

Having image candles on the altar is ok if the spirits who walk with you (such as the Lucky Indian Spirit, La Madama, or the 7 African Powers) ask for them. Statues and dolls are also put on or around the altar that are gifts for them to work through. This is a separate altar from where you practice witchcraft.

If you have gods and goddesses, they need a separate altar. Keep your spirit guides and ancestral spirits separated from anything else you do. The only exception being lighting white vigil candles for others or running Novenas. In the old days traditionally, people would bury their dead loved ones in their home! The Norse, the Taino, and many different cultures buried them under the house or hung them from the ceilings in bowls. The Taino's would keep the skull, two arms bones, and a part of the rib cage in a calabash strung up outside the house. This practice influenced Palo Mayombe in that there are human remains that are used to create the Prenda (spiritual pot worked by the Polaro). Today people keep the ashes of their cremated loved ones in their home on a shelf or over the fireplace to honor them. This is the same idea. This is where we pray, meditate, say the Rosary, do mantra, and interact with our spirits.

But I am adopted! How can I honor my ancestors? You are lucky enough to honor all of them. When you are adopted into a family you are and always will be family. But if you do not know your birth parents get a DNA test so you can see the migration patterns of your people. Also be aware that if you do get the ancestry.com DNA test they will show you matches of people who might be relatives. That is my trigger warning! But it is worth finding out what is in your blood and where you spirits might be from. A spiritualist or medium can totally help with that!

**Working with your guides**

After you have constructed your Ancestral altar, you must use it. Remember that your Ancestral altar is a special place to commune with your spirits. You are opening yourself up for intimate contact with your ancestors and spirit guides. You will pray and meditate here to create a secure bond with your spirits. This is private time between you and your guides.

When you step before the altar, knock three times on it or ring your bell. You can make the sign of the cross if you like and say a prayer to God for thanks. Then call down your Holy Guardian Angel, your spirit guides, and ancestral spirits. Take the Florida Water on the table and splash some on your hands. Do a "dray bath" running your hands around the head, around the arms, down the legs, and around the back. Put some Florida Water on the back of the neck. Put your hands on the goblet or bowl and ask your spirits to remove any negative energy or spirit attachments that might be clinging to you.

Close your eyes and take a deep breath. Let go of any unnecessary thoughts and emotions. Stay focused on being present. Say your prayers. That can be praying the Rosary, the Selected prayers, or just talking from the heart. When you are finished with your prayers, talk to your spirits. Tell them how you feel. You can tell them what you need, but they already know. Ask them to protect you and guide you. Ask them for dreams. Ask them to make it clear to you what you should do next to improve the quality of your life as you draw closer to God. After you have finished talking to your spirits, thank them for helping you and continuing to help you. Sit for a few minutes and listen. Then journal about your experience.

**Prayers to be said from the "Collection of Selected Prayers" by Allan Kardec are:**

Act of Contrition

Prayer to the good spirits

Praise to God the Father

Prayer for every day

Prayer for peace in the home

Prayer for the medium

Prayer for your guardian angel for spiritual protection

Prayer to distance from negative spirits

The above-mentioned prayers are included in this book. You need to be able to train your senses and perception. You must discipline your mind and body. You need to be aligned and attuned to the energy around you while working with your spirits. You need to create a strong bond between you and your spirits, one so strong that nothing can come between you. You also must start learning how to sense subtle energies around you while you work at your altars. You cannot do that if you are not clear.

**But what if I am talking to demons?**

I hear this all the time. It is very popular for people to push this concept that when you pray to your Ancestors and spirit guides, they will not hear you and you will be conversing with malefic spirits. That is bullshit. When a Jew, Christian, Muslim, Hindu, or Buddhist says their prayers do you think that they think twice as to who is listening to them? Colonization worked because it destroyed African and Indigenous people's faith in their ancestral spirits and gods. You have to have faith when you talk to your spirits, they are listening to you. A lot of spirits might be listening to you but trust that your Holy Guardian Angel is ALWAYS with you. It is their Divine assignment to stand by you and help you in this game of life. Here is the thing about recognizing the difference between which spirits are around and are not. When you work with your spirits you should feel at peace. You should feel balanced, protected, and harmonized with them. When you encounter a spirit that does not belong you will sense it along with fear and anxiety. You will never feel fear when working with your spirits no matter the form they come to you in. It is what it is.

## Your Principal Spirit Guide

The concept of a Holy Guardian Angel is not unique to Christianity. This spirit has been called many things in many cultures. In ancient Greece, it was an individual's Daimon. The great philosopher Socrates spoke of his Daimon as a voice that would warn him of danger. In the IFA, Yoruba, and Santeria religion, it is called the Ori. In Haitian Vodou, it is called the Met Tet or the Master of the Head. Of all the saints and spirits within your Spiritual Court or "frame," the most important one to bond with is your Principal Spirit Guide. It is this spirit who is the leader of your Spiritual Court. From here on out, we will refer to this entity as your Principal Spirit Guide or Principal Guide. Your Principal Guide accompanies you through life from the time of your birth until the time of your death. In Spiritism, it is believed that God appointed you to this spirit and its sole purpose is to guide and assist you in your spiritual development. Your Principal Guide has many functions, but the most important is helping you evolve spiritually. As this guide helps you grow, it elevates itself and is rewarded.

The Principal Guide speaks to us through dreams and our inner voice, the voice that tells you right from wrong. Pray to your Guide, telling them your thoughts and feelings. Then practice contemplative prayer (meditation) to hear their response. Each person's Spiritual Guide is unique for that particular person. No one else has your Principal Guide in their Court. The most important thing to remember is that your Personal Guide will never encourage you to do something immoral or harmful. Your spirits will never tell you to kill another person or torture animals. I cannot emphasize enough the importance of keeping yourself mentally and emotionally balanced.

The spirit world is dangerous and not a joke. Individuals

who suffer from mental illnesses, especially depression, are protected by their Spiritual Court, but also need to find professional help in order to maintain their balance. Spiritism never replaces healthcare for physical or mental illness. Spiritism works on the spiritual level and assists in healing on the mental, emotional, and physical level. It will not prevent you from experiencing sickness, sorrow, and death. Finding a therapist and a doctor who respect your religious beliefs is very important. Remember that the goal of Spiritism is enlightenment, elevation, and love. Your Guides would never tell you to stop taking your medication or encourage you to inflict harm on yourself or others. Those kinds of thoughts are "demonic" and should be banished. When a message like that comes through, it's time to clean your house. That does not mean if you have a negative thought, you should be afraid of yourself or the world. It does mean that you need to tighten up your ship and examine yourself. First, determine if it's an emotional, mental, or physical imbalance. If you have concluded that it is an external influence, send it packing. This book's Materia medica will give you all the tools you need to do that. Take a spiritual bath, do a simple fast, and pray the Rosary if you feel you need immediate protection.

## Your Spiritual Court

Your Principal Guide is the captain of your Spiritual Court. The Spiritual Court is composed of other spirits who have been assigned to help you, ancestral spirits, or spirits you have attracted along your way. They are also referred to as "commissions" or "emissaries" sent to minister to you. Your court can change throughout your life. Some spirits might come into your life to accomplish a mission and then leave when it is finished. Again, we elevate these spirits as we elevate ourselves. The only spirit that will be with you from cradle to grave is your Principal Guide. We live in a world full of spirits born from every nation on earth. Some are more intelligent than us, while some are less intelligent. Just think about the world we live in. The spirit world is no different. Your Principal Guide and other protective spirits are often ancestral spirits or familiar spirits from past lives and are connected to you through your bloodline.

Maintaining a strong bond between you and your Spiritual Court is vital for your protection. These spirits are here to help carry you through this life. If a person's morals start to break down, so will their Court. When I use the word "moral," I mean if a person starts to become envious, jealous, spiteful, ungrateful, angry, harmful, abusive, or violent, they will lose contact with these elevated spirits. They will begin to detach themselves from us. When this happens, negative and harmful spirits have a way to influence us. Evil entities will enter and then our lives start going downhill if not spiral off into chaos. What I have learned on my journey is that I have to worry about myself, my spiritual health, and my connection to my spirits. I cannot and do not have time to worry about what other people are saying or doing. Our time here is too short. Worry about yourself and your spirits.

## Words of Caution

"Shamanistic experiences" can resemble psychosis, but a person who is in good mental and spiritual health will be able to distinguish reality from visionary thoughts. It's my belief there are people who have psychic gifts that are being wasted because they have been misdiagnosed by doctors with mental illness. When starting on this path, try to gain support from family, friends, and maybe even a therapist who will be able to check in with you and give you feedback on your behavior. The ideal would be to find other practitioners to stay in contact with. If you have ever used the phrase, "I swear that happened, I know I am not crazy!" — you're not. People who suffer from mental illness do not realize that they have the disease. I want to say that when a person loses control over their reality, they start to fall into psychosis. That could be a temporary loss of reality, but that does not mean you are schizophrenic.

If you go on a shamanic journey that is drug induced by magic mushrooms, ayahuasca, or DMT, after the experience is over you are able to reflect on it and process it in the real world. If those symptoms continued, it could be a sign there is some dysfunction going on. Be smart, but do not be paranoid. Oh, and I am not encouraging drug use by any means. However, anyone who has had experiences with entheogens will concur that the magical powers of plants are no joke. Teaching plants will humble you and "bring you to Jesus". Anybody who makes fun of herbalists or herbal magic needs to take a heroic dose of psilocybin and come back and talk to me.

The point is it's up to you at the end of the day to make sense of how you experience reality. Remember psychic experiences are subjective, they are something you experience alone. Trying to explain yourself to others is exhausting. Keep a good head on your shoulders. If you feel the need, then get a therapist who can talk with you and help you keep yourself grounded. You are good for nothing if you allow the world of spirits to take over your entire life. And you have to be able to determine if the spirits leading you have your best interests in mind. As you go through all the gifts in this book, you will read about the gift itself, what it is, and what it does. Then there is a prayer that asks God to enhance your natural gifts.

# HOW TO PRAY THE MOST HOLY ROSARY

Praying the Rosary is a spiritual cleanse. Witches that lived and practiced Folk Magic in Catholic countries went to Mass. They still do actually. Many practitioners of African diasporic traditions honor the Catholic elements that were used during slavery. Many Rootworkers say removing the Biblical elements used in Hoodoo takes out the Juju. If you have an aversion to Christianity like I do, the idea of praying to Mother Mary might seem ridiculous. The truth is it is a prayer just like any Hindu or Buddhist mantra chanted with a pair of Mala beads. Your intention matters here and if your intent is to be respectful to the Divine and honor your ancestors you can do it without associating your personal feelings about the political organization known as the church. There is a difference between spirituality and religion. Even witches and Babalawos can be as blindly dogmatic and visceral as any Christian or Muslim can be. Because truly spiritual people can see the positive aspects to any spiritual practice.

When you sit down to pray the Rosary you will meditate on a different Mystery depending on the day.

**The Joyful Mysteries** are said on Mondays and Saturdays.

**The Luminous Mysteries**, or mysteries of light, are said on Thursdays.

**The Sorrowful Mysteries** are said on Tuesdays and Fridays.

**The Glorious Mysteries** are said on Wednesdays and Sundays. We will go over all the mysteries together, what to meditate on while reciting the prayers, and what your affirmation should be when praying them.

To say the rosary makes the sign of the cross and kiss the crucifix.

Begin by reciting the "Apostles Creed" on the crucifix then say the "Our Father" on the first large bead.

Say three "Hail Mary's" on the next three beads followed by one "Glory Be" and one "Oh My Jesus".

Then announce the first of the five mysteries being contemplated that day. Recite the "Our Father" again on the next large bead followed by ten "Hail Mary", a "Glory Be", and an "Oh My Jesus".

After you have completed all five mysteries say the "Hail Holy Queen" and "Final Prayer".

After you have finished with the Rosary prayers you can say the prayer to St. Michael the Archangel. Then you have completed praying the Most Holy Rosary.

Let's go over all the mysteries now. While praying each "decade" of the Rosary, when done correctly, you will be meditating on a scene from the Gospel announced. Each meditation inspires an affirmation to imitate the faith of Mary and Jesus.

**The Joyful Mysteries**

**The Annunciation:** The angel Gabriel announces to the Virgin Mary that God wishes her to become the mother of his son. Mary obeys with humility and joy. (Luke 1:26-38)

Affirmation: I will be humble and courteous towards all.

**The Visitation:** Mary visits St. Elizabeth who will become mother of Saint John the Baptist. She remains with Elizabeth lovingly for three months. (Luke 1:39-56)

Affirmation: I will help my neighbor in need.

**The Nativity:** Jesus Christ the Son of God is born in a stable. His mother places him in a manger. He's visited by shepherds and Wise men. (Luke 2:1-14)

Affirmation: Christ became man, I will become Christlike.

**The Presentation of the Child Jesus in the Temple:** In obedience to the law of Moses, Mary and Joseph take the infant Jesus to the temple in Jerusalem to present him to his Heavenly Father. (Luke 2:29-32)

Affirmation: I will obey the laws of God as Jesus, Mary, and Joseph did.

**The finding of the child Jesus in the temple:** On having lost Jesus Mary and Joseph seek him. After three days, they find him in the temple talking to the Learned men. (Luke 2:48-52)

Affirmation: I will fulfill my daily duties.

**The Luminous Mysteries**

**Jesus is baptized in the Jordan River:** Jesus appears in the Jordan and insists that John baptize him. As this occurs the Holy Spirit descended upon him in the form of a dove as God proclaims, "This is my beloved son". (Matthew 3:13-17)

Affirmation: As Christ was baptized, I will also submit to his Father's will.

**Jesus self-manifestation at the wedding of Cana:** When Christ changed water into wine, we see you marry in guise of a teacher and intercessor as you urged the servants to do what Jesus commands. (John 2:1-12)

Affirmation: As Mary tells people to "do whatever he tells you", I will do what Christ wants of me.

**Jesus proclaims the Kingdom of God:** As Jesus announced the Kingdom, he called all to conversion and forgiveness of sins, saying, "I came not to call the righteous, but sinners." (Mark 1:14;2:17)

Affirmation: I will strive to be worthy to enter Christ's

Kingdom through his example.

**The Transfiguration:** The Transfiguration shows the glory of the Godhead shining forth from the face of Christ. Peter, James, and John witness Jesus' face and clothes become dazzling with light, as he spoke with Moses and Elijah. (Luke 9:28-36)

Affirmation: God revealed himself to us. I will always live my life for Christ.

**Jesus' institution of the Holy Eucharist:** Christ offers bread and wine as symbols of his body and blood instituting a sacrificial memorial of his death and resurrection for the salvation of the world. (Mark 26:17-35)

Affirmation: I will receive Christ regularly at Holy Mass and consecrate myself to him forever.

### The Sorrowful Mysteries

**Agony in the garden:** Jesus prays in the garden of Gethsemane. The Thought of his coming sufferings and of our sins causes him to sweat blood. (Matthew 26:38-39)

Affirmation: Jesus, I will pray with all my heart.

**The Scourging:** Our Lord Jesus Christ is stripped, bound to a pillar, and cruelly scourged until his innocent body is covered with wounds and blood. (John 19:1)

Affirmation: Jesus I will keep my body pure.

**The Crowning of Thorns:** A crown of thorns is pressed into the head of Jesus. His eyes are filled with tears and blood. His executioners mock and spit on him. (Mark 15:16-17)

Affirmation: Jesus, I will banish unclean thoughts.

**The Carrying of the Cross:** Weighed down by the cross, Jesus patiently walks the road to Calvary. Mary makes the stations of the cross with her dying son. (John 19:17)

Affirmation: I will bear my cross patiently.

**The Crucifixion:** Fastened to the cross by nails, Jesus, after three hours of agony dies in the presence of his Mother. (John 19:28)

Affirmation: I accept the death God has prepared for me with all the pains that may accompany it.

**The Glorious Mysteries**

**The Resurrection:** Jesus rises from the dead, glorious and immortal, on Easter Sunday. He conquered death and opens the gates of heaven. (Mark 16:6-8)

Affirmation: I will live with Christ so that I may rise with him.

**The Ascension:** Forty days after his resurrection, Jesus ascends, in the presence of his Mother and his disciples into heaven. (Acts 1:10-11)

Affirmation: I will follow the example of Christ on earth, because I hope to be with him in heaven.

**The Descent of the Holy Spirit:** Ten days after the ascension, the Holy Spirit descends in tongues of fire upon Mary and the disciples. (Acts 1:4)

Affirmation: I will love God and my neighbor.

**The Assumption:** The Apostles go to the tomb where they had laid the body of the Mother of God. They find that the angels had borne their Queen to Heaven. (Song of Songs 2:3-6)

Affirmation: I will praise Mary through the rosary.

**The Coronation:** The Mother of God, to the joy of all the angels and saints, is crowned Queen of Heaven and Earth by her Divine Son. (Luke 1:51-54)

Affirmation: I will love Mary as my queen and mother.

**Our Lady's Promise**

"I promise to assist at the hour of death with the graces necessary for salvation all those who on the first Saturday of five consecutive months, go to confession and receive Holy Communion, recite the Rosary, keep me company for a quarter of an hour, while meditating on the mysteries of the Rosary, with the intention of making reparation."

**The Holy Rosary Prayers:**

**Sign of the Cross**

In the name of the Father, and of the Son, and of the Holy Spirit. Amen.

**Apostles' Creed**

I believe in God, the Father almighty creator of heaven and earth and in Jesus Christ, His only Son, our Lord, who was conceived by the Holy Spirit, born of the Virgin Mary, suffered under Pontius Pilate, was crucified, died, and was buried. He descended into hell. On the third day he rose again from the dead. He ascended into heaven and is seated at the right hand of God, the Father almighty. He will come again in glory to judge the living and the dead. I believe in the Holy Spirit, the Holy Catholic Church, the communion of saints, the forgiveness of sins, the resurrection of the body, and the life everlasting. Amen.

**Our Father**

Our Father, who art in heaven, hallowed be thy name; thy kingdom come; thy will be done on earth as it is in heaven. Give us this day our daily bread and forgive us our trespasses as we forgive those who trespass against us; and lead us not into temptation but deliver us from evil. Amen.

**Hail Mary**

Hail Mary, full of grace. The Lord is with thee. Blessed art thou amongst women, And blessed is the fruit of thy womb, Jesus. Holy Mary, Mother of God, Pray for us sinners, Now and at the hour of our death. Amen. Glory Be Glory be to the Father, and to the Son, and to the Holy Spirit. As it was in the beginning, is now, and ever shall be, world without end. Amen.

**Oh, My Jesus**

Oh, my Jesus, forgive us of our sins. Save us from the fires of hell. Lead all souls into heaven, especially those in most need of thy mercy. Amen.

## Hail Holy Queen

Hail Holy Queen, Mother of Mercy, hail our Life, our Sweetness, and our hope. To your do we cry out, poor banished children of Eve. To you we send up our sighs, mourning and weeping in this vale of tears. Turn then most gracious advocate, Your eyes of mercy towards us, and after this, our exile, show unto us, the blessed fruit of thy womb, Jesus. O clement, O loving, O sweet Virgin Mary. Pray for us Oh Holy Mother of God, That we may become worthy of the promise of Christ. Amen.

## Final Prayer

Oh God, by the life, death and resurrection of your only begotten son you purchased for us the rewards of eternal life; grant, we beseech you, that while meditating upon the mysteries of the Holy Rosary, we may imitate what they contain and obtain what they promise. Through the same Christ Our Lord. Amen.

## Espiritismo's Core Beliefs

**Espiritismo believes in one God** — the supreme intelligence, the Good, the One above all, the Creator of all things, and the Mother and Father of all things. In Spanish it is called Papa Dios (Father God), and in Creole it is Bondye (Good God). God the spirit is so advanced and infinite that we cannot comprehend or put into words God's nature. God created other spirits that do rule over us and act as intermediaries for God. Everything that comes from God is just and good.

**Espiritismo believes in the immortality of the soul**, and it also believes in reincarnation. That means the soul of an individual can return here on Earth many times in different life cycles. Each life cycle is an opportunity for the soul to grow and evolve — similar to Yoga and Buddhism.

**Espiritismo believes in the progression of the soul**, that the spirit always evolves within many incarnations, and it never de-evolves or goes backwards. That means a human will not be reincarnated as a dog. When a person dies, their soul leaves the body and the spirit maintains its unique individuality.

**Espiritismo believes that those who pass into the spirit world can still communicate with the living**

At some point they will incarnate again in a new body to experience the world.

**Spiritism believes in karma, the law of cause and effect.**

Karma is God's merciful way of allowing us to learn right and wrong from our actions and experience their repercussions. Espiritismo rejects the doctrine of eternal hellfire and punishment for erring souls.

**A soul will continue to reincarnate as many times as it has to in order to find enlightenment.**

After an unlimited number of life cycles, if enlightenment is achieved, the soul has no need to incarnate again and will remain in the spirit realm. A spirit can choose to come back to act as a person's spirit guide. Hence, each person's Spiritual Court.

**Ancestors are not composed of the recently deceased. They are very old spirits who have crossed over the abyss where they reside in the realm of the ancestors**

Heaven, Summerland, or whatever you want to call that realm of existence. They are ancient elevated spirits who have lived many lifetimes and no longer have the need to incarnate. Your dead grandparents are not your ancestors, nor any dead relatives who have lived in the past few hundred if not thousands of years.

**Spiritual progress and growth are the reason we are here.**

Similar to Eastern spiritual traditions, our primary goal is to perfect ourselves and become more compassionate, empathetic, forgiving, and merciful.

Espiritismo's view on morality is Christian based. Allan Kardec's Spiritism aligns itself with Christian morality and views. Creolized Spiritism also holds to Christian principles, but considers the natural state of man as embodied by the peaceful, democratic, and hospitable Tainos as the ideal.

### Differences between an Espiritista and a Necromancer

A Necromancer is a conjurer of the dead who compels the dead to perform black magic with bribes and payments either to steal something, kill someone, or commit another immoral deed. Fear of sorcery and witchcraft traditionally stems from the necromancer's ability to call forth infernal spirits, or intranquil spirits, for the purpose of sending harm to others. They also use their knowledge of herbalism to make poisons, cause abortions, or turn people into living zombies. The conjuring of the dead for malicious purposes is not approved of in Puerto Rican Espiritismo. Remember that everything you think, everything you say, and everything you do vibrates throughout the entire universe. You are not required to believe these doctrines to practice Espiritismo. But over time, by practicing, you might come to believe them.

# THE SELECTED PRAYERS

**Act of Contrition**

Jesus my redeemer, pure spirit that came into the world to show us the true doctrine of the Eternal Father, I am sorry if I have offended you in any way. I have fallen short of obeying your commandments — that is to love my neighbor as myself. I believe in your compassion and ask for your intercession to the merciful Father to forgive me, a repentant sinner. I pray that I may be granted the strength to bear the trials and tribulations this life has placed before me. Amen.

**Prayer to the Good Spirits**

Praise be to you the pure spirits of our Father; I elevate my heart and thoughts to you. Guide me in the path of truth and instruct me in the divine precepts, so that I may be worthy of the good fortune afforded to an obedient child. I call on your divine influence at this moment to fortify me. Amen.

**Praise to God the Father**

I call on you Heavenly Father for your blessings and also to the elevated spirits of your celestial court; they are your sublime emanations of all that is infinitely good. Oh, elevated spirits whose virtues emanate perfection and receive instruction from our God omnipotent, help me know his Fatherly love. Sing to me a new song I can learn to chant in my heart as I strive toward the heavenly reward. I glorify you Heavenly Father. Only through your mercy can I enjoy the light of truth and the embrace of your love. I suffer with patience through my trials and tribulations for your infinite goodness. I come to understand the magnitude of your infinite knowledge that defines my mission on Earth. Thank you for your blessings! Guide me, messengers of God, and illuminate me with knowledge that my soul may be purified with the benefit of your influence. Bring an end to my pilgrimage and consider me a dove resting at the foot of the throne of the King of Kings requesting forgiveness. Please sing with me his praise. Amen.

## Prayer for Every Day

God of infinite goodness and mercy, Lord Omnipotent, I pray for grace with the assistance of my guardian angels. I ask that you distance me from negative influences, so that I may concentrate on the development of my soul so I can elevate my spirit to your presence. I ask for blessings upon the whole human race, so that our bonds of fraternal love can be strengthened. Give me compassion for my enemies, consolation in my affliction, and prudence in all my actions. Give me the light of truth that illuminates the path of Divine happiness. Please instruct my guardian angels that they may protect and watch over me. I pray for light and progress and for the light and progress of my parents, brothers, sisters, friends, and enemies. I also ask for health for the sick and enlightenment for the unilluminated. I ask you to cast your light on negative spirits that surround me and have compassion for those who are influenced by their negativity. Also compassion for those in jail and prison. I ask for forgiveness for my persecutors also. Amen.

## Prayer for Peace in the Home

Heavenly Father, I am surrounded by darkness and imperfection all the time. I understand the extent of your mercy and wish to walk in your righteous path. I therefore have repented of my sins and ask for your forgiveness. I therefore elevate my thoughts to you and ask you to grant my home peace. May my mind be illuminated and my thoughts glow with the Spirit of your peace. My hope is to seek elevation for my assigned spirit guides in your magnificent celestial territory. Oh, Sacred Peace, strengthen my heart with your holy influence and do not forsake me. Magnificent One, I also ask you to strengthen all of my family members so that only your peace resides in our home. Lord Jesus, you who during your pilgrimage here on Earth taught us peace, help me preserve peace and harmony in my home. Grant me the gift of peace and tranquility. Minimize my guardians' distress, so that my home can become a sanctuary of your peace. Amen.

## Prayer for the Medium

All Powerful God allow your enlightened spirits to assist me in the communication I seek. Protect me from attacks by evil entities and distance me from egotistical thoughts that could deter me from accomplishing my purpose. If I should err, implant in me a thought that would advise me of my mistake. Instill in me the humility that would allow me to recognize criticism for my continued spiritual advancement. Should I for some reason become abusive or vain while exercising my spiritual ability, I pray that you assist me to resist negative influences before they can deter me from my principal purpose. Amen.

## Prayer to the Good Spirits

Benevolent and thoughtful spirit guides, messengers of the Almighty, loving sentinels charged with the mission of helping me grow in wisdom and love, I ask you to give me your support as I face each day's challenges. Help me oh spirit guides to have the fortitude of character to resist harmful thoughts and to resist the temptation to listen to the voices of evil entities who would induce me to err. Illuminate my thoughts and help me recognize my defects, remove the veil of ignorance from my eyes so I may recognize my faults. To you who I in particular acknowledge as my spirit guides and all other good spirits who take an interest in my well-being, I pray that I might be worthy of your consideration. You know my needs. I therefore ask that you help me improve the quality of my life as I become closer to God. Amen.

**Prayer to Distance Negative Spirits**

In the name of God Almighty, may the negative spirits be distanced from me and may enlightened spirits replace them and assist me in the battle against them. Negative spirit who inspires bad thoughts, treachery, and lies in the minds of God's people, I refute you with all of my strength. Above all, I desire that God grant you His mercy. Enlightened spirits who God has assigned to assist me, grant me the strength to resist the influence of negative spirits, and the necessary light so that I do not become the object of their perverse intentions. Amen.

# DIVINATION WITH PLAYING CARDS

Divination is an absolute requirement for being a witch. You can read Tarot, runes, bones, shells, whatever you want. If you do not like Tarot, buy oracle cards instead. But I am including my personal interpretations for reading a regular pack of bicycle playing cards. I have had kids and teens ask me how to practice witchcraft while under the control of intolerant parents. If you are one of those kids that cannot wait to get out of your parent's house to have your witchy stuff learn how to read playing cards. It is more impressive to me when someone reads me with playing cards.

Some Witches prefer playing cards because they are simple and to the point. For a deeper inspection into a person's spiritual needs, a Witch would cast a birth chart and analyze the cosmic forces at play in their life. Use this book as your guide and memorize the simple explanations. Pick one card a day and meditate on its meaning until you memorize the entire pack. Casting a simple three card spread of past, present, and future will give you everything you need to assess the situation.  To get a yes or no answer from your deck, designate one card as the "yes" card and one as "no". Make sure you have explained this out loud to your spirit guides so everyone is on the same page. After I finish reading, I shuffle the cards several times to clear the tool of that reading's energy.

**Hearts (cups)**

Hearts represent the realms of emotions and feelings. Heart

cards cover not just love but the whole range of human emotion, from despair and powerlessness to contentment and joy. Hearts very often also represent relationships, because relationships engender the full range of emotions.

### Ace of hearts

All aces are the fully realized manifestation of the suite and in general this card represents emotions, intimacy, and love. Expressing your feelings, developing intimacy, and establishing deep bonds are in order. It might mean to conduct your affairs in a forgiving and loving manner and being sympathetic and showing kindness to others. This card also means trust your gut instincts.

### 2 of hearts

The 2 of hearts card is always about romantic love or close relationships between people. The relationship can be one of intimacy, unconditional love, or the love shared between soulmates. This card may be a call for you to forgive or grow close to someone you care about. The long-term stability of the 2 of hearts is not set in stone. Relationships take work.

### 3 of hearts

The 3 of hearts card is about friendship and communities. Social structure, families, friendships, and other groups that you are intimately tied with. This card may signal the need for you to find a community or companions that you can rely on to help you meet your goals. It can also mean the need to learn and trust other people.

### 4 of hearts

The 4 of hearts card represents someone who is withdrawn, introspective, or self-absorbed. You may be feeling apathetic, disengaged, or unmotivated. This card is a warning to look at your relationships and make sure that you are showing gratitude and appreciation for what you have. This card encourages you to change your attitude and perspective.

## 5 of hearts

The 5 of hearts card is about loss, sadness, grief, and disappointment. It can mean you are overcome with grief. This card can signal any type of loss, such as a home, person, relationship, friend or a pet. It is anything that would make you feel remorse. Loss happens for a reason. The 5 of hearts encourage us to pay attention and take stock of what we have left. It's time to let go.

## 6 of hearts

The 6 of hearts card is about positive memories from the past often associated with childhood. It's about reminiscing about the good times, having positive memories and experiencing the joys of childhood. This kind of reflection is positive and uplifting and it can also be about spending more time with children, or relatives. It represents innocence generally.

## 7 of hearts

The 7 of hearts card represents delusions and fantasy. Daydreaming that can lead you away from committing yourself fully to your situation. If you're too uptight it might signal that you need to relax and engage in something to unwind. This card represents that your feet are not planted firmly on the ground or being in touch with reality. Another interpretation can be that you have many possibilities or many options in front of you: Some good and bad and to be careful in what you choose because not everything is as it appears.

## 8 of hearts

The 8 of hearts is about moving on. You might be stagnant in your situation and feel drained and burned out. The 8 of hearts card suggests you need to recognize it's time to walk away and that change is difficult. It cautions that making yourself stay in the situation will only get worse in the long run. You might feel the need to retreat from society for a short time to seek deeper truth and reexamine your life and where it's headed.

## 9 of hearts

The 9 of hearts card is a very positive card to draw, because it has been called the wish card, signaling that your hopes, desires, and dreams will come true. It can also refer to your emotions, and this card may indicate contentment or happiness with the way things are currently. This card also may indicate that its time to enjoy what the world has to offer, and your dreams might soon become a reality

## 10 of hearts

The 10 of hearts card is about finding happiness and gaining contentment from the simple things in life. It also indicates being surrounded by family, friends, and spending time with each other. It also means lasting peace and harmony. This card is asking you to develop lasting peace and joy and know that it's attainable. You should enjoy your good fortune and happy times and do not take what you have for granted.

## Jack of hearts

The Jack of hearts card has both positive and negative qualities. On the positive side it reflects introspection since it could refer to someone who is aware of other people's feelings and responds deeply to those emotions. They may be a poet, artist or someone who draws upon their emotions for strength. He can also mean someone who is emotional, and has no restraint and is melodramatic, completely unrealistic and emotional, If you draw this card, you need to ask yourself is the Jack of hearts making the situation better or worse

## Queen of hearts

The Queen of hearts card is emotional, intuitive, spiritual, motherly, and compassionate. She is able to sense others' emotional state and even psychic abilities. She might be a lover of the arts or very artistic since she's associated with mothers. There are negative qualities to this card also, where she can be too emotional, weaker, and dependent on others for her happiness. You should think carefully about this card and whether you are too emotional or not emotional enough.

### King of hearts

The King of hearts card is about strong leaders that are in touch with their emotions and they lead calmly. The king is emotionally stable, and tolerant of others' opinions and actions. He's caring, understanding, and a supreme diplomat. He may be someone involved in healing, clergy, therapy, or charity work. He also represents a balance between the emotions and intellect which is something the card might suggest you work toward.

### The Suit of Clubs (wands, rods, batons, or staves)

Clubs are action cards. Clubs may be a called to action in the realms of creativity, business, intellect, or relationships. They represent action, adventure, risk-taking, or competition. They can also refer to physical or spiritual energy, inspiration, intuition, ambition, and growth.

### Ace of clubs

Ace of club's card is full of energy, adventure, courage, excitement, and personal power. It's about bold enthusiasm and a seed that may sprout into an idea. It may be a gift or an opportunity. This card is about creativity and invention and your chance to create something unique and original. You should trust your creative potential.

### 2 of clubs

The 2 of clubs represents individual courage, greatness, personal power, and invigorating forces that give you the courage and strength to accomplish your goals. This card represents the wisdom necessary to accomplish goals. This card bestows the extra daring sense that you can move forward unafraid to make your goals a reality. This card can also represent a union with others or cooperating in a joint venture. You should use this ability wisely, as it could represent a manifestation.

## 3 of clubs

The 3 of clubs represents successful plans and ventures. The card shows progress on a project or goal. This card may demonstrate the need for his help. The 3 of clubs is about exploring the unknown and seeking uncharted waters and possibly doing something new to expand your horizons or doing something different. It means you need to be a visionary and see the big picture. Because of this, the card is about leadership and providing direction by setting an example and showing others how to walk a path.

## 4 of clubs

The 4 of clubs represent celebrations, rejoicing, marriage, graduation, and promotion. The 4 of clubs ask one to take time to reflect upon your accomplishments, formal ceremonies, and the exciting time period you are in. This card can also represent finding freedom to break into new areas and letting go of that which binds you to be in an emotional state, personal situation, or profession. This card encourages you to be free and escape oppressive or negative situations which you find yourself in.

## 5 of clubs

The 5 of clubs represents conflicts, disagreements, competitions, or going against an opponent or enemy rivalry. This card also represents lack of cohesion, leadership or strategy or bureaucratic debates impeding your progress such as trivial hassles. This card shows you what kind of obstacles or setbacks can get in your way. It means you have to be innovative and find another way to resolve your situation and overcome your obstacles.

## 6 of clubs

The 6 of clubs represent victories and triumphs. This card indicates that you have achieved success and come out on top and have the moral high ground. It also means you have overcome your obstacles. It can also indicate someone who is proud of themselves in the work that they do and that they enjoy their success.

## 7 of clubs

The 7 of clubs is a card about being brave and taking a stand. You stand up for what you believe in and have firm convictions and viewpoints. I may also represent bravery. The 7 of clubs can indicate that aggressive action could be the best course of action however do not rush off foolishly without knowing exactly what you're fighting for. The 7 of clubs also indicates that you have the high ground despite the fact that you are outnumbered, and you are right in your convictions and must face your fears and take a stand.

## 8 of clubs

The 8 of clubs is about communication and taking swift and decisive action to make your move and declare your intent. If you have been holding off waiting for something don't wait any longer. Now is the time to act especially if any events are already in motion. The 8 of clubs also indicates that you should proceed rapidly. This card can also indicate that something is coming to a quick conclusion. The 8 of clubs can also announce that an important message is coming that will give the necessary information one needs or fill in a missing link.

## 9 of clubs

The 9 of clubs is about stamina and perseverance. The 9 of clubs also indicates that you can have unexpected setbacks and disappointments, however this card tells you to persevere in the face of setbacks and continue to work on your goals. The 9 of clubs also indicate that you may be thinly spread and need to regroup. This card may also indicate that you're on the defensive and must remember that you have the power to stay strong in order to overcome the obstacle.

### 10 of clubs

The 10 of clubs represents that the individual is being burdened and overtaxed. You've taken on too much. You're not able to say no. It can also mean the inability to relax or someone who's dumped on repeatedly and left to clean up the mess. If this card presents, you should cut back and lighten your duties and let others help you. Remember life is an uphill struggle and you must do your best to maintain your strength and avoid people that take advantage of you.

### Jack of clubs

The Jack of clubs represents positive and negative qualities and the willingness to take risks, and act boldly. It also represents ambition and passion. On the other hand, the Jack of clubs may indicate a person is too confident in himself and acts hasty, quick to act without thinking, restless and hot tempered. You should ask yourself whether or not the appearance of this card is making the situation better or worse. The cards around it will indicate whether the Jack of club's energy will help or hinder the situation.

### Queen of clubs

The Queen of clubs represents an attractive, compassionate, confident, dedicated, poised, and gracious female. She has many admirers, and she is the center of attention. She is determined and passionate about what she does. This card may indicate a person who is a lover or a friend but never an enemy. The Queen of clubs represents someone who is passionate, always moving and involved in projects or someone who is cheerful, energetic and self-assured.

### King of clubs

The King of clubs represents power and authority or a charismatic leader that is dominant and passionate. He can be forceful concerning things he cares about. He is the center of attention and cares not what people think of him and can be overwhelming to those around him. He is liked and respected by others and may have the tendency to be creative, artistic, and innovative. If this card presents in the reading you should ask yourself whether or not the energy that the King of clubs brings is helping or harming the situation.

### Spades (swords)

The Spades represent all aspects of thinking and communication or 'head-stuff'. The Spades rule over truthfulness or lack of truthfulness, writing, studying, and decision-making. Spades and swords are also associated with taking (constructive or destructive) action, for example making changes, using force, asserting power, displaying ambition, having courage, or facing conflict.

### Ace of spades

The Ace of spades represents the potential to do good or evil. It encourages you to seek the truth, and to be just and use your power for the greater good. The Ace of spades represents discovering the truth and coming to a clear understanding about a situation. This card could mean seeking Justice or fighting for a good cause or freeing others from oppression. It is about fighting intelligently and using logic to analyze a situation before proceeding further. The Ace of spades may represent a challenge you are about to face as well.

### 2 of spades

The 2 of spades represent the potential for good and evil. The two sides may represent balance or that they are unequal. The 2 of spades may also show a stalemate or impasse and no movement in a situation at the current time. This card can also represent a defensive barrier placed around the person, or that the person is hiding true emotions or feelings and refusing to let those around them see what is going on with them. The 2 of spades may also indicate a person is closed off from the truth in matter or ignoring warning signs where the truth is relevant. If the 2 of spades presents it may be a warning that the person should seek the truth in a situation and take down barriers to avoid a stalemate otherwise the situation will remain the same.

## 3 of spades

The 3 of spades represents betrayal, heartbreak, pain, and loneliness. This card represents situations where one may feel betrayed to find that someone has cheated, been dishonest or disloyal. It's a warning that something in your life is wrong and you are unaware or unwilling to believe or accept the truth. The 3 of spades cautions you to pay attention to your situation and trust your instincts. This card brings with it considerable pain that can eventually lead to positive growth and change.

## 4 of spades

The 4 of spades represents temporary relief and a period of peace and rest. It represents a time to heal and find peace and quiet and take a step back. This card asks you to reassess your life and prepare for what is coming. The 4 of spades may also indicate that you should tie up loose ends and save money. This card warns of a storm ahead that might present difficulties or that the person has weathered the storm. The 4 of spades also indicates that you can succeed after the storm has passed, but that you should rest and recover before proceeding.

## 5 of spades

The 5 of spades may indicate defeat or failure involving a project, mental or emotional defeat or financial ruin. On the other hand, this card may represent a small victory by aggressively pursuing your goals despite struggles. The 5 of spades may also represent one's self-interest and the inability to look out for oneself after suffering a defeat. This card indicates that one should make sure to make self-care a priority.

## 6 of spades

The 6 of spades indicates one is stuck in stagnant water. The individual is in quicksand and unable to move out of a situation or is unhappy where they are. The 6 of spades may represent that this stagnation is causing depression because the individual has worked hard but receives nothing in return. This card indicates that it is time to pick up the pieces and start focusing on bringing yourself to a more positive place in your life by taking a trip or journey to gain a fresh perspective.

## 7 of spades

The 7 of spades indicates that there is a situation that involves cunning, trickery, or deceit. This card indicates that someone may have used trickery, lying or deception to defeat someone. Or that one has been tricked by secrecy and backstabbing. The 7 of spades may be indicating that someone is hiding the truth from you or someone who avoids responsibility. The 7 of spades warns of someone trying to take something from you by employing trickery, deceit and cautions to be wary of backstabbing.

## 8 of spades

The 8 of spades indicates powerlessness, restriction, and confusion. There may be a situation that is beyond your control or you may feel trapped in a situation. This card may indicate that the individual feels hopeless and there is not movement in a positive direction. The 8 of spades can indicate that the individual feels victimized.  However, this card indicates that you still have the power to change your current situation by clearing the fog from your mind or thoughts and release yourself from what binds you.

## 9 of spades

The 9 of spades represents mental anguish, guilt, or turmoil. The key is that all the pain, suffering, and anguish comes from within. You may be going over an issue in your mind dwelling on it night and day. It's about guilt and the unwillingness to forgive yourself. You have focused on what you have done wrong. This keeps you up at night and sends you into deep depression. The situation may be approaching you or you might already be in it, but you can't go back in time and you can't change what happened. Look and think carefully about changes and moving on.

## 10 of spades

The 10 of spades represents true destructive nature, is severe and represents someone who has hit rock bottom or the lowest point of one's life. The 10 of spades warns of a dark hour coming or that one is facing the dark hour currently. This card can represent that one has been the victim of a horrific event or action. The 10 of spades represents self-pity or hopelessness and it can also mean being a martyr for a cause.

## Jack of spades

The Jack of spades represents pure logic or someone who is frank, honest, direct in their communication and behavior. This person may be blunt, show no discretion, and have no tact. He may act with discreteness, boldness, certainty, be overbearing, heavy handed, and forces his positions on others. The Jack of spades while a master of logic, may possess character traits that make him uncaring and aloof – cut off from emotions. This could also represent someone who is prone to narcissistic abuse.

## Queen of spades

The Queen of spades represents a woman who is brutally honest and logical. She has a sharp wit and good sense of humor. The Queen of spades offers honesty because she is experienced and has the ability to understand emotions. She has the ability to see the truth in situations. The Queen of spades may present as a mentor or coach and is able to convey the truth to the person while being loving and caring while doing so.

## King of spades

The King of spades represents a man who is intelligent, and analytical. The King is able to articulate the most difficult topics to others with ease. He is able to correct the course of action and works in the best interests of those he loves. The King of spades represents a person who works against corruption, lies, and confusion. He may represent someone who is also a fair judge. He is someone others can trust and a leader who is willing to act and will strike the first blow in the name of Justice.

## Diamonds (pentacles, coins, or discs)

Diamonds reflect all practical, material aspects, including home, work, business, projects, property, and money—all the things we can touch, and yes again, relationships, but from a practical viewpoint. Diamonds may also indicate health issues.

## Ace of diamonds

The Ace of diamonds represents possibilities concerning luck, prosperity, wealth, fortune, hard work, and determination that payoff. This card is about being practical and working with your strengths that include using common sense and realistic outlooks about your goals. Is also about trust and security and putting your faith and trust in your support system. It's about feeling protected and may indicate a good time to begin a new project.

## 2 of diamonds

The 2 of diamonds indicates that one may be juggling projects or about perpetual change. The 2 of diamonds is about maintaining balance in your life with everything you have going. This card also reminds us to be sure of the commitments we make, because it may require flexibility, and adapting quickly. This card may also be a warning to avoid new projects because you may become overburdened with taking on a new task. You may have to let go of other projects in order to take on something new.

### 3 of diamonds

The 3 of diamonds represents teamwork, cooperation, and planning. This card may signal that a group effort is required to accomplish a goal where each person contributes to the overall goal. The three of diamonds indicates that the team must prepare and plan for contingencies through teamwork and paying attention to details. The 3 of diamonds warns one not to rush blindly into a project without a plan especially with a group of people. This card can also represent the ability to get a job done with the skill, knowledge, and resources.

### 4 of diamonds

The 4 of diamonds indicates control and possession. It can signify someone who is greedy and piling up acquisitions or saving up money or keeping hold of what he or she has. The 4 of diamonds may indicate the need to save up for the future, or unexpected occurrences may make you feel the need to be in charge to set limits or rules. This card can also indicate that there is pressure from someone to control you from creativity or new approaches to a problem. The 4 of diamonds can indicate that an individual may be blocked or obstructed by someone holding them back. This card represents that the need to control forever is impossible and you must restrain the desire to infinitely control a situation.

### 5 of diamonds

The 5 of diamonds represents those hard times may be coming bringing about financial difficulty or the struggle to make ends meet. The hard times expressed in this card could be the product of material problems that are caused by illness or emotional difficulty. Someone's health might be suffering. The 5 of diamonds can also indicate feelings of rejection may be involved or that one may be about to enter a period of hard times. If this period has not happened yet you may be able to work to lessen the effects. Start planning and storing up now and draw upon your inner strength to get through the possible rough times ahead.

## 6 of diamonds

The 6 of diamonds represents the availability of resources and giving and receiving. This card encourages you to dig deeper and recognize that it's easy to flip from having everything to having nothing and vice versa. The Six of diamonds encourages one to take what is offered or to give freely to those in need. This card represents change.

## 7 of diamonds

The 7 of diamonds represents risk of the reward and assessing possible future actions. This card might represent reaping the results of a hard effort and earning the fruit of your labor. Now might be the time to sit back and enjoy your rewards and take a break from your daily toils to reflect upon your success and consider alternative approaches. The 7 of diamonds may indicate the need to reflect upon what has been done. This may lead to change of direction and questioning your past choices.

## 8 of diamonds

The 8 of diamonds represents paying attention to detail and being diligent in your work. This card may signal the need to double down in your efforts and remain focused on a goal.

## 9 of diamonds

This card is all about being self-reliant. It is about security and finding independence. It is time to enjoy the fruit of your labor. The cards invite us to self-reflect and find our own worth. Having a positive sense of self is required to overcome difficult situations and obstacles.

## 10 of diamonds

This card is about financial stability. It is also a sign that if you have been experiencing hard times that you are about to get some support. The ancestors will be bringing you a blessing so be ready to receive it.

### The Jack of diamonds

The Jack of diamonds might indicate that a person is realistic, cautious, and encourages others to proceed carefully. The Jack of diamonds might indicate that a person can stay grounded keeping true to their beliefs, however with the stability can come stubbornness, obstinance, refusal to listen or to compromise. Generally, this card indicates that a person does not know how to relax and is a workaholic.

### Queen of diamonds

The Queen of diamonds indicates a caring, nurturing, generous and kind mother, caretaker or home maker. The Queen of diamonds can manifest as someone who is dedicated to helping and caring for others. The Queen of diamonds is resourceful, sensible, and able to handle all problems and come up with solutions quickly. The Queen of diamonds can indicate that this person can be overprotective and sometimes obsessive.

### King of diamonds

The King of diamonds represents a person who is reliable, trustworthy, willing to take responsibility and keeps all his promises. He acts quickly in a crisis and has a stabilizing effect on the problem. The King of diamonds works calmly but diligently towards his goals and is always successful at what he does. He is not a risk taker or innovative person, and he relies on the tried-and-true method of success.

### Playing Cards and Astrology

"Cards of Destiny" is a system of divination that uses a standard deck of 52 playing cards. The system is based on mathematical formulas and cycles of the calendar, with each card representing a certain period within the year. It's akin to astrology, but instead of planets and stars, it uses the symbolism inherent in a deck of cards. In this system, each person has a birth card based on their birthday, and this card is said to provide insights about their life path, personality traits, and destiny. The system also includes yearly spreads, which are believed to offer predictions about the coming year. "Cards of Truth" is a system of divination and life understanding developed by Ernst Wilhelm. The system combines multiple esoteric disciplines including astrology, numerology, and card reading. The card reading aspect is based on a standard deck of 52 playing cards, similar to the system developed by Olney H. Richmond.

Olney H. Richmond was an American author and mystic who lived in the late 19th and early 20th centuries. He is best known as the creator of the Mystic Test Book, a system of divination using playing cards, also known as the "Cards of Destiny." He also founded the Order of the Magi, a spiritual organization based in Detroit, Michigan, which emphasized the spiritual significance of the mathematical principles found in a deck of cards. Despite his influence in certain esoteric circles, Richmond and his work remain relatively unknown in the mainstream. In the "Cards of Truth" system, each card corresponds to specific periods in a person's life and can provide insights into their personality, life events, and personal development. The system also incorporates astrological principles, adding another layer of interpretation to the cards. You can actually take an online course to study the Cards of Truth system of divination.

# USING ASTROLOGY DICE

Astrology dice are a divination tool used by astrologers and those interested in astrology. They typically come in a set of three dice. One die has the 12 astrological signs (Aries, Taurus, etc.), the second has the planets (Mars, Venus, etc.), and the third has the 12 astrological houses. When rolled, the combination of symbols on the dice is interpreted to answer questions or provide insights about the user's life, similar to a horoscope.

**To use astrology dice for divination, you follow these steps:**

**Set Your Intent:** Before you roll the dice, have a clear idea of what you are seeking guidance on. This could be a specific question, or a general area of your life you want insight into.

**Roll the Dice:** Roll all three dice at once.

**Interpret the Dice:** Each die represents a different aspect of the astrological chart as follows:

**The Planet Die:** This represents the energy or action at play.

**The Sign Die:** This represents how the action or energy is expressed or the qualities it has.

**The House Die:** This represents the area of life where this energy or action is likely to manifest.

For instance, if you roll and get Venus (planet of love, beauty, and values), Scorpio (intense, passionate, investigative sign), and the 10th house (career, public image), you might interpret this as a time to bring more passion and intensity into your career, or perhaps you're about to enter into a business partnership that will be deeply transformative. Remember, astrology and divination are highly personal. It's important to consider your own intuition and feelings when interpreting the dice. The above interpretation is a very simplified example, and interpretations can get very complex depending on your knowledge of astrology.

# HOW TO BECOME
# A BETTER HUMAN

Becoming a better Witch involves self-reflection, understanding your values, and taking consistent action to improve yourself. Here are some suggestions to help you on your journey:

**Develop self-awareness:** Reflect on your thoughts, emotions, and actions. Identify your strengths and weaknesses, and consider how they impact your relationships and personal growth.

**Set personal goals:** Establish clear, realistic goals for self-improvement in areas that are important to you. Break them down into manageable steps and track your progress.

**Cultivate empathy and compassion:** Strive to understand the feelings and perspectives of others. Practice active listening and offer support when needed.

**Be open to change:** Recognize that personal growth requires adaptability and a willingness to let go of old habits or beliefs that no longer serve you.

**Practice gratitude:** Regularly express appreciation for the positive aspects of your life. Cultivating gratitude can improve your well-being and help you maintain a positive outlook.

**Develop healthy habits:** Take care of your physical, mental, and emotional health through regular exercise, a balanced diet, and stress management techniques.

**Foster positive relationships:** Surround yourself with supportive, like-minded individuals who encourage your growth. Nurture existing relationships and seek out new connections that align with your values and aspirations.

**Communicate effectively:** Develop strong communication skills to express your thoughts and feelings clearly and respectfully. Practice active listening when engaging with others.

**Be responsible and accountable:** Take responsibility for your actions, and learn from your mistakes. Make amends when necessary and strive for continuous improvement.

**Contribute to the well-being of others:** Volunteer your time, share your skills, or offer support to those in need. Acts of kindness and generosity can help create a positive impact on the lives of others and foster personal growth.

Remember, becoming a better person is an ongoing process that requires patience, persistence, and self-compassion. Embrace the journey of personal growth and celebrate your progress along the way.

# HOW TO HAVE A SUCCESSFUL LIFE

Living a successful life can have different meanings depending on individual values, beliefs, and goals. There is no universal definition of success, as it is largely subjective and varies from person to person. However, some common elements that people often associate with a successful life include:

**Personal fulfillment:** Pursuing one's passions, interests, and talents, and feeling a sense of accomplishment and satisfaction from one's endeavors.

**Happiness and well-being:** Experiencing overall contentment, maintaining a positive outlook on life, and nurturing emotional and mental health.

**Financial stability:** Achieving financial security, being able to meet personal and family needs, and having the freedom to make choices based on personal values rather than financial constraints.

**Healthy relationships:** Building and maintaining strong connections with family, friends, and loved ones, while fostering a sense of belonging and support.

**Personal growth:** Continuously learning, evolving, and developing as an individual, including expanding one's knowledge, skills, and self-awareness.

**Giving back:** Contributing to the well-being of others and making a positive impact on society through acts of kindness, philanthropy, or community involvement.

**Work-life balance:** Balancing professional achievements with personal commitments, hobbies, and leisure time to maintain overall well-being and prevent burnout.

**Professional accomplishment:** Achieving career goals, making meaningful contributions in one's field, and gaining recognition or respect from peers.

Ultimately, defining and pursuing a successful life is a personal journey that depends on your individual values, priorities, and aspirations. Reflecting on what success means to you and setting clear goals can help you navigate your path toward a fulfilling and meaningful life.

# CONCLUSION

Thank you for buying this book. I gave you as much ammunition as I could to go start practicing magic today. Just remember that the spiritual "map" is not the actual territory. I could lay a map of the Amazon rainforest down on a table and stare at it, but it will never be the experience of walking in that rainforest itself. That includes all the danger I will face exposed to raw unrelentless Nature. Do not confuse the spiritual map with the actual spiritual terrain. You have to DO THE WORK to become a Witch... bitch.

Philip Ryan Deal

# RECOMMENDED READING

Yoga of the Planets: Their Mantra and Philosophy Andrew Foss

The Vedic Astrology Deck by Jeffery Armstrong

Karma: A guide to cause and effect by Jeffery Armstrong

Art and Science of Vedic Astrology Volumes 1 and 2 by Ryan Kurczak

The Nakshatras: The Stars beyond the Zodiac by Komilla Sutton

Rahu and Ketu: Our Karmic Destiny by Joni Patry

Shodasha Varga the 16 Divisional Charts of Vedic Astrology by Komilla Sutton

Beneath a Vedic Sky by William R. Levacy

The Nakshatras: The Lunar Mansions of Vedic Astrology by Dennis Harness

Vedic Astrology and the Vedas: A Complete Guide to Jyotish by Manjula Tara

An Introduction to Western Sidereal Astrology 2nd Edition by Kenneth Bowser

Ancestral Medicine by Daniel Foor

Badass Ancestors by Pati Wigginton

The Shamanic Journey: A beginners guide to shamanic journeying by Gerry Starnes

Advanced Magick for Beginners by Alan Chapman

Taino's and Caribs: The aboriginal culture of the Antilles by Sebastian Robiou Lamarche

Astonishment & Power: The eyes of understanding Kongo Minkisi by Wyatt Macgaffey and Renee Stout

Palo Mayombe: The Garden of Blood and Bones by Nicholaj De Mattos Frisvold

Dreaming Mother Earth by Jose Barreiro

New Devotionary Spiritist Collection of Selected Prayers by Allan Kardec

Creole Religions of the Caribbean by Margarite Fernandez Olmos and Lizabeth Paravisini

Divine Horseman: The Living Gods of Haiti by Maya Deren

West African Religion by Georfrey Parrinder

Working Conjure by Hoodoo Sen Moise

Earth Power by Scott Cunningham

Earth, Air, Fire, Water by Scott Cunningham

Sons of the Goddess by Christopher Penczak

The Inner Temple of Witchcraft by Christopher Penczak

Made in the USA
Las Vegas, NV
17 September 2024

95443911R00184